SHAKESPEARE'S
LATE PLAYS

CHALLENGING MINDS. INSPIRING SUCCESS.   CITY COLLEGE **NORWICH**

In memory of
Gareth Roberts,
a generous colleague, teacher and friend

SHAKESPEARE'S
LATE PLAYS

New Readings

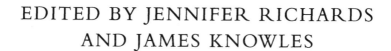

EDITED BY JENNIFER RICHARDS
AND JAMES KNOWLES

EDINBURGH UNIVERSITY PRESS

© Edinburgh University Press, 1999
Copyright in the individual chapters is
retained by the authors.

Transferred to Digital Print 2010

Edinburgh University Press
22 George Square, Edinburgh

Typeset in Bembo
by Koinonia, Bury, and
Printed and bound in Great Britain by
CPI Antony Rowe, Chippenham and Eastbourne

A CIP record for this book is available
from the British Library

ISBN 0 7486 1152 5 (hardback)
ISBN 0 7486 1153 3 (paperback)

The right of the contributors to be identified
as authors of this work has been asserted in
accordance with the Copyright, Designs and
Patents Act 1988.

CONTENTS

CONTENTS

LIST OF ILLUSTRATIONS

ACKNOWLEDGEMENTS

Shakespeare's Late Plays: New Readings sprang from the enthusiasm of our students for the plays, and from our shared sense of a need for such a collection, but it would not have come to fruition without the efforts, professionalism and patience of all its contributors and our editor at Edinburgh University Press, Nicola Carr. Our first thanks, then, go to these.

Although the volume was several years in the planning, it came together at a two-day symposium on the late plays held at the University of Newcastle in October 1997. We would like to thank in particular Rowena Bryson, whose organisational skills contributed so much to the smooth running of the event, and the English department's postgraduate students, Janie Mills, Lorraine McNeil and John Wheeling, for managing registration, coffee and lunch. Thanks, too, are due to the participants at the symposium, whose questions and discussion have informed the writing of these chapters. Finally, the symposium could not have taken place without a grant from the University of Newcastle, and without the support of colleagues in the department of English.

Jennifer Richards and James Knowles
University of Newcastle
September 1998

TEXTS AND EDITIONS

In all the chapters the following editions are used unless otherwise stated:

Pericles	in *William Shakespeare: The Complete Works*, eds S. Wells and G. Taylor (Oxford: Clarendon Press, 1988)
The Winter's Tale	ed. S. Orgel (Oxford: Clarendon Press, 1996)
Cymbeline	ed. R. Warren (Oxford: Clarendon Press, 1998)
The Tempest	ed. S. Orgel (Oxford: Clarendon Press, 1987)
Henry VIII (or *All is True*)	ed. R. A. Foakes (London: Methuen, 1957) [Arden 2]
The Two Noble Kinsmen	ed. L. D. Potter (London: Routledge, 1997) [Arden 3]

Citations to other works by Shakespeare are taken from Wells and Taylor, *Complete Works* (as above).

Citations to Theobald's version of Fletcher and Shakespeare's *Cardenio* are taken from *Double Falshood; or, The Distrest Lovers ... Written Originally by W. Shakespeare; and now Revised and Adapted to the Stage by Mr. Theobald*, facsimile ed. K. Muir (London: Cornmarket Press, 1970). References are by act, scene and page number.

NOTES ON CONTRIBUTORS

—◆◇◆—

Julia Briggs, Professor of English and Women's Studies, DeMontfort University, Leicester, has written *The Stage Play World* (1983, revised edition 1997) and *E. Nesbit: A Woman of Passion* (1987). She is general editor of the Penguin Modern Classics reprints of Virginia Woolf's writings and has edited *Virginia Woolf: Introductions to the Major Works* (1994). Her edition of *The Second Maiden's Tragedy* is forthcoming in the Oxford Works of Thomas Middleton, and she is currently writing an intellectual biography of Virginia Woolf and a study of feminist readings of Shakespeare.

Helen Hackett, Senior Lecturer in English, University College, London, is the author of *Virgin, Mother, Maiden, Queen: Elizabeth I and the Cult of the Virgin Mary* (1995) and '*A Midsummer Night's Dream*' for the Writers and their Work Series (1997). She is currently writing a book on women and romance in the English Renaissance.

Margaret Healy, Lecturer in English, School of English and American Studies, University of Sussex, has written '*Richard II*' for the Writers and their Work Series (1997) and is currently completing a monograph entitled 'Fictions of Disease: Bodies, Plagues and Politics in Early Modern Writings'.

Thomas Healy, Reader in Renaissance Studies, Birkbeck College, London, is the author of books on Crashaw (1986) and Marlowe (1994) and *New Latitudes: Theory and Renaissance Literature* (1992). He has edited the Longman Critical Reader on Andrew Marvell (1998) and co-edited *Literature and the English Civil War* (1990) and *The Arnold Anthology of British and Irish Literature in English* (1997). He is currently completing a book entitled 'The English Boat: The Poetics of Sectarianism in Early Modern England'.

James Knowles, Lecturer in English, University of Newcastle upon Tyne, has edited *Four City Comedies* (1999) and writes on Jonson and the masque. His edition of *The Entertainment at Britain's Burse* appears in *Representing Ben Jonson* (forthcoming) and he is currently writing a monograph, 'The Theatrical Closet', and editing the entertainments and masques for the Cambridge edition of the Works of Ben Jonson.

Gordon McMullan, Lecturer in English, King's College, London, has co-edited *The Politics of Tragicomedy* (1992), edited *Renaissance Configurations* (1998) and authored a monograph, *John Fletcher and the Politics of Unease* (1994). He is currently editing *Henry VIII* for the Arden edition.

Willy Maley, Senior Lecturer in English, University of Glasgow, has written *Salvaging Spenser: Colonialism, Culture and Identity* (1997) and has edited *A Spenser Chronology* (1994). With Brendan Bradshaw and Andrew Hadfield he has co-edited *Representing Ireland: Literature and the Origins of Conflict, 1534–1660* (1993) and with Andrew Hadfield *Spenpflr: A View of the State of Ireland* (1997). In addition he has co-edited *Postcolonial Criticism* with Bart Moore-Gilbert and Gareth Stanton (1997).

Jennifer Richards, Lecturer in English, University of Newcastle upon Tyne, has published articles on Sidney and Castiglione. She is currently editing Elizabeth Rowe's *Poems on Several Occasions*, and completing a monograph study of 'Courtliness and Rhetoric in Early Modern England'.

Gareth Roberts was Senior Lecturer in English, University of Exeter until his death in March 1999. He wrote *The Open Guide to Spenser's Faerie Queene* (1992) and *The Mirror of Alchemy* (1994). With Lawrence Normand he edited *Witchcraft in Early Modern Scotland: James VI and the North Berwick Witches* (1999). At his death he was editing *Errors* for Arden III and translating Ovid's *Fasti* with Peter Wiseman.

Alan Stewart, Lecturer in English, Birkbeck College, London, is the author of *Close Readers: Humanism and Sodomy* (1997) and (with Lisa Jardine) of *Hostage to Fortune: The Troubled Life of Francis Bacon, 1561–1626* (1998). He is a member of the editorial board for the Clarendon Press Works of Francis Bacon and he is currently completing Volume 5 'Writings 1608–1612'.

Alison Thorne, Lecturer in English, University of Strathclyde, has written a monograph, *Vision and Rhetoric in Shakespeare* (1999), and is currently editing the Macmillan New Casebook on 'Shakespeare's Romances'.

Richard Wilson, Professor of Renaissance Studies and Director of the Shakespeare Programme at Houghton Tower, University of Lancaster, is author of a monograph on *Julius Caesar* (1992) and of *Will Power* (1993) and has co-edited *New Historicism and Renaissance Drama* (1993). His Longman Critical Reader on Christopher Marlowe will appear in 1998, and he is currently preparing 'Shakespeare and Politics' for the Oxford Shakespeare Library. A new collection of essays called 'Gothic Shakespeare' will be published shortly.

Introduction:

SHAKESPEARE'S LATE PLAYS

Jennifer Richards and James Knowles

Shakespeare's late plays have generated different responses: from one perspective they are 'meanly written', from another, unrealistic (the product of a playwright '[b]ored with people, bored with real life, bored with drama, bored, in fact, with everything except poetry and poetical dreams'), and from yet a third, 'myths of immortality'.[1] But what exactly are the 'late' plays? They are usually identified as those plays written mainly by Shakespeare between 1607 and 1613–14, the 'romances' *Pericles* (written with George Wilkins), *The Winter's Tale* (*c*.1609–10), *Cymbeline* (1610), and *The Tempest* (*c*.1610–11),[2] and the 'last' plays,

1. Dryden, 'Defence of the Epilogue', in *Essays*, 1: 165; Strachey, *Literary Essays*, p. 12; Wilson Knight, *The Crown of Life*, p. 30.
2. *The Winter's Tale* is probably the earliest of these plays, dating from *c*.1609–10, with *Cymbeline*, a closely related play, in 1610 (Wells and Taylor, *Textual Companion*, p. 131). Orgel prefers 1611 for *The Winter's Tale*, arguing that the play was new when Simon Forman saw it on 15 May 1611, but computerised tests on the frequency of colloquialisms and rare words suggest that *The Winter's Tale* predates *Cymbeline* (*The Winter's Tale*, ed. Orgel, p. 80). *Cymbeline* may be dated before autumn 1610, if Roger Warren's arguments about the indebtedness of Heywood's *The Golden Age* to the play are correct (*Cymbeline*, ed. Warren, p. 63). *The Tempest* must be the last of this group, since it cannot predate September 1610, when William Strachey's letter describing Sir William Somers' expedition arrived (possibly the source for the 'still-vexed Bermudas' of I, ii, 229). *Pericles* is the problem here: it is usually dated to *c*.1606–7 or perhaps 1607, decisively earlier than the other 'romances', but it shares

1

written in collaboration with John Fletcher, *Cardenio* (*c*.1613), *Henry VIII* (or *All Is True*) (*c*.1613) and *The Two Noble Kinsmen* (*c*.1613).[3] Their study, although riddled with questions about authorship, textual integrity and genre, has been one of the central contributions of the twentieth century to Shakespeare scholarship, as critics have moved away from earlier dismissals of them to a greater appreciation of their distinctive qualities.

The late plays are often considered to form a distinct group because they share common themes and motifs – death and rebirth, family unity, repetition, time, riddles – a theatrical emphasis on spectacle and music, and a reconciliatory or optimistic mood. There are, however, many problems in this grouping, not only in its 'thematic' coherence (itself a matter of interpretation), but particularly in the key matters of dating and naming which themselves shape these interpretations. For instance, if we accept an early date for *Pericles* (1607), it precedes both *Coriolanus* (1608), a play which seems antithetical to normal critical perceptions of the late plays, and the revised (Folio) version of *King Lear* (*c*.1610), which, in its use of 'British' history, its themes of family (dis)unity, redemption and providence, and its use of tragicomic and romance forms, shares much with the late group.

Similar problems follow their classification. We describe them here as 'late' Shakespeare, but we would like to distinguish between the early plays in this group, the so-called 'romances', and the three 'last' plays identified above. Elsewhere, however, they are variously depicted as Shakespeare's later, last or final plays, the romances, the late comedies,

---

themes, ideas and sources with those plays, and the later scenes (x–xxii) have many stylistic affinities with the late plays' (Wells and Taylor, *Textual Companion*, pp. 132, 130; *The Tempest*, ed. Orgel, p. 63).

3. The exact order of these plays is controversial, but the lost play *Cardenio* (or *Cardenno* or *Cardenna*) may well have been written first, since on 20 May 1613 John Heminge was paid for its performance at court during the previous winter season. A further performance was given before the Duke of Savoy's ambassador on 8 June 1613 (see Chambers, *The Elizabethan Stage*, vol. IV, pp. 127, 128, 180). *Henry VIII*, under its title *All Is True*, was the play being performed when the Globe burned down on 29 June 1613. The reference to the King's Men's 'losses' in the prologue to *The Two Noble Kinsmen* (l. 32) is usually taken to refer to the destruction of their playhouse on that occasion, although *The Two Noble Kinsmen* is also linked to an earlier event, since the morris dance (III, v) corresponds closely to the second antimasque of Beaumont's *Masque of the Inner Temple and Gray's Inn*, performed to celebrate the marriage of Princess Elizabeth to Frederick, Elector Palatine, on 20 February 1613 (ed. Edwards, *A Book of Masques*, pp. 131–42, and reprinted as Appendix 3, *The Two Noble Kinsmen*, ed. Potter, pp. 240–9).

and the tragicomedies. All of these nominations are retrospective, and they have become the foundations for very different and highly influential interpretations of the shape and trajectory of Shakespeare's career.

The terms 'late', 'last' and 'final', for instance, invite us to structure the Shakespeare canon in different ways. In particular, the adjectives 'last' and 'final' imply an intention of closure not apparent in the temporally less specific 'late'. Which play, we may well wonder, is Shakespeare's *last*, and in what way does its identification affect our judgement of his dramatic career? Can we even speak of a 'last' play, given that Shakespeare lived until 1616, and given, too, that there is no way of knowing whether he saw these years as the final phase of his dramatic writing? When G. Wilson Knight wrote about *Shakespeare's Final Plays* in 1947, he depicted them as 'the culmination of a series', shaped from the middle of his career, and as the 'inevitable development of the questioning, the pain, the profundity and grandeur of the plays they succeed'.[4] In his view, it is *Henry VIII* which provides a properly 'satisfying' end to the Shakespeare canon because it offers a revived interest in 'national and contemporary themes' and a 'less visionary and enigmatic conclusion' to its rival, *The Tempest* – often preferred because Prospero's 'retirement' seems consonant with Shakespeare's own (pp. 256–7). Wilson Knight was writing against earlier critics who tended to dismiss the 'final' plays as the 'freaks of a wearied imagination'. In the place of such distaste, though, he imagines Shakespeare as the elder statesman of Elizabethan and Jacobean drama, whose experience and collected insights herald a new era of dramatic writing. The apparent conciliatory mood of the late plays he explains as an 'expression, through the medium of drama, of a state of mind or soul in the writer directly in knowledge – or supposed knowledge – of a mystic and transcendent fact as to the true nature and purpose of the sufferings of humanity' (p. 22).

Wilson Knight's views have proved popular and found a variety of supporters. In a similar way, the structuralist critic Northrop Frye, writing in 1965, argued that Shakespeare's 'last phase represents a genuine culmination' of his dramatic career, displaying his attainment of insight into the cyclical pattern that governs the natural world and the life of man, while Bethell (1947) found a Christian resonance to *The Winter's Tale* in particular, identifying the restoration of Hermione at its end as a 'carefully prepared symbol of spiritual and actual resurrection in which alone true reconciliation may be attained'.[5] On these views, the

---

4. Wilson Knight, *The Crown of Life*, p. 9.
5. Frye, *A Natural Perspective*, p. 7; Bethell, *'The Winter's Tale'*, p. 103.

progression of the Shakespeare canon – from comedy to tragedy to lyrical romance – reveals a playwright on a personal journey from immaturity to maturation and death, matched (allegorically) by a spiritual journey through struggle and conflict to reconciliation.[6] Such emphases reflect the post-war mood but they also belong to a Romantic tradition of Shakespeare criticism which rejected the neoclassical tastes and naturalistic expectations of eighteenth-century critics such as Samuel Johnson. In notes on *The Tempest*, for instance, the Romantic critic Samuel Taylor Coleridge reminds us 'that drama is an *imitation* of reality, not a *copy*', and he compares the theatre to 'dreaming', allowing him to expand our conception of 'reality' to encompass the 'imaginative faculty', and prompting later critics to search the plays for new 'planes' of meaning and spiritual autobiography.[7]

In such a tradition, the temporal adjectives 'last' or 'final' establish the plays written between 1607 and 1613–14 as a valedictory gesture, a meditated closure of an established body of dramatic writings which somehow exists as an independent imaginative world in its own right. Historicist rereadings of the plays from the 1960s may have questioned the integrity of this world, but they still treat the Shakespeare of this period as a 'mature' figure, albeit as a political conservative rather than a spiritual guide. Historicist critics may disagree with Coleridge's view that Shakespeare 'never promulgates any party tenets', but they tend to agree with Coleridge's less self-aware characterisation of the playwright as 'a philosophical aristocrat', who 'delight[s] in those hereditary institutions which have a tendency to bind one age to another' (p. 122). In *Shakespeare's Last Plays: A New Approach* (1975), Frances Yates sought to provide spectators and readers of the plays with the very context neglected by critics such as Wilson Knight. For her, though, they embody a profound nostalgia for an Elizabethan triumphalism, albeit in the service of the Jacobean state. Her reading of *Cymbeline*, moreover, is based on topical identification (Cymbeline refers to James, and his two sons and daughter correspond to James's actual family, Henry, Charles and Elizabeth), pointing to the fact that the *approach* to the plays remains unchanged: spiritual allegory becomes topical analogy.[8] Even David Bergeron's more careful contribution to an historicised Shakespeare

---

6. See Barroll, *Politics, Plague*, pp. 1–7.
7. Coleridge, 'Notes on *The Tempest*', in *Shakespearean Criticism*, vol. I, p. 116. On the plays' distinct 'planes of reality' see Tillyard, *Shakespeare's Last Plays*.
8. Yates, *Shakespeare's Last Plays*, Chs 1 and 2, esp. p. 48. See also Jones, 'Stuart *Cymbeline*', Kurland, '*Henry VIII* and James I', and Tennenhouse's study of the romances and the Jacobean family in *Power on Display*, pp. 149–86.

seems unable to escape the 'received teleologies' implicit in allegorism.[9] Though Bergeron may be critical of the kind of topical identification practised by Yates, and prefers to consider James and his family as a '"text" that Shakespeare "read"' (just as he read *Pandosto* or Chaucer's *Knight's Tale*), his argument serves only to reinforce our perception that Shakespeare 'idealized ... royal families'.[10]

To what extent, though, do these plays represent a coherent, and mature, body of work? Historicist work of a different kind – textual scholarship – offers a rather different view of the heterogeneity of these plays. Studies of the origins of the First Folio texts, for example, remind us of their textual instability: four of the 'late' plays, *Cymbeline*, *The Winter's Tale*, *The Tempest* and *Henry VIII*, survive as texts only in the form 'tidied' for print by the editors (sometimes identified as Hemmings and Condell). Two texts, *Cymbeline* and *The Tempest*, were copied by Ralph Crane, a scrivener who elaborated the stage directions in the copies to such a degree that we cannot regard their stage action as 'Shakespearean' in any clear sense. Finally, and most problematically, the labyrinthine *Pericles*, is known only from the presumed 'bad' quarto of 1609.[11]

Renewed emphasis on Shakespeare's collaborative practices also jeopardises the assumption that the late plays offer a considered gesture of finality, or a fitting conclusion to the grand master's dramatic *oeuvre*.[12] Of the romances, *Pericles* was long considered to be the effort of at least one

---

9. See Palfrey, *Late Shakespeare*, p. 5.

10. Bergeron, *Shakespeare's Romances*, pp. 19–22. One important exception to these royalist readings is Leah Marcus's study of *Cymbeline* in *Puzzling Shakespeare*, in which she discovers a 'different kind of topicality' in its failure 'to make sense at the level of Stuart interpretation', prompting an 'unease' with James's style self-authorship, and highlighting its tendency to 'work against the communication of its [own] Stuart message' (Marcus, *Puzzling Shakespeare*, pp. 109, 110, 117). See also Potter, who criticises topical readings of the late plays on the basis that 'political meaning' is always 'a matter of context' (Potter, 'Topicality or politics?', p. 90).

11. See Wells and Taylor, *Textual Companion*, pp. 36–8 and 556–60, and see Roberts, 'Ralph Crane', and Jowett, 'New created creatures'. Marcus is attentive to how the presentation and arrangement of *Cymbeline* in the first folio might affect our reading of it; she concludes her essay with a study of the differences between the quarto (1608) and folio *King Lear* (1623), noting that '[w]hat we have in the 1608 quarto and the 1623 folio are two "local" versions of *King Lear* among other possible versions which could have existed in manuscript, promtpbook, or performance without achieving the fixity of print' (Marcus, *Puzzling Shakespeare*, pp. 106–110, 148–59, 151).

12. On the question of authorship see Hoy, 'The shares of Fletcher and his collaborators'; Hope, *The Authorship of Shakespeare's Plays*; McMullan, '"Our whole life is like a play"', and Masten, 'Beaumont and/or Fletcher'.

other author (George Wilkins) because of its untidy character, while critics have argued from internal evidence that Shakespeare worked with John Fletcher around 1613 on the play-text of *Henry VIII* and, from external evidence, on the lost *Cardenio* and *The Two Noble Kinsmen*. In naming *Henry VIII* as Shakespeare's final play, Wilson Knight chose to dismiss the question of authorship, claiming to support his argument from close textual readings alone. But we should question the credibility of an account of Shakespeare's 'last' phase which seeks deliberately to protect the integrity not just of the canon itself, but of its authorship too. Because *The Two Noble Kinsmen* first appeared in print in 1634, and proclaimed its authors to be 'the memorable worthies of their time, Mr John Fletcher, and Mr William Shakespeare', and also – as Julia Briggs argues in this collection (p. 214) – because it does not share the upbeat mood of the other plays, it has tended not to be included in critical considerations of the late plays. Yet its consideration will lead us to recognise a darker side to the late plays, and perhaps to stress less emphatically their distance from Shakespeare's Jacobean tragedies, while the broader question of his collaboration in the 'last' plays suggests that they represent less a valediction to his art than a desire to find a suitable successor,[13] or even the dramatic experimentation of a playwright at the peak of his career.

GENRE

Critics instinctively feel that there is something different about the late plays, though the nature of that difference – as we have already suggested – often proves difficult to locate and describe. This is evident in attempts to identify their generic traits. We find, for example, that the plays have been variously designated romances, late comedies and tragicomedies, and that each term indicates a new way of looking at them. 'Romance' recalls the strangeness of the plays – their distant and far-away locations, their apparent attachment to chivalric values, their delight in riddles and expansive time scales, and, above all, their distinctiveness as a grouping. Alternatively, the term 'late comedy' proposes their kinship with Shakespeare's famous comedies of the 1590s, such as *Midsummer Night's Dream*, *Much Ado About Nothing* or *As You Like It*, or the Jacobean comedies and problem plays, such as *All's Well* and *Measure for Measure*. In contrast again, the term 'tragicomedy' suggests Shakespeare's possible awareness of the dramatic experiments of Giovanni Battista Guarini, and reminds

---

13. Proudfoot, 'Shakespeare and the new dramatists', p. 248.

us too of his collaboration with John Fletcher, whose *The Faithful Shepherdess* (1609), identified in its preface 'To the Reader' as a 'pastoral tragi-comedy', made its own distinctive contribution to English experiments in the genre.[14]

The problems with defining the late plays through genre, however, are exacerbated by our uncertain understanding of generic types themselves. *Shakespeare's Later Comedies* (1971), a collection of essays which discusses the Jacobean comedies and the 'romances', assumes a generic link between the plays which requires repeated qualification. The editor finds that he needs to distinguish between the '"last"' plays (here the romances), which 'are shown to represent an almost visionary remoteness from reality', and the Jacobean comedies, which display 'stronger ethical concerns', 'deeper ironies' and more 'resonant rhetoric'. He also discovers diversity *within* the two groups, making 'attempts to formulate a single pattern for each type of comedy encounter the awkward truth that Shakespeare constantly varied and remoulded the forms he worked with'.[15] Different problems are encountered by Jonathan Hope and Gordon McMullan in relation to the term 'tragicomedy'. In their introduction to *The Politics of Tragicomedy*, they observe the dependence of Renaissance critics for a 'working definition of the genre' on John Fletcher's brief prefatory address 'To the Reader', mentioned above. Critics mistakenly assume that his definition can be applied to a range of works, including Shakespeare's late plays, when in fact it is necessary to distinguish between what Fletcher identifies as 'pastoral tragicomedy' – indebted to the experiments of Guarini – and the more general Elizabethan and Jacobean use of the term 'tragicomedy' to indicate a mixed genre, one which included 'tragic and comic elements'.[16]

The problem becomes apparent as soon as we attempt to establish a definition of 'tragicomedy'. One would think that the search would be helped by the existence of contemporary definitions (no such explanations, for instance, exist for 'romance'). Indeed, we possess not only Fletcher's observation in the preface to *The Faithful Shepherdess* that '[a] tragie-comedie is not so called in respect of mirth and killing, but in respect it wants deaths, which is enough to make it no tragedy, yet brings some near it, which is enough to make it no comedy' (p. 242), but also the more detailed description by Guarini himself in *The Compendium of Tragicomic Poetry* (1599). For Guarini:

---

14. Fletcher, *The Faithful Shepherdess*, in *Select Plays*, p. 242.
15. Palmer, *Shakespeare's Later Comedies*, p. 9.
16. McMullan and Hope, *The Politics of Tragicomedy*, introduction.

he who makes a tragicomedy does not intend to compose sepa-
rately either a tragedy or a comedy, but from the two a third thing
that will be perfect of its kind and may take from the other parts
that with most verisimilitude can stand together. ... [Tragicomedy]
has two ends, the instrumental, which is the form resulting from
the imitation of tragic and comic affairs mixed together, and the
architectonic, which is to purge the mind from the evil affection of
melancholy, an end which is wholly comic and wholly simple.[17]

The absence of critical consensus concerning the interpretation of
these apparently clear definitions and their applicability to Shakespeare,
however, indicates that they are far from straightforward. While Philip
Edwards finds Guarini's definition of 'tragicomedy' a suitable model for
Shakespeare's late plays, David L. Hirst emphasises its remoteness, arguing that Shakespeare seems to aim at very different 'tragicomic' effects,
and that only *The Tempest* approximates to the Guarinian form. Moreover,
Hirst notes the differences between Fletcher and Guarini themselves. He
suggests that the influence of Guarini on Fletcher is evident in the unity
of the latter's dramatic action, but notes, too, that Fletcher took his
themes from Sidney and Spenser, suggesting that he 'was writing for a
very different kind of audience from Guarini's'.[18] In contrast again,
Barbara A. Mowat distinguishes between tragicomedy as a dramatic
form which derives from mystery and morality plays ('a form in which
the dramatic kinds are freely mixed'), a 'tragedy with a happy ending',
and the Guarinian *and* Fletcherian version, which constructs a 'third
dramatic kind'. Like Edwards, she finds that Guarini's definition offers
itself as a model by which Shakesperean tragicomedy – whether the
problem comedies or late romances – 'may be judged'.[19]

What does emerge helpfully from this contradictory advice, however,
is that the late plays are generically *mixed*, and that a tendency in that
direction is apparent – although explored differently – in Shakespeare's
earlier plays. Such a recognition is more important than trying to
establish that the plays share a set of formal features. For as Rosalie Colie
has taught us to recognise, 'generic inclusionism ... is integral to Renais-

---

17. Guarini, *The Compendium of Tragicomic Poetry*, pp. 507, 522.
18. Edwards, Ch. 7, 'Tragicomedy' in *Shakespeare: A Writer's Progress*; Hirst, *Tragicomedy*, p. 22.
19. Mowat, 'Shakesperean tragicomedy', pp. 82–3. For other discussions of tragicomedy see McMullan and Hope, introduction to *The Politics of Tragicomedy*; Maguire, *Renaissance Tragicomedy*; Riskine, *English Tragicomedy*; and Waith, *The Pattern of Tragicomedy*.

sance literary criticism'.[20] As Colie argues, mixed genres involve a way of perceiving the world, or 'mode of thought', indeed, an attempt to represent 'a collective vision', and 'culture as a whole' (pp. 19–20, 21). We might note alongside this that one of the characteristics of a mixed genre is its capacity for social 'inclusion' (what the courtier-poet Philip Sidney disparagingly observed as a tendency to 'mingl[e] kings and clowns'),[21] a recognition which invites us to pay attention to the cultural and political implications of tragicomedy, rather than its formal characteristics. Might Shakespeare's turn to 'tragicomedy' in the later 1600s be a gesture of social inclusion, or is he merely harnessing a form which is intrinsically 'royalist', a mode 'useful to Renaissance courts celebrating their own successful or hoped-for dominion over adversity'?[22] This question is relevant to that other mixed genre associated with Shakespeare's late plays: romance.

ROMANCE

Undoubtedly, 'romance' is the term most popularly attributed to the late plays, although its use is fraught with difficulties. First, it applies strictly speaking only to *Pericles, Cymbeline, The Winter's Tale* and *The Tempest*, although *The Two Noble Kinsmen* is based on a chivalric romance, Chaucer's *Knight's Tale*. Secondly, as Stanley Wells reminds us, Shakespeare never used the word 'romance' in his writings, let alone to describe the plays themselves, while the first large-scale printing of his collected works in 1623 publishes the late plays variously (and only) as 'comedies', 'histories' and 'tragedies'.[23] *The Tempest* and *The Winter's Tale* are classified as comedies, *The Famous History of King Henry the Eighth* as a 'history' and *Cymbeline* as a 'tragedy', while *Pericles* and *The Two Noble*

---

20. Colie, *The Resources of Kind*, p. 29; see also *The Tempest*, ed. Orgel, p. 4: '[t]o find a new category for a play was not, for the Renaissance critic, to abandon the old ones. J. C. Scaliger describes the *Oresteia* as both tragedy and comedy; analogously, the Quarto of *Troilus and Cressida* declares it witty "as the best comedy in Terence or Plautus", while the Folio editors included the play among the tragedies'. Also cited in *The Winter's Tale*, ed. Orgel, p. 3.

21. Sidney, *Apology for Poetry*, p. 135. See Hall, who notes from the evidence of the preface to *The Faithfull Shepherdess* that for Fletcher 'tragicomedy is a form in which one can mix people of various social stations and still keep decorum' (*Renaissance Literary Criticism*, p. 182), and Yoch on Guarini's comparison of tragicomedy to a republic ('The Renaissance dramatization of temperance', p. 115).

22. See also Potter, '"True tragicomedies"', p. 198, and Yoch, 'The Renaissance dramatization of temperance', p. 116.

23. Wells, 'Shakespeare and romance', p. 49.

Kinsmen are conspicuous by their absence. Thirdly, romance connotes not just an historical kind, but, as Northrop Frye has argued, a distinct artistic phase or 'tendency' which is informed by an understanding not just of the 'ordinary cycle of nature' but of the 'nature God intended man to live in', and which was lost after the Fall – 'a world of perpetual fertility where it was spring and autumn at once'.[24] Unsurprisingly, one recent editor of *The Winter's Tale* and *The Tempest* is distinctly uneasy with the term romance, conscious as he is of its debt to this 'Romantic' tradition.[25] Yet 'romance' is still a useful description of some of these plays when understood as an historical mode, for it links the plays to the prose romances of the 1580s and 1590s, such as Sidney's *Arcadia* (from which Shakespeare borrowed the plot for *King Lear*), Spenser's *The Faerie Queene* and Robert Greene's *Menaphon* and *Pandosto* (the source for *The Winter's Tale*), and to the heroic romance dramas popular in the public theatres, such as *Sir Clyomon and Sir Clamydes*, *George a Greene*, *The Rare Triumphs of Love and Fortune* and *Mucedorus*.

Howard Felperin comes close to capturing the spirit of the term 'romance' when he describes it broadly as 'a success story in which difficulties of any number of kinds are overcome, and a tall story in which they are overcome against impossible odds or by miraculous means'.[26] Romance, though, can also be understood as a series of motifs and patterns of action. In Shakespeare's late plays many of these derive from Greek romance, and they include a sense of a higher power organising the action, the breakdown – and reunion – of family units, and the eventual recovery of royal daughters and preservation of a dynastic line.[27]

---

24. Frye, *A Natural Perspective*, p. 136. See esp. Frye's discussion of the masque at IV, i, in *The Tempest*, which he claims states fully the concerns of Shakesperean romance, presenting a vision of a new world 'where there is a *ver perpetuum*, where spring and autumn exist together'. In this moment, 'ordinary experience disappears', reality and illusion are finally separated, and 'masque time has become the rhythm of existence, the recovery by man of the energy of nature' (*A Natural Perspective*, p. 157).

25. Orgel prefers to identify *The Tempest* and *The Winter's Tale* simply as 'tragicomedies'. For him, romance is an 'invented … category' which springs from our belief 'that certain kinds of seriousness are inappropriate to comedy and because we are made uncomfortable by the late plays' commitment to non-realistic modes'. It is notable, though, that his understanding of romance derives entirely from the nineteenth-century tradition: he cites Coleridge's identification of *The Tempest* as a romance in his 'Notes on *The Tempest*', and calls attention to Dowden's first naming of *Pericles*, *Cymbeline*, *The Winter's Tale* and *The Tempest* as 'romances' (*The Tempest*, ed. Orgel, p. 5). The same discussion can be found in *The Winter's Tale*, ed. Orgel, pp. 2–5.

26. Felperin, *Shakespearean Romance*, p. 10.

27. See Wells, 'Shakespeare and romance', pp. 50ff.

But we need to remember, too, that romance involves a way of seeing the world — what Colie calls 'a mode of thought' — and that for many readers its emphasis on dynastic triumph and its celebration of an innately virtuous nobility make it an appropriate vehicle for specifically 'aristocratic' values. This is evident, for example, in Sidney's *Arcadia*, which seems to affirm the 'natural' superiority of its two princely protagonists, Pyrocles and Musidorus. In one incident, Musidorus, disguised as a shepherd, is pitted against his clownish 'master', the herdsman Dametas, in a jousting exercise. His beloved Pamela retells the story:

> O how mad a sight it was to see Dametas, like rich tissue furred with lamb-skins! But O, how well it did with [Musisdorus], to see with what a grace he presented himself before me on horseback, making majesty wait upon humbleness … in effect so did he command [his horse] as his own limbs; for though he had both spurs and wand, they seemed rather the marks of sovereignty than instruments of punishment … The sport was to see Dametas, how he was tossed from the saddle to the mane of the horse and thence to the ground, giving his gay apparel almost as foul an outside as it had inside.[28]

Despite his disguise, Musidorus' native nobility shines through. His horsemanship proclaims not just his actual social status (after all, as a herdsman Dametas is unlikely to be practised in this art), but his natural authority, that is, his ability to master his passions (represented here by his horse). In contrast, the foolish Dametas manages only to confirm that he is truly 'foul' *and* subordinate.[29]

The description of four of the late plays as romances, then, might appear to support the popular view that they constitute 'courtly' or 'aristocratic' drama. Yet romance does not perceive its social world in any simple sense. Colie's characterisation of genre as a 'mode of thought' allows us to perceive how romance itself can be 'thoughtful' and self-reflective, and even view its world from a variety of perspectives. A romance might 'view state affairs from below' as with *George a Greene the Pinner of Wakefield* (1590), or Robert Greene's prose fictions.[30] Equally, it might explore familiar topoi, or offer an appraisal of its social and

---

28. Sidney, *Arcadia*, pp. 247–8.
29. See also the use of mummerset to distinguish 'low' characters in *Sir Clyomon and Sir Clamydes*.
30. Gibbons, 'Romance and the heroic play', pp. 225ff. We are grateful to Katherine Wilson for sharing some of her ideas on Robert Greene with us.

political milieu. In 'The Legend of Courtesy' (*The Faerie Queene*, Book VI), Spenser offers contradictory attitudes towards innate nobility, as if this issue were being debated in the course of the narrative journey.[31] In much the same way, Shakespeare also engages with the generic conventions he inherits, rather than following a set of rules. In particular, we might want to ask of his late plays whether they affirm the familiar romance topos that beauty is a guide to moral integrity and social status. After all, characters such as Cloten in *Cymbeline* and Autolycus in *The Winter's Tale* repeatedly remind us to distrust outward show and perceived social status.

THE POLITICS OF STAGING

Shakespeare's supposed 'late' attachment to the court has had a major influence on, and in turn been influenced by, discussions of staging. In particular, the growing importance of the 'private' hall stages (as opposed to the 'public' amphitheatres, such as the Globe) has been regarded as crucial in determining a stylistic and theatrical shift to appeal to a coterie audience. Knowledge of court performances for *The Winter's Tale*, *Cymbeline*, *The Tempest* and *Cardenio*, reinforced by the presumed influence of masques (in features such as Prospero's masque, the potential allusion to *Oberon* in *The Winter's Tale* (IV, iv, 332), and the spectacular, 'masquelike' staging of Posthumus's vision (*Cymbeline*, V, iii)), has been used to further this argument, as have Shakespeare's collaborations with John Fletcher, seen as one of the new dramatists of the coterie tradition. In turn, more historicist critics suggest that the impact of royal incorporation on the King's Men (and on other theatre companies such as the Admiral's Men) was to confirm a growing court and elite influence on the late plays.[32] Shakespeare's own position as a 'Groom of the Chamber' and his later self-gentrification have been seen to confirm this transformation of Elizabethan vagabond players into royal servants and mouthpieces.[33]

31. In one instance, the narrator moralises that 'For a man by nothing is so well bewrayd, / As by his manners, in which plaine is showne / Of what degree and what race he is growne', but he proceeds to offer the story of a 'lusty' knight who, 'though meaner borne, / And of lesse livelihood and hability, / Yet full of valour, the which did adorne / His meanesse much' (*Faerie Queene*, VI, iii, 1, Book VI, iii, 7).
32. See Gurr, *The Shakespearian Playing Companies*, pp. 114–15 and 122–36, for a more nuanced account.
33. Orgel mistakes Shakespeare for a Gentleman of the Chamber (*The Tempest*, ed. Orgel, p. 43). For a critique of this perspective see Holderness *et al.*, *Shakespeare Out of Court*, pp. 129–35.

Although this trend, conflating historical, theatrical and interpretative criticism, began with figures such as A. H. Thorndike, E. E. Stoll and H. Granville-Barker in the early twentieth century, it received major impetus with Bentley's 'Shakespeare and the Blackfriars Theatre', which argued that the opening of the new, smaller, indoor, 'private' theatre in the Blackfriars gave a new direction to Shakespeare's writing.[34] The most extreme version of this argument is offered by Gary Schmidgall, who distinguishes between *Pericles* (performed at the Globe), 'intended for the delight of what Jonson called "grounded judgements"', and the courtly 'high aesthetic' of *The Two Noble Kinsmen* (performed at Blackfriars).[35]

Such approaches can be challenged, especially as work on the constituent elements (staging, history and interpretation) have refashioned our sense of Jacobean theatre. The studies of Andrew Gurr and Martin Butler have questioned the idea of a coterie or privileged audience divided off from the popular amphitheatre tradition.[36] Both have demonstrated the longevity of socially mixed audiences in the amphitheatres and of a popular tradition which thrived in both amphitheatre and hall theatre. Moreover, many of the staging devices formerly attributed to court influence, especially through the masque, have been shown to be the product of commercial staging technique rather than masque machines. Equally, although we know that the Blackfriars was smaller in its capacity (about 700–800 seated as opposed to 2,500–3,000 seated and standing at the Globe) and probably created a more intimate space with gallants seated on stage and the auditorium more a curved u-shape than an oblong, such spatial arrangements may have increased the radical impact of texts transferred from the public stage.[37] Thus, in the case of *The Tempest*, as Gurr points out, much of the effect of the play derives from the explosive introduction of large-scale public stage effects into the smaller auditorium, shattering decorum and conventions, literary and social.[38]

In particular, in the case of the late plays, *Pericles* predates any move to the Blackfriars, while *The Winter's Tale*, *Cymbeline* and *Henry VIII* are known to have been staged at the Globe, although it is likely that all the late plays were played at both houses, with only *The Two Noble Kinsmen* attributed solely to the Blackfriars (due to the 1613 burning of the

34. Bentley, 'Shakespeare and the Blackfriars Theatre'.
35. Schmidgall, *Shakespeare and the Courtly Aesthetic*, pp. 114–15.
36. Butler, *Theatre and Crisis*, Appendix II, and Gurr, *Playgoing in Shakespeare's London*.
37. For the Blackfriars, see Gurr, *The Shakespearean Stage, 1574–1642*, pp. 154–64, and Orrell, *The Human Stage*, Ch. 12.
38. Gurr, 'The *Tempest*'s tempest at the Blackfriars'.

Globe). Moreover, even though *The Winter's Tale*, *Cymbeline*, *The Tempest* and *Cardenio* all received court stagings in the mid-Jacobean period, the idea of a *specific* court staging style is highly problematic, given that there were as many as three royal households mounting plays in different locations. Even within the purlieu of James VI and I's household, the Twelfth Night masques and associated plays could be mounted in any number of locations, ranging from the Banqueting Hall at Whitehall to Wilton House in Wiltshire, or other spaces in other palaces, such as the Hall at Hampton Court. Spaces and resources would vary in each of these places, so the key word was adaptability rather than a homogeneous style. Additionally, recent historical scholarship has contrasted the diversity of James VI and I's court with that of his predecessors,[39] and many of the aesthetic policies, such as the pursuit of classicism, which have been associated with Jacobean absolutism can be shown to be generated by the aristocratic grandees and factions as much as by the crown.[40]

Similarly, we need to question the quasi-materialist conception of patronage as central to the production of culture, which underpins 'elitist' readings of the plays. Patronage was not simply power diffused downwards, it was a transaction dependent upon the exchange of power, gifts, favours, benefits and material objects, and involved a complex web of mutual bonds, duties and rights. Of course, patronage was not an ideal relation, and it may have operated ultimately to serve the patron, but this advantage often had to be achieved through complex negotiations and manoeuvrings which shaped and defined patterns of behaviour. Quite simply, to be a King's Man does not establish that Shakespeare was solely the cultural servant of the king.

The diversity within seventeenth-century culture, which encompassed a wider range of class, regional and gendered voices than we realise, means that plays sought to appeal to a broad cross-section of society. The implications of this imperative are neatly illustrated in Dekker's spoof courtesy-manual, *The Gull's Horn-Book* (1609):

> The theatre is your poet's Royal Exchange upon which thrive their Muses – that are now turned to merchants – meeting, barter away that light commodity for a lighter ware than words – plaudits … Players are their factors who put away the stuff and make the best of it they possibly can … Your gallant, your courtier and your captain had wont to be the soundest paymasters … when your

39. Smuts, 'Cultural diversity and cultural change', pp. 104–5
40. See Gent, *Albion's Classicism*.

> groundling and gallery commoner buys his sport by the penny and like a haggler is glad to utter it again by retailing.[41]

The passage not only shows the social heterogeneity of many audiences but how the shift from elite patronage and markets ('paymasters') to a more plebeian commercialism (a 'factor' was a merchant) was recognised. The passage strikingly evokes the fluidity of the social and cultural interaction that occurs within theatre, making it a 'Royal Exchange' (just like Gresham's Royal Exchange in Cornhill Street). This quality of exchange makes theatre one of the most important institutions in early modern London, not just because of the economic forces implicit in 'exchange', but because it involves a variety of different kinds of transaction, especially between spoken and written cultures, between audiences made up of spectators and auditors.

Finally, the emphasis on spectators in late plays' criticism has usually been designed to highlight their exclusivity, yet the visual is as much associated with popular theatre as with court aesthetics. Thus *Henry VIII* with its complex stage pageants looks back to Elizabethan popular theatre and its pageantry, while moments such as the vision in *Cymbeline*, in its metrical use of fourteeners, have an archaic and nostalgic quality. Rather than simply seeing the spectacular staging as a sign of vapid courtly interests, we should recognise, as contemporaries did, that spectacle might operate in different ways, either *exclusively*, as in the Jonsonian masque, or more *inclusively*, as part of a wider public discourse which itself belonged to the emblematic and visual culture of the period. Such a distinction is made by Jonson himself in *The Magnificent Entertainment*:

> it is to be noted, that the *Symboles* vsed, are not, neither ought to be, simply *Hieroglyphickes*, *Emblemes* or *Impreses*, but a mixed character, partaking somewhat of all, and peculiarly apted to these more magnificent Inuentions: wherein, the garments and ensignes deliuer the nature of the person, and the word the present office. Neither was it becoming ... the dignitie of these shewes (after the most miserable shift of the Puppits) to require a Truch-man, or ... one to write, *This is a Dog*; or, *This is a Hare*: but so to be presented, as vpon the view, they might, without cloud, or obscuritie, declare themselues to the sharpe and learned: And for the multitude, no doubt but their grounded iudgements did gaze, said it was fine, and were satisfied.[42]

---

41. Cited in McLuskie, 'The poets' Royal Exchange', p. 53.
42. Jonson, *The Magnificent Entertainment*, ll. 253–67, in *Ben Jonson*, vol. VII.

This differentiation *within* spectacle, between Jonson's learned symbolism and the 'debased' iconography used by his collaborators (the popular dramatists Dekker and Middleton), is compared to what Jonson regarded as the lowest form of popular entertainment, the puppet show. Spectacle need not belong to the court; if the writers choose, it can be understood by the 'multitude'.

This distinction within spectacle, which allows it may operate to include as much as exclude, can fruitfully be associated with the verbal dimension of the late plays. As Andrew Gurr has noted, 'there is no English term which acknowledges the full experience of both hearing and seeing the complete "action" of a play', but this absence itself is suggestive of two different emphases within early modern drama, on the 'auditor' and the 'spectator'.[43] Like 'spectacle' and spectatorship the concepts of the 'audience' and 'auditors' can operate to include or exclude, so that a non-literate or semi-literate audience can hear rehearsed the kind of argument it cannot read. Theatre, literally, acts as an exchange between oral and written cultures. In the case of the late plays, where so much critical emphasis has been placed upon spectacle and emotion at the expense of 'argument', it is important to recognise their commitment to such 'exchange', and to emphasise, too, their engagement with ideas and their deployment of rhetoric – the very things which might appeal to their 'auditors'.

WHAT'S PAST IS PROLOGUE: NEW READINGS OF SHAKESPEARE'S LATE PLAYS

The essays which appear in this collection are inevitably indebted to the rich and complex critical tradition prompted by the late plays. Yet they also offer new emphases. Our 'late' plays are not just 'mystical' reflections on the cyclical patterns of the natural world, or spectacular celebrations of the Jacobean state. Indeed for us, their 'planes of reality' are properly sublunary, and they are deeply interested in issues of rhetoricity and interpretation, which in turn inform their engagement with Jacobean ideology. Many of the essays in this collection, then, offer new cultural and intellectual contexts to the plays. In 'Pericles and the Pox', for instance, Margaret Healy explores this play's representations of early modern syphilis as a vehicle for a critique of James's arrangement of political marriages, while in 'Postcolonial Shakespeare' Willy Maley

---

43. Gurr, *Playgoing in Shakespeare's London*, p. 86.

explores a less critical *Cymbeline* as a 'nativity' play, which deals with the 'birth of Britain' as it struggles to throw off, and assume in a new form, Roman (Catholic) imperialism. In contrast again, Gordon McMullan explores representations of manliness and mannerliness in *Henry VIII* as a background to a critique of Henry as an 'intemperate monarch', and Alan Stewart asks us in '"Near akin"' to consider *The Two Noble Kinsmen* through the conflict between classical-humanist and chivalric modes of male friendship and the realities of complex kinship relations in Jacobean England: *The Two Noble Kinsmen* is not a failed play about 'idealised male friendship', he argues, but a play about 'a failed attempt at male friendship'. With a different emphasis, James Knowles questions the presumed courtly style of the late plays, and explores the different debts of Prospero's masque in *The Tempest* to the public theatre and to the independent tradition of aristocratic masque.

Other contributors emphasise the plays' interest in rhetoric and hermeneutics. Helen Hackett picks up the plays' generic self-consciousness in '"Gracious be the issue"', when she explores how their evocation of 'maternity' often appears 'as a metaphor for a distinctive kind of narrative': tragicomic romance. In a different way, Alison Thorne notes in "To write and read / Be henceforth treacherous" that *Cymbeline* is acutely concerned with issues of interpretation, and 'reflects ironically on the question of its own illegibility'. Thomas Healy questions the extent to which 'all is true' in *Henry VIII*, and suggests that the play participates in a Reformation debate about the uses (and interpretation) of history. On his view, *Henry VIII* is part of a sceptical and interrogative public discourse, not an affirmation of royalist historiography. Gareth Roberts also develops such sceptical implications, considering how *The Winter's Tale* and *The Tempest* both celebrate and demystify the idea of magic and illusion, while Jennifer Richards explores how Shakespeare's invocation of the experience of being 'outside' and 'inside' in *The Winter's Tale* invites us to reflect more carefully on its presumed courtly elitism or exclusivity.

Yet perhaps the most contentious inclusion in this collection is Fletcher's and Shakespeare's *Cardenio*.[44] Although this play is 'lost', so that any discussion remains to some extent speculative, the availability of Lewis Theobald's *Double Falshood*, published in 1728 and claimed as a reworked version of Shakespeare and Fletcher's play, raises unexpected

---

44. See Wells and Taylor, *Textual Companion*, p. 132 for a discussion of the textual status of *Cardenio*.

implications for the 'closure' of the Shakespeare canon.[45] Like other 'lost' plays, such as *Love's Labour's Won*, this text offers a tantalising version of another Shakespeare beyond the one we know, and invites us to reconsider the shape of the canon and its relation to our perception of his career. In particular, the darker mood of *Cardenio*, apparent too in *Henry VIII* and *The Two Noble Kinsmen*, encourages us to place a new emphasis on the pessimism of the 'last' plays, while the inclusion of such an 'unstable' text discourages a different kind of speculation concerning Shakespeare's 'final' gesture.

CARDENIO AND DOUBLE FALSHOOD

Many scholars have regarded *Double Falshood* as simply another eighteenth-century forgery, but there has been a strong counter-tradition which has characterised the text as an authentic, if mangled, redaction of the lost *Cardenio*. As Kenneth Muir has argued, if Theobald's story about his ownership of three manuscripts of the play can be verified then 'there would be strong reason to believe that *Double Falshood* was a debased version of *Cardenio*, and equally strong reasons for believing that the original authors were Shakespeare and Fletcher. With few exceptions, critics have endeavoured to escape from this conclusion.'[46] Since the late 1980s interest in *Cardenio* has gradually grown, with prominent discussions in the Oxford *Shakespeare* and Gary Taylor's attempted reconstruction of an acting version of the play.[47]

In Theobald's version Henriquez (son of Duke Angelo), having raped Violante (I, iii; II, ii), falls in love with his friend Julio's beloved, Leonora. Although her father coerces her into the match (II, iii), Julio interrupts the ceremony (III, i; III, ii) and Leonora, who had planned to commit suicide, faints and later conceals herself in a nunnery (III, ii). Julio goes insane seeking vengeance against his former friend (IV, i), while the ravaged Violante exiles herself, disguised as a boy, amongst the shepherds

---

45. Although the play was entered in the *Stationers' Register* in 1653 by the bookseller Humphrey Moseley as 'The History of Cardenio, by Mr. Fletcher & Shakespeare', the text disappeared: see Freehafer, '*Cardenio*, by Shakespeare and Fletcher', pp. 501–3. Theobald's text is a revision of a Restoration stage version of a Jacobean original.
46. Muir, *Shakespeare as Collaborator*, p. 159.
47. Wells and Taylor, *Complete Works* (also *Textual Companion*). In a recent popular summary of Shakespeare scholarship Jonathan Bate discerns traces of 'the faint cry of a Shakespeare and Fletcher original trapped below the layers of rewriting' (*Genius of Shakespeare*, pp. 75–81, 81). It is possible that a version of *Cardenio* may be edited for Arden 3.

in the wilds (III, iii). Mistaken for a boy, she is almost raped again (IV, i). Roderick, the virtuous brother of Henriquez, is persuaded by him to help abduct Leonora (using the hearse), but his plans are frustrated when he is denounced to Roderick by the two women (V, ii). The play concludes when Henriquez repents and marries Violante, while Julio (having regained his sanity) marries Leonora.

The most intriguing aspect of this version of the Cardenio story lies in the name changes, as Cardenio becomes Julio, and Cervantes' villain Don Fernando becomes Henriquez, while many of the complex layers of irony and the inset narrative are stripped out from the Spanish version. Despite this there are strong parallels between the plot structure of the play and *Two Noble Kinsmen*, for instance in the rejection of Violante (Dorothea in Cervantes) due to her low birth, which matches the Jailer's daughter's situation, and the madness of both Julio (Cardenio) and the daughter have many resonances (see Julia Briggs, pp. 221–2 below).[48]

Even in the mangled form the text does have some remarkable echoes.[49] The play clearly relates to the 'broken nuptials' genre, while links to *The Winter's Tale*, *Cymbeline* and *All's Well* can also be found.[50] In terms of the play's style it appears to fall into two parts, with Acts I and II more pronouncedly Shakespearean, and Acts IV and V particularly close to Fletcher's style, which was more likely to survive Restoration and eighteenth-century 'improvement'.[51] Many passages seem to relate

---

48. Frey, "'O sacred, shadowy, cold and constant queen'", esp. pp. 309–11, explores the plot similarities.

49. The most problematic aspect of *Double Falshood* lies in the provenance of the text. As Muir notes, if indeed Theobald can be trusted about his ownership of three copies of the play then the claims must be taken seriously, and John Freehafer has shown the likelihood not only that Theobald owned these manuscripts, but that his connections would have given him access to the right circles, where such materials might have descended from the King's Men or from those connected to Restoration theatre (Freehafer, '*Cardenio*, by Shakespeare and Fletcher', pp. 502–3). Moreover, the gradual rehabilitation of Theobald's reputation as a Shakespearean scholar (see Seary, *Lewis Theobald*) has also encouraged scholars to reconsider the authenticity of *Double Falshood*, and, indeed, perhaps most tellingly, as Muir noted, forgery by Theobald based on knowledge of Moseley's *Stationers' Register* entry seems unlikely as, logically, he would have used the entry to support his claims of the authenticity of the play (instead Theobald tried to deny that Fletcher had a hand in the text). It is the appearance of a text, however mutilated, attributed to Shakespeare at a point when his collaborations were unrecognised and the existence of *Cardenio* unknown, which makes the possibility that *Double Falshood* embodies the ghost of Shakespeare and Fletcher's play so likely.

50. Leech, *The John Fletcher Plays*, pp. 152–3.

51. Kukowski, 'The hand', pp. 81–9.

to Shakespearean lines, and Muir isolates several examples in I, i, and I, ii, which are 'either Shakespearian or remarkably good imitation'.[52] Equally striking are the parallels with Fletcher's work.[53] Indeed, beyond these general similarities with the other last plays, *Double Falshood*'s language supports the idea of a Jacobean ur-text beneath the layers. For instance, the play follows Shelton's translation of *Don Quixote* down to the verbal details,[54] and Kenneth Muir highlighted the use of 'absonism' as 'the kind of word [Shakespeare] did use in his late period'.[55] Recent studies which explore the use of non-stylistic linguistic markers provide further support for the presence of two hands in the play, with traces of Shakespearean influence most clearly found in I, ii, and up to II, ii, and Fletcherian parallels clearest in II, iii, IV, i, and V, ii.[56]

Two essays in this volume approach the issue of *Double Falshood/ Cardenio* from different positions. Richard Wilson seeks to place the play within its Jacobean context of 1611–13, specifically the tensions between Prince Henry and King James, along with the mourning which accompanied the prince's death, which was intermingled with celebrations of the marriage of Princess Elizabeth to the Elector Palatine. Using Theobald's text directly and treating it as *Cardenio*, Wilson traces the tragicomic aspects of the play to the mood of this period, and the intrigue brewing around Frances Howard. In contrast Julia Briggs examines the continuities and, indeed, the discontinuities with other plays in the canon. Briggs locates a growing mood of pessimism in the last plays, which differentiates *Cardenio*, *All Is True (Henry VIII)* and *The Two Noble Kinsmen* from the 'earlier' late plays (*Cymbeline*, *The Tempest* and *The*

52. In I, i, the punning on 'weighing ... unweighed course' (p. 2), Julio's speech 'Urge not suspicion ... Freedom quit me' (I, ii; p. 6) and 'I do not see ... one constant Heat' (I, ii; p. 5).
53. Kukowski, 'The hand', pp. 81–2 and 89. Muir, *Shakespeare as Collaborator*, p. 153, notes the similarity of Violante's plaint (IV, ii; p. 49) and Apsatia's speech in *The Maid's Tragedy*, IV, ii. Of course, reading *Double Falshood* may prompt us to ponder how much of the original was Shakespearean: it is interesting to note that in 1653 Fletcher was listed as the first author.
54. Freehafer, '*Cardenio*, by Shakespeare and Fletcher', pp. 501–2. Thus verbs like 'bobb'd' (V, ii; p. 59) highlighted by Richard Wilson in his essay (p. 204) may be echoes of the Shelton text beneath the layers of the revised *Cardenio*. 'Bob' can mean 'to deceive' (OED 1), 'to mock' (1c), 'to strike' (2) and 'to fish for' (OED 4). Shelton is cited at OED 2, although the implication in V, ii; p. 59, seems to be more sexual.
55. Functional transformations of nouns to verbs like 'heirs' in *Double Falsehood* (I, i; p. 2) can be compared to 'urned' in *The Two Noble Kinsmen*, I, ii, 44. OED cites Chapman's *Illiads* (1611) as the earliest use of 'heirs', which given the likely date for *Cardenio* presents an interesting coincidence.
56. Hope, *The Authorship of Shakespeare's Plays*, p. 100.

Winter's Tale). Although she places less reliance on Theobald's text of *Double Falshood*, looking back at Shelton's translation for guidance about the likely shape of *Cardenio*, she also highlights the strange mixed mood of the play and the hearse trick, but rather as a recurrent idea also traceable in *The Two Noble Kinsmen* and the nuptials interrupted by funerals, and in the brutality of *Henry VIII* with its unresolvable marital tensions. For her, *The Two Noble Kinsmen* extends elements inherent in *Cardenio* but encompasses a bleak vision of a world of 'uncomprehending submission' in which 'For what we lack / We laugh, for what we have are sorry' (*The Two Noble Kinsmen*, V, iv, 132–3).

PART I

MATERNITY AND MANLINESS

1

'GRACIOUS BE THE ISSUE': MATERNITY AND NARRATIVE IN SHAKESPEARE'S LATE PLAYS

Helen Hackett

The fact that maternity is a theme and a problem in Shakespeare's late plays has often been recognised. The most obvious instances are the very visible on-stage presence in *The Winter's Tale* of the heavily pregnant body of Hermione, and the birth of Marina to Thaisa at sea in *Pericles*. *The Winter's Tale*'s final regenerative Acts also offer the persistent celebration of 'great creating nature' (IV, iv, 88). Even plays where mothers are physically absent share with all the late plays a persistent invocation of mothers, both in person and through imagery. In *The Tempest*, for instance, Miranda's mother is a significant guarantor of identity and inherited chastity – 'Thy mother was a piece of virtue, and / She said thou wast my daughter' (I, ii, 56–7). She is opposed to another dead mother, Sycorax, from whom Caliban derives his claim and his unregeneracy, and whose frequent naming makes her a shadow which haunts the play. In *The Two Noble Kinsmen*, not only does Emilia repeatedly worry that the combat between Palamon and Arcite will bereave at least one mother and draw maternal curses upon her (III, vi, 245; IV, ii, 4–6), but, as Walter Cohen has noted, the final scenes are fraught with imagery of sexuality and reproduction.[1] This is especially striking since these scenes have a predominantly tragic tone, deploying tropes of fertility to express grief and loss: the combat reaches a 'consummation'

---

1. *The Norton Shakespeare*, gen. ed. Greenblatt, p. 3198.

fulfilling Emilia's fears that 'Palamon would miscarry', and Hippolyta's eye 'conceives a tear, / The which it will deliver' (V, v, 94, 101, 137–8).

Such use of maternal imagery to heighten moments of distress, and the fact that mothers are so often dead or believed dead in these plays, has raised difficult questions as to how far the maternal is being celebrated, falling in with the general theme of rebirth, and how far it is being repressed or excluded. Pericles, on recovering the mother, Thaisa, in the daughter, Marina, declares that 'I am great with woe, and shall deliver weeping' (xxi, 95). Cymbeline, at the restoration of his three lost children, asks: 'O, what am I? / A mother to the birth of three? Ne'er mother / Rejoiced deliverance more' (V, vi, 370–2). Prospero describes how, when tossed on the sea with the baby Miranda, he wept and 'Under my burden groaned' (The Tempest, I, ii, 156). Henry VIII laments that his 'issue's fail' has given him 'Many a groaning throe' (II, iv, 195–6). In all these crucial and climactic scenes the central male protagonist and authority-figure appropriates the maternal to express the heightened emotion at a turning point between grief and joy.

A question this provokes is whether identification with the maternal role by male protagonists serves to venerate the maternal or to repress it. Primarily negative interpretations of maternity in the late plays have been advanced, from different perspectives, by Janet Adelman and Richard Wilson. For Adelman, using a psychoanalytic approach, the figuration of mothers throughout Shakespeare's works is punitive, epitomised by Hamlet: the problematic maternal body is 'made into a monster or a saint, killed off or banished from the stage', yet 'remains at the center of masculine subjectivity, marking its unstable origin'. Adelman sees the romances in terms of a schematised response to this psychic problem: 'the sanctified mother who can bless is recovered in Thaisa and Hermione, the witch-mother reemerges in Cymbeline's Queen and in Sycorax'.[2] Meanwhile Richard Wilson, taking a historicist approach, has valuably shown how the late plays' emphasis on maternity foregrounds the dependence of identification of the father upon women's unverifiable reports, and coincides with movements to take midwifery out of the realm of women and folklore and into the realm of men and empirical science.[3]

While recognising that a foregrounding of the maternal may speak as much of masculine anxiety as of celebration, it is worth remembering that, even from a feminocentric point of view, motherhood and birth

2. Adelman, Suffocating Mothers, pp. 36–7.
3. Wilson, 'Observations on English bodies'.

can connote not only joy and hope but also possible mortality and tragedy. This remains true today, but of course had even more force in the early modern period. Childbirth was a charged moment in that it not only potentially brought forth life, but was also quite likely to bring the death of the mother and/or the child, or to produce the profoundly feared result of a malformed baby. Autolycus' pack of ballads satirically reminds us of this even in the middle of the fertility-celebrating shepherds' feast:

> Here's one to a very doleful tune, how a usurer's wife was brought to bed of twenty money-bags at a burden, and how she longed to eat adders' heads and toads carbonadoed ... Here's the midwife's name to't. (*The Winter's Tale*, IV, iv, 260–6)

This is clearly an absurd and far-fetched tale, yet it draws directly upon a thriving Elizabethan and Jacobean tradition of ballads about 'monstrous' births. The Huth collection at the British Library contains a number of such broadsides from the 1560s, including accounts of a child born with slanting eyes, pointed ears, and a frill around its neck; another born with 'Ruffes' of flesh around the neck; a pair of Siamese twins; a baby boy born with no hands, feet, tongue or penis; and another with 'the left leg growing upward toward the head, and the ryght leg bending toward the left leg, the foote therof growinge into the buttocke of the said left leg'.[4] Each of these asserts itself as a 'true description', supplied with exact details of date, place, parents and sometimes witnesses. The same formulae are used for descriptions of deformed pigs or of 'a marveilous straunge Fishe' caught in the English Channel, filed alongside in the Huth collection;[5] all alike are 'monsters', sententiously interpreted in the accompanying ballads as warnings from God. Grotesque woodcut illustrations are given; as one ballad has it:

> No Carver can, nor Paynter maye
> The same so ougly make

---

4. John D., *A Description of a Monstrous Chylde* (1562) [Huth 50/33]; H. B., *The True Discription of a Childe with Ruffes* (1566) [Huth 50/34]; John Mellys, *The True Description of Two Monstrous Children* (1566) [Huth 50/35]; Anon., *The True Reporte of the Forme and Shape of a Monstrous Childe* (1562) [Huth 50/36]; Anon., *The Forme and Shape of a Monstrous Child* (1568) [Huth 50/38].

5. W[illiam] F[ullwood], *The Shape of Two Monsters* (1562) [Huth 50/37]; Anon., *The Description of a Monstrous Pig* (1562) [Huth 50/39]; C. R., *The True Description of this Marueilous Straunge Fishe* (1569) [Huth 50/41]; I. P., *A Meruaylous Straunge Deformd Swyne* (n.d. [?1570]) [Huth 50/42].

As doeth it self shewe at this daye
A sight to make the quake.

But here thou haste by Printing arte
A signe therof to se
Let eche man saye within his harte
It preacheth now, to me.[6]

In some of the accounts the baby died a few hours after birth; in others, like that of the boy born without hands, feet, penis or tongue, he is reported to be feeding vigorously, 'And at the makynge hereof was living, and like to continue'.[7]

While these broadsides present their contents as occasions for wonder, horror and moral reflection, behind that very horror and reflection lies the essential appalling truth that any pregnancy might potentially produce malformed, damaged or lifeless offspring. David Cressy has written of how sixteenth- and seventeenth-century religious services for the 'churching' of new mothers were concerned less with purification, as is often supposed, than with thanksgiving for a successful outcome:

> The service announced the woman's deliverance and preservation from 'the great danger of child-birth'. Its words, including the majestic Psalm 121 – 'I have lifted up mine eyes unto the hills, from whence cometh my help' – have more to do with survival than cleansing.[8]

Ulinka Rublack, in a study of pregnancy and childbirth in early modern Germany, has similarly concluded that these 'were highly unstable and risky processes for mother and child – "rough passages" indeed. The threat of death was closely linked to the ability to give life.'[9] Rublack's legal source material includes two cases of 'monstrous' births, one attributed to a shock to the mother-to-be, the other to the cursing and beating of the pregnant woman by her drunken husband (pp. 95–6, 100). Further cases show an awareness that child-bearing could be made to go tragically wrong by imprisonment or other forms of political or legal persecution: cases manifesting the vulnerability of pregnant women to such fear and anxiety imposed by external authorities 'generated statements about the role of force in marital, social and political relationships:

6. John D., *A Description of a Monstrous Chylde*.
7. Anon., *The True Reporte of the Forme and Shape of a Monstrous Childe*.
8. Cressy, 'Purification', p. 119.
9. Rublack, 'Pregnancy', p. 109.

they affected attitudes, diversely, to the execution of justice and to husbands' abuse' (pp. 109–10). This bears fascinatingly upon Leontes' role in *The Winter's Tale* as simultaneously abusive husband, unjust judge and tyrannical monarch to Hermione immediately before and after she gives birth, and its tragic consequences; and upon the general use of motifs of maternity in the late plays as not simply an incorporation of feminine forces, but an index of the propriety of masculine behaviour in both husbands and rulers.

Helen Wilcox's reading of Shakespeare's tragicomedies – both the problem plays and the late plays – foregrounds the extent to which these texts show maternity as a hazardous and obstructed process. She concludes that it is exactly its mingling of regenerative and tragic potential that makes maternity central to Shakespeare's blend of apparently opposing genres:

> motherhood in early modern England consisted of many paradoxes, relating to chastity and fertility, absence and presence, life-threatening and life-giving qualities. Thus it is entirely apt that maternity should epitomize the paradoxical complexity of the tragic/comic mix in these plays, and exemplify a genre which brings both death and new life into its cycle of action.[10]

In brief, she suggests that we can usefully think of tragicomedy as a maternal genre.

Thus maternity in the late plays can be considered not merely in terms of the presence or absence of maternal characters, but as a metaphor for their distinctive kind of narrative. In fact it is striking how often within the plays maternal metaphors are used for narrative itself. The word 'issue' is insistently repeated, signifying both children and narrative outcome.[11] Antigonus mistakenly designates Perdita 'the issue / Of King Polixenes', and Polixenes laments that his actual 'issue', Florizel, has not proved gracious (*The Winter's Tale*, III, iii, 42–3; IV, ii, 26). Cymbeline greets his lost sons with the question 'How, my issue?' (V, vi, 333). But alongside these are numerous examples of the term in relation to narrative event and consequence: in *The Winter's Tale*, Hermione's waiting woman Emilia expects 'a thriving issue' of Paulina's goodness (II, ii, 48); the envoys to the oracle at Delphos head for home with the wish 'gracious be the issue' (III, i, 22); and Autolycus invites the narrative of Perdita's restitution with the words 'I would most gladly know the issue

---

10. Wilcox, 'Gender and genre', p. 137.
11. I am grateful to Sarah Wintle for pointing this out to me.

of it' (V, ii, 8). In *Henry VIII* the Old Lady who seeks more reward for saying that Henry's child is like him asserts 'I'll put it to the issue' (V, i, 177).

These two senses of the word 'issue', as both progeny and event, frequently come together. The penitent Leontes believes that 'the heavens, taking angry note, / Have left me issueless' (*The Winter's Tale*, V, i, 172–3). Queen Katherine's womb has been a tomb to Henry VIII's 'male issue', and must be replaced by the fruitful womb of Anne (*Henry VIII*, II, iv, 188). Arcite and Palamon in prison lament, before they see Emilia, that they will have 'no issue know us' (*The Two Noble Kinsmen*, II, ii, 30–2). In such instances, the playwright implies that to be without children is to be unable to move forward in story, locked into sterility and stasis. Fertility is the underlying motor of narrative, and masculine desires to secure futurity can only be fulfilled by means of union with a womb-bearing woman.

Other tropes specifically ground tragicomic romance narrative in the maternal body. In *Pericles*, Gower undertakes to show 'Th'unborn event' (xv, 45), while in *The Winter's Tale* the truth is 'pregnant by circumstance' (V, ii, 30–1). Wolsey reflects that the 'poor man that hangs on princes' favours' suffers 'More pangs and fears than wars or women have' (*Henry VIII*, III, ii, 368–71). Time, the great restorative force in tragicomic romance, can be understood as the time of parturition; waiting to give birth is a time of profound awareness of human subjugation to time. Hermione's lady in waiting, noting that 'She is spread of late / Into a goodly bulk', wishes 'good time encounter her' (*The Winter's Tale*, II, i, 20–1); instead Leontes' tragic intervention causes her to be 'something before her time, delivered' (II, ii, 28). Even the sea, which so persistently appears in these plays either as a place of actual shipwreck or as a metaphor for turbulent fortune, can be understood as a kind of amniotic fluid from which characters supposed dead are reborn.

All such examples can support the idea that tragicomic narrative structures are inherently maternal. I want to place alongside this a consideration of how far the prominence of maternal narrative tropes in Shakespeare's romances can be associated with his source genre of prose romance. Only one of his late plays, *The Winter's Tale*, has a clear and direct source in a single Elizabethan prose romance – Robert Greene's *Pandosto*, 1588. However, the *Two Noble Kinsmen* derives from Boccaccio via Chaucer, and *Pericles* – disdained by Ben Jonson as a 'mouldy tale'[12] –

---

12. 'Ode to Himself', l. 21, in Jonson, *The New Inn*, pp. 204–8; see Scragg, *Shakespeare's Mouldy Tales*.

from a lost late classical Latin or Greek romance via Gower; both exactly the kinds of sources drawn upon by Elizabethan authors of prose romance. Indeed, all the late plays announce their affinity to the genre through their repeated motifs of shipwrecks, lost children, marvellous visions and the workings of providence. Another distinguishing feature of Elizabethan prose romance was that its authors proclaimed themselves to be producing idle tales for the entertainment of women. Thus John Lyly began *Euphues and his England* (1580), the sequel to *Euphues: The Anatomy of Wit*, with an epistle 'To the Ladies and Gentlewomen of England', beseeching them to 'take the pains to read it, but at such times as you spend in playing with your little dogs', and to have 'Euphues … as often in your hands, being but a toy, as lawn on your heads, being but trash'. Barnaby Rich included a similar dedication 'To the right courteous gentlewomen' in *Rich's Farewell to Military Profession* (1581), explaining that he had turned away from military pursuits in favour of the more fashionable entertainment of ladies. His title page declared his tales to have been 'Gathered together for the onely delight of the courteous Gentlewomen … for whose onely pleasure thei were collected together'.[13]

From Louis B. Wright in 1935 to recent feminist critics like Caroline Lucas and Tina Krontiris, there has been a tendency to take literally these presentations of romance as women's reading.[14] Most recently, however, Wendy Wall and Juliet Fleming have drawn attention to the ideological loading of gender tropes in Renaissance authorial prefaces, and Lorna Hutson has shown how romances in which women appear to be prominent may in fact be more concerned with the construction of masculinity.[15] Indeed such evidence as we have of women's reading in the late sixteenth and early seventeenth centuries does not support the idea that they were avid consumers of romances.[16] The most we can say

---

13. Lyly, *Euphues and his England*, pp. 200–1; Rich, *Rich's Farewell*, p. 1.
14. Wright, *Middle-Class Culture*; Lucas, *Writing for Women*; Krontiris, 'Breaking barriers'.
15. Wall, *The Imprint of Gender*; Fleming, 'The ladies' man'; Hutson, *The Usurer's Daughter*.
16. Romances are completely absent from the extensive reading recorded by Lady Margaret Hoby in her diary for 1599–1605, and by Lady Grace Mildmay in her journals for 1570–1617. Both women principally read devotional texts; Mildmay also read herbals (Hoby, *Diary*; Weigall, 'An Elizabethan gentlewoman'). The journals of Lady Anne Clifford for the period 1616–19, and her 'Great Picture' of 1646, both include some romances (Clifford, *Diaries*, pp. 48, 61; Parry, 'The Great Picture', pp. 210, 217), but these form only a fraction of the wide-ranging reading matter catalogued in both sources. Similarly, works dedicated to women of the Russell family over the period 1570–1620 included the likes of Robert Greene's *Penelope's Web*, but also embraced religion, geography, history, travel, modern languages and Montaigne's *Essays* (Clarke, 'The Russell women').

with certainty is that the authors of romances, who were all male, designated romance as feminine material – perhaps because non-serious reading of matters of love and courtship, as distinct from instructive reading of wars and other public affairs, lent itself to a metaphorical gendering as feminine.

Another possible reason for the cultural construction of romance as feminine may lie in traditional myths about women as storytellers. *Penelope's Web*, 1587, another work by Robert Greene, the author of *Pandosto*, claimed to give men access to the kinds of tale which women tell one another in private. Greene informed gentlemen readers that 'I was determined at the first to have made no appeale to your favorable opinions, for that the matter is womens prattle, about the untwisting of Penelope's Web' – the book depicts Penelope and her ladies telling one another stories while they unweave her web in her chamber by night in order to keep her suitors at bay. However, he changed his mind on 'considering that *Mars* wil sometime bee prying into *Venus* papers, and gentlemen desirous to heare the parlie of Ladies'.[17] The stories of Penelope's ladies are described as 'merrie chat' designed to 'beguyle the night with prattle'; they are entertainments which enliven time which would otherwise pass slowly (pp. 152, 154, 162). The activity of narration is also closely identified with the archetypal feminine activities of spinning and weaving: one of Penelope's maids is described as 'applying as well her fingers to the web as her tongue to the tale', while later when Penelope takes her own turn at storytelling her maids listen 'setting their hands to the Web, and their eares to hir talke' (pp. 155, 162). The 'endlesse web' of cloth (p. 233), whose ravelling and unravelling makes time stand still and seems able to go on forever, becomes in effect a metaphor for the generation of a potentially limitless thread of female story.[18]

This analogy invokes other myths of women who literally wove narratives, such as Philomel and Arachne.[19] Their stories combine positive and negative aspects of spinning or weaving metaphors for female storytelling. Philomel was able to tell the truth about her rape, even though her tongue had been cut out, by depicting it on cloth; female weaving is thereby represented as equivalent to a female voice, and as a vivid means of communication. Arachne defeated Minerva in a weaving contest by her depiction of the many affairs of the gods, associating female storytelling with the capacity to draw upon an abundant fund of

17. Greene, *Penelope's Web*, pp. 144–5.
18. See Parker, *Literary Fat Ladies*, p. 26.
19. Ovid, *Metamorphoses*, Book VI, ll. 572ff, ll. 5ff.

story. The idea of making an intricate narrative fabric from a thread also suggests skill in plotting. On the other hand, though, thread connotes linearity and a tendency to run on and on, such that the metaphor can represent women's narration as the undirected, unlimited and unthinking flow of a 'natural' facility. This is emphasised by Minerva's punishment of Arachne: she metamorphoses her into a spider, an image which does invoke the intricate structure of a web but also reduces spinning, and the female narrative for which it stands, to the status of a spontaneous bodily emission.

The idea that women were especially liable to tell idle and foolish tales was well established by the sixteenth century and was already described in the phrase 'an old wives' tale'. In *Amadis de Gaule*, the heroine Oriana, on being parted from her newborn baby, fears that his wetnurse might 'sit gossipping with her neighbours, telling vaine tales and fruitlesse fables'.[20] In Marlowe's *Doctor Faustus*, the protagonist scoffs at Mephistopheles's talk of hell and damnation with the words 'Tush, these are trifles and mere old wives' tales.'[21] George Peele's play *The Old Wives Tale* (c.1593) is, just as its title suggests, grounded upon this idea of the fantastical women's story. Three pages named Antic, Fantastic and Frolic who are lost in a wood are taken in by a smith and his wife, Madge, whom they address as 'gammer' (that is, 'godmother', 'old woman'). They entreat her to tell them a story:

> antic   … methinks, gammer, a merry winter's tale would drive away the time trimly.
> Come, I am sure you are not without a score.
> fantastic   I'faith, gammer, a tale of an hour long were as good as an hour's sleep.
> frolic   Look you, gammer, of the giant and the king's daughter, and I know not what. I have seen the day, when I was a little one, you might have drawn me a mile after you with such a discourse.[22]

Madge accedes to their request with the words 'So I am content to drive away the time with an old wives winter's tale' (ll. 98–9), accepting their evaluation of her story as merely better than doing nothing. However, she puts up a little resistance to their accompanying evaluation of it as

20. Anon., *Ancient … History of Amadis de Gaule* (1619), Book III, pp. 29–30; O'Connor, '*Amadis de Gaule*', p. 135.
21. Marlowe, *Doctor Faustus*, A-text, II, i, 138.
22. Peele, *The Old Wives Tale*, ll. 85–93.

equivalent to a sleep: she asks 'that you will say hum and ha to my tale, so shall I know you are awake' (ll.110–11). Her story begins:

> Once upon a time there was a king or a lord or a duke that had a fair daughter, the fairest that ever was; as white as snow and as red as blood; and once upon a time his daughter was stolen away, and he sent all his men to seek out his daughter. (ll. 113–17)

It is no coincidence that this could serve pretty well as a synopsis of one of Shakespeare's late plays. Madge narrates in this style for a while, then the characters appear on stage to act out the tale, but with periodic interruptions from the pages and Madge to remind us of the oral narrative frame of teller and audience.

Madge is shown actively making choices between formulaic motifs which she puts together to construct a plot. The motifs are common to both fairy tale and printed literary romance, like the beautiful princess, the lost child and the quest. Their familiarity is part of their entertainment value; originality is not a measure of worth in this context. Madge's ongoing selection suggests that she is rummaging in a bottomless chest of such motifs. The indecisions, muddles and loops in her narratorial style also evoke a spontaneous oral delivery: she frequently interrupts herself with phrases like 'O Lord, I quite forgot! ... O, I forget!', which provide occasions for elaborations and digressions (ll. 122–8).

Margaret Spufford gives examples from the seventeenth and eighteenth centuries of women's involvement in various oral traditions like ballad singing and the sharing of bawdy tales and jokes, as well as fairy tales and folk tales.[23] Such evidence often takes the form of affectionate reminiscences of childhood pleasures, just as Frolic in *The Old Wives Tale* nostalgically recalls 'when I was a little one'; as Spufford notes, John Clare remembered that in his rural childhood 'the old women's memories never failed of tales to smooth out labour; for as every day came, new Giants, Hobgoblins and Fairies was ready to pass it away' (p. 4).

These depictions and recollections are no doubt partly a reflection of real life: since women were less educated and literate than men, their storytelling was likely to take oral forms and to be relatively 'foolish'. Equally, it was usually women who looked after children, and who would therefore seek to occupy them with stories; and the boring yet often communal nature of women's tasks like weaving and spinning would lend themselves to simultaneous storytelling. All the same, I think

---

23. Spufford, *Small Books*, pp. 4–6, 12–13, 59, 62, 79–80, 172.

we can surmise that the association between women (especially older women) and oral fantastical stories became an entrenched cultural construction because of its power as a fantasy of maternal origin. My use of this phrase is adapted from Janet Adelman, who writes of how in Shakespeare's plays from *Hamlet* on:

> the problematic maternal body can never quite be occluded or transformed: made into a monster or a saint, killed off or banished from the stage, it remains at the centre of masculine subjectivity, marking its unstable origin. For the contaminated flesh of the maternal body is also home: the home Shakespeare's protagonists long to return to, the home they can never quite escape.[24]

Fantastical tales elicited in Shakespeare's period a similar ambivalent combination of contempt and affection. Their mingled characteristics of simplicity, familiarity and wonder meant that they were readily identified with a vaguely remembered past, a primitive time of beginnings, something which could be sunk back into comfortably but from which the individual had to move on; all of these qualities made them readily identifiable with a child's relationship with its mother. Moreover, the idea of these stories as unstructured, boundless, and indeed oral conceptualised them almost like a biological flow – something which just pours out; and women have historically been identified with the fluxes of the body, especially mothers, who personify bodily sources of production.

The tales of 'monstrous' births which I discussed earlier also illustrate how maternity itself could be a source of marvellous narrative. While claiming to be 'true descriptions', these are at the same time presented as tales of the extraordinary, bringing something of the romance world of hobgoblins and changelings into contact with here-and-now experience. They are not only tales about women as mothers, but also often tales with female sources, since the named witnesses are frequently midwives or other women in attendance at the childbed. The claim to veracity thus contains its own potential undermining, since the accounts could easily be doubted, while still enjoyed and gasped over, as 'old wives tales'. The proverbial unreliability of midwives is implicit both in Autolycus' assertion that his ballad of a 'monstrous' birth has 'the midwife's name to it' *(The Winter's Tale, IV, iv, 266)*, and in the response of the Old Lady who attended on Anne Boleyn's childbed to her disappointing reward: 'Said I for this the girl was like to him? I'll / Have more, or else unsay't' *(Henry VIII, V, i, 175–6)*.

---

24. Adelman, *Suffocating Mothers*, p. 36.

Just as *The Winter's Tale* is the late Shakespearean play which most graphically shows the maternal body on stage, so this is the play which most frequently foregrounds the idea that idle and fantastical narrative is the province of women, especially women in maternal or quasi-maternal roles such as midwife or children's nurse. It is Mamillius who declares that 'A sad tale's best for winter. I have one / Of sprites and goblins' (II, i, 26–7), but he is a child shown as literally still at his mother's knee, living like most small children in an intimate circle of nurturing women. His close bond with his mother is shown not only by the fact that he whispers his tale in her ear and later drops dead when she is abused, but also by his very name, Mamillius, which is a diminutive of the Latin word for breast. When the idea of the winter's tale is picked up again in the latter scenes of the play, it is overtly associated with the female in the form of first the return of Perdita, who personifies the return of the mother in the daughter, then the return of Hermione supervised mid-wife-like by Paulina. The news of Perdita's restoration is 'so like an old tale that the verity of it is in strong suspicion ... Like an old tale still, which will have matter to rehearse though credit be asleep and not an ear open' (V, ii, 61–3). Paulina confesses of Hermione, 'That she is living, / Were it but told you, should be hooted at / Like an old tale' (V, iii, 116–18).

Elsewhere, however, although the late plays embrace the fantastical, digressive and time-filling narrative principles of romance, they do not so comfortably embrace the idea of this as feminine or maternal. In *Henry VIII* the effect of the reversion of the Old Lady who acts as midwife to Anne Boleyn to the stereotype of the unreliability and disreputability of the old wives' tale is to revive the fearful unknowability of paternity, with which Leontes' troubles began. This play as a whole invokes the idea of old fantastical story, only carefully to distinguish itself from it. The knights at the Field of Cloth of Gold are reported to have jousted so well 'that former fabulous story / Being now seen possible enough, got credit / That *Bevis* was believed' (I, i, 36–8). Later, the porter's assistant at the christening of Princess Elizabeth, overwhelmed by the popular crowds forcing their way in, protests that 'I am not Samson, nor Sir Guy, nor Colbrand, / To mow 'em down before me' (V, iii, 21–2). Similarly, the prologue to *The Two Noble Kinsmen* expresses anxiety that if the play is unsuccessful, Chaucer will complain that its author 'my famed works makes lighter / Than Robin Hood' (ll. 20–1). In naming popular romances these late plays invoke them as a frame of reference but at the same time claim their own elevation above them.

However, the idea of idle story and its pleasures does remain very much present. The prologue to *The Two Noble Kinsmen* proposes that the

play will 'keep / A little dull time for us' (ll. 30–1); the epilogue refers to
it not as a play but as 'the tale we have told' (l. 12). Gower introduces
scene xviii of *Pericles* with the words 'Thus time we waste' (l. 1). It is
notable, though, that Gower is a *male* custodian of old, time-filling story.
In fact despite the kinds of configuration I have described, there is no
example in the late plays of a woman actually telling a story. It is
invariably gentlemen who relate to one another the miraculous reunions
and other wondrous off-stage events. In *Cymbeline*, it is Belarius who has
told tales of courts and princes (III, iii, 1–15), and his warlike adoptive
sons, living in all-male seclusion, worry about their own narrative
capacities:

> What should we speak of
> When we are old as you? When we shall hear
> The rain and wind beat dark December, how,
> In this our pinching cave, shall we discourse
> The freezing hours away? (III, iii, 35–9)

The choric figure of Time in *The Winter's Tale*, which on the face of it
could readily be female as the birth-giver to event, is definitely male,
referring to 'himself' (IV, i, 31), and drawing on the patriarchal icono-
graphical tradition of Time as the Old Father to his daughter Truth.[25] In
The Tempest it is Prospero who narrates her origins to Miranda and who
is the organiser of narrative event for all the other characters.

In the end, then, just as maternity is often invoked only to be taken
away from women, when patriarchal characters like Pericles, Cymbeline,
Prospero and Henry VIII are given maternal tropes to express their own
moments of heightened tragicomic emotion, so authority over narrative
is frequently appropriated to male figures. An idle and digressive narrative genre is plundered for its pleasures, but placed in the hands of
ordering patriarchs, as if to leave it to women like Peele's Madge would
be to risk an uncontainable, unstructured and disorderly flow of story.
Let us not forget, after all, that these are plays by a man or men (that is,
Shakespeare and Fletcher) whose careful attention to form is apparent
beneath the surface digressiveness, just as the Elizabethan romances
which announced themselves to be directed by the interests of ladies
and gentlewomen were composed by male authors who took them
more seriously than they pretended. The idea of Shakespeare's tragicomic romances as maternal in genre is fruitful in so far as maternity is

---

25. As used in Elizabeth I's coronation pageants; see Anon., *The Quenes Maiesties Passage*,
    sigs C2ᵛ–D1ᵛ.

inherently tragicomic, but the tradition which connects maternity with the actual *generation* of romance narrative is present in most of these plays only in repressed form.

An exception to this is *The Winter's Tale*, especially in the role of Paulina. Eleven of Shakespeare's plays have what Dennis Kay has called 'postponed endings' – the postponement of full explanatory narrative beyond what is shown on stage.[26] While, as Kay shows, the effects of this vary, they often include the sense of an abundance and fertility of narrative spilling over beyond the confines of the five Acts we have seen. In a few cases, it is female characters who lead their companions away for further narrative: these are Paulina in *The Winter's Tale*, along with the Abbess in *The Comedy of Errors* (V, i, 396–402), Portia in *The Merchant of Venice* (V, i, 295–9), and Mistress Page in *The Merry Wives of Windsor* (V, v, 233–4). Among these *The Comedy of Errors*, an early play (1591–2?), especially anticipates many of the concerns of the late plays, sharing one of its sources, Gower's romance tale of Apollonius of Tyre in the eighth book of his *Confessio Amantis*, not only with *Pericles* but possibly also with the statue scene in *The Winter's Tale*.[27] Among Shakespeare's female presiders over postponed endings, it is the Abbess in *The Comedy of Errors* who in her closing words most overtly draws together the themes of maternity and narrative which we associate with the late plays:

> Renownèd Duke, vouchsafe to take the pains
> To go with us into the abbey here,
> And hear at large discoursèd all our fortunes,
>
> …
>
> Thirty-three years have I but gone in travail
> Of you, my sons, and till this present hour
> My heavy burden ne'er deliverèd.
> The Duke, my husband, and my children both,
> And you the calendars of their nativity,
> Go to a gossips' feast, and joy with me.
> After so long grief, such nativity![28]   (V, i, 396–8, 403–9)

The burden which she delivers after a thirty-three-year labour is both her 'reborn' sons, and the story of her motherhood and self-concealment.

---

26. Kay, "'To hear the rest untold'".
27. I am grateful to Gareth Roberts for pointing this out to me.
28. *The Norton Shakespeare* gives 'festivity'; but the 1623 Folio, the only source for *The Comedy of Errors*, gives 'nativity'. Editors have often felt a need to emend this because it repeats the last word of the last line but one. See *The Comedy of Errors*, ed. Foakes, note on V, i, 406.

Such direct linking of maternity and narrative would be entirely appropriate in any of the late plays, yet is not openly stated there. The nearest we get to it is in the role of Paulina as a sort of midwife of events. When she bursts into the tragic, masculine world of the first half of *The Winter's Tale* with Hermione's baby in her arms, Leontes frantically abuses her with just about every term popular culture offers for a woman who talks too much: she is Dame Partlet, Lady Margery, 'a callat / Of boundless tongue', and a midwife to boot (II, iii, 76, 91–2, 160). The play ends, however, with her receiving his gracious submission: 'Good Paulina, / Lead us from hence, where we may leisurely / Each one demand and answer to his part' (V, iii, 152–4). It is Paulina who is invited to preside over the narratives which will fill the 'wide gap of time' (l. 155) and which spill over abundantly beyond the end of the story as shown.

The Winter's Tale is the late play in which the female body both before and soon after childbirth is most graphically shown on stage; and in which the invocation of 'old tales' is most frequent; and in which 'great creating nature' is most present; and in which the term 'issue' with its dual sense most often occurs. Accordingly it is the late play in which the female generation of story comes closest to being openly recognised and surrendered to, rather than taken under the charge of an organising male figure.

2

'THOU HAST MADE ME NOW A MAN': REFORMING MAN(NER)LINESS IN *HENRY VIII*

Gordon McMullan

I

'Thou hast made me now a man', Henry tells Cranmer after the arch-bishop has spoken prophetic words over the baby Elizabeth in the christening scene at the close of *Henry VIII*, announcing 'never before / This happy child did I get anything' (V, iv, 64–5). This claim of the king's that his masculinity has only now finally been established by his father-ing (or perhaps more accurately, by Cranmer's christening) of a baby girl is a puzzling one, and one which has generally been ignored by critics. Yet Henry's appalling treatment of the two of his wives who are repre-sented in the play, Katherine of Aragon and Anne Bullen, requires us to examine his (and the play's) definitions of what it means to 'be a man', to assess the relationship the play sets up between manliness and manner-liness – between the social parameters for appropriate conduct and the construction of masculinity – and to analyse the play's representation of

I am grateful to Richard Proudfoot for inviting me, a fair while ago now, to edit *Henry VIII* for Arden 3 and thereby obliging me to become involved with a fine and complex play I had previously tended to ignore; to Lorna Hutson for discussion of early modern temperance; to Alan Stewart for organising a conference on early modern masculinity at Birkbeck College, London, in 1997 during which I had initial thoughts about Henry's sexuality; and to Jenny Richards and James Knowles for providing the 'tyme of dede mete' to give shape to those thoughts.

Henry VIII as an intemperate monarch. In the process, we can begin to establish an understanding of the play's attitude both to the history it represents and to its present, and specifically its attitude to the state of the Reformation in both Henrician and Jacobean England.

II

As David Kuchta has noted in a useful essay, '[t]wo public definitions of masculinity competed with each other in Renaissance England', definitions which were inherited, unsurprisingly, from ancient Greece and Rome.[1] The Renaissance male courtier looked, as you would expect, to classical texts for his self-fashioning, but he found conflicting advice. On the one hand, manliness was defined by way of display, of conspicuous consumption, expenditure and excess; on the other, it was defined in terms of restraint and moderation. In a sense, both definitions depend upon a sense of the appropriate. The first definition relied upon a clear sense that 'dress and manners were not mere externals: they were manifestations of internal worth, graceful supplements to nobility' (p. 235). Such forms of display functioned by way of what Michel Foucault has called 'a hierarchy of analogies', by a clearly defined relationship between outward appearance and social standing. It would thus be as inappropriate for a nobleman *not* to indulge in conspicuous consumption as it would be for a commoner to borrow the nobleman's clothes.

But the boundaries between appropriate expenditure and excess were, not surprisingly, unclear in a period of considerable economic fluidity, and the second definition emerging from courtly culture in a sense reaches the opposite conclusion from the first on the same premises. Conspicuous consumption could equally easily be seen as the activity of the intemperate prodigal – and, in England, of corrupting foreign influences – and a model of moderation and temperance set up in opposition. Certainly, as Kuchta notes:

> [p]uritans, mercantilists, and country gentlemen opposed the import of Italian ideals of courtesy and the Italian (and later French) fashions which accompanied them … [These groups] linked effeminacy with sumptuous display and political dependence: manly simplicity signified political autonomy; restraint symbolized freedom. In this politicized vision of masculinity, fashion was merely an external imposition by tyrannical and arbitrary custom. (p. 234)

---

1. Kuchta, 'Semiotics of masculinity', p. 234.

In the second definition, then, a 'good man' was a moderate, temperate man, who was defined as 'stronger than himself', that is, as someone who is able to harness and manage his various appetites and to present himself to the world as a model of restraint and self-control, and a 'bad man' as a prodigal, who was defined as 'weaker than himself', that is, as someone who is unable to resist his own material – and, for that matter (and this, as I will suggest, is crucial), sexual – urges. Manliness and mannerliness are thus closely equated: masculinity is defined oppositionally in terms both of fashionable excess and of restraint and temperance.

I would argue that these two competing definitions of masculinity are set against each other in *Henry VIII*, and that the equation of manliness and mannerliness is central to an adequate understanding of the position of the king in the play's moral structures. In the terms of the first definition of manliness, Henry's enjoyment of occasions such as the celebrations for his meeting with the king of France at the Field of Cloth of Gold or the great masque at Cardinal Wolsey's house serves to confirm his status as a truly manly Renaissance ruler. At the Field of Cloth of Gold, we gather, the two kings, Henry and Francis, competed for grandeur and the two courts emulated each other, climbing on the shoulders of the other's self-display to produce still grander displays of consummate courtly expenditure. 'Each following day / Became the next day's master', we are told:

> till the last
> Made former wonders, its. To-day the French,
> All clinquant all in gold, like heathen gods,
> Shone down the English; and to-morrow they
> Made Britain India: every man that stood
> Show'd like a mine ...
> The two kings
> Equal in lustre, were now best, now worst,
> As presence did present them: him in eye
> Still him in praise, and being present both,
> 'Twas said they saw but one, and no discerner
> Durst wag his tongue in censure. (I, i, 16–22, 28–33)

These are two Renaissance rulers at the height of their splendour: the visit to France makes it abundantly clear that the king of England can hold up his head in the company of the most spectacularly splendid of Continental rulers. Yet as the last line I quoted suggests, not everyone was happy with this glorious exercise in conspicuous consumption, even if they did not actually dare object. And we rapidly learn both that the agreements reached in France have fizzled out to nothing and that the grand, masculine display that dominated the celebrations has placed English manhood, at least from certain perspectives, under severe threat from an incursion of foreign manners and customs.

'New customs', the unglamorous Lord Sands exclaims, 'Though they be never so ridiculous / (Nay, let 'em be unmanly) yet are follow'd' (I, iii, 2–4). And the bluff English lords demonstrate, through their nervous humour at the expense of their frenchified colleagues, a distinct anxiety about the feminising effect of French manners on the English court. 'I would pray our monsieurs / To think an English courtier may be wise, / And never see the Louvre', the Chamberlain says, querulously, and he goes on to make a telling connection between foreign fashion and spiritual decline: 'Death my lord', he says, 'Their clothes are after such a pagan cut to't / That sure th'have worn out Christendom' (I, iii, 21–3, 13–15). This religious fear is a persistent element in the courtiers' resistance to French customs, as they talk of the 'reformation' of French-influenced courtiers and the requirement that they 'renounc[e] clean / The faith they have in tennis and tall stockings' (I, iii, 19, 29–30). More to the point for the purposes of this chapter, Sands makes it extremely clear that the influx of French custom has had a detrimental effect on English manhood. 'The devil fiddle 'em', he shouts, 'I am glad they are going, / For sure there's no converting of 'em', adding that 'now / An honest country lord as I am, beaten / A long time out of play, may bring his plain-song, / And have an hour of hearing' (I, iii, 42–6). There is thus considerable resistance within the play to the first of the two classical definitions of manliness, because within the grand displays characteristic of Continental courts are perceived the seeds of destruction both of English manhood and of the English Reformation.

This anxiety focuses, inevitably, on the king. Repeatedly in the play, in the terms of the second definition, Henry is seen to fail to adopt appropriately masculine modes and therefore to threaten both the realm and the Reformation. Henry's manhood is at stake right from the first time we see him, as his anxiety obliges him to accept the evidence against the duke of Buckingham despite its apparent fictionality. He acknowledges his former position of feminised subordination in respect of Buckingham, 'when we / Almost with *ravish'd* list'ning, could not find / His hour of speech a minute' (I, ii, 119–121; my italics). 'Ravish'd list'ning' is surely, in these terms, a female activity (or, perhaps better, passivity), certainly not an appropriate posture for a king. And this sense of subordination to a subject must put Henry's royal status on the line (or at the very least hark uncomfortably back to the weakness of a

Henry VI). But his principal problem remains his inability to father a healthy male heir. This failure to demonstrate his manliness by assuring the continuation of the royal line is, of course, something he shares with the royal protagonists of other 'late plays': Prospero's 'birthpangs' on the boat; Pericles' loss of his daughter and consequent adoption of the lifestyle of a hermit; Leontes' immoderation, which leads to the death of his son. But Henry's crisis of masculinity is in a certain way more fundamental, more quietly persistent, than those of the protagonists of these other plays.

The king's conscience is the principal battleground. We first hear Henry discussing his conscience in curious terms in Act II, when he is momentarily regretting his decision to divorce Katherine: 'O my lord', he says to Wolsey, 'Would it not grieve an able man to leave / So sweet a bedfellow? But conscience, conscience; / O 'tis a tender place, and I must leave her' (II, ii, 140–3). It is fairly clear that Henry is thinking of Katherine in sexual terms, boasting of his 'ability' and leading us to wonder in particular what exactly he is implying here by the phrase 'tender place'. One apparent answer to this question is given in the next scene (and underlined by the way in which Anne's opening line 'Not for that neither' (III, i, 1) can be played as a direct rejection of Henry's hypocrisy if the two scenes are played in rapid succession),[2] in which Anne's ostensible innocence is undermined by her dialogue with a knowing Old Lady, who speaks with heavy innuendo of 'the capacity' of Anne's 'soft, cheverel conscience' to receive the king's gifts, if she 'might please to stretch it' (II, iii, 31–3). As Judith Anderson has noted, there is a quite explicit sense in which the king's conscience begins to seem almost physically feminised, curiously indistinguishable in his own imagination from his wife's vagina.[3]

The failure of his masculinity is at its clearest in the awkward narrative Henry offers in explanation of his 'conscientious' decision to part from Katherine on the grounds that he has now decided, rather belatedly, that he should never have married her in the first place, since she was his brother's widow. The narrative focuses again on his conscience, on the debilitating effect that his failure to produce a male heir has had on his internal presence of mind. He begins nervously – 'Now what mov'd me to't' (to the divorce, that is), 'I will be bold with time and your

---

2. I am immensely grateful to Greg Doran for giving me the chance to attend rehearsals of his 1996 RSC production of *Henry VIII* and thus to become aware of a range of staging possibilities for moments such as this.

3. Anderson, *Biographical Truth*, pp. 128–9.

attention: / Then mark th'inducement: thus it came; give heed to't' – and then he tries to explain:

> My conscience first receiv'd a tenderness,
> Scruple and prick, on certain speeches utter'd
> By th'Bishop of Bayonne, then French ambassador,
> Who had been hither sent on the debating
> A marriage 'twixt the Duke of Orleans and
> Our daughter Mary: i'th'progress of this business,
> Ere a determinate resolution, he
> (I mean the Bishop) did require a respite
> Wherein he might the king his lord advertise
> Whether our daughter were legitimate
> Respecting this our marriage with the dowager,
> Sometimes our brother's wife. This respite shook
> The bosom of my conscience, enter'd me,
> Yea, with a spitting power, and made to tremble
> The region of my breast, which forc'd such way
> That many maz'd considerings did throng
> And pressed in with this caution. First, methought
> I stood not in the smile of heaven, who had
> Commanded nature, that my lady's womb
> If it conceiv'd a male-child by me, should
> Do no more offices of life to't than
> The grave does to th'dead: for her male issue
> Or died where they were made, or shortly after
> This world had air'd them. Hence I took a thought
> This was a judgment on me, that my kingdom
> (Well worthy the best heir o'th'world) should not
> Be gladded in't by me. Then follows that
> I weigh'd the danger which my realms stood in
> By this my issue's fail, and that gave to me
> Many a groaning throe: thus hulling in
> The wild sea of my conscience, I did steer
> Toward this remedy whereupon we are
> Now present here together. (II, iv, 165–200)

Henry's masculinity is under direct threat here. We have already seen the connotation of 'tenderness', and the word 'prick' would have had the same alternative signification for the Jacobean audience as it does for us. As he recounts events, it is clear that doubt about Mary's legitimacy has had a penetrating effect on his selfhood: it impales him, 'enters' him 'with a spitting power', once again remodelling the conscience in vaginal terms. As a result, he even adopts a curiously maternal stance, as his need for an heir resolves itself into a kind of phantom pregnancy, the 'danger' that gives him 'many a groaning throe'. The effect of this speech must have been quite shocking to those in the audience tuned in to the language of the king's explanation, both because it thoroughly compromises the king's manliness and because, despite its acknowledgement of the symptoms of the problem, there is no suggestion that Henry is aware that the cause might be his own immoderation rather than Katherine's supposed inability to produce male offspring.

Early modern man inherited certain anxieties about sexual intercourse from classical tradition, anxieties (in Foucault's words) about 'the very form of the act [and] the cost it entailed'.[4] Greek medical and philosophical texts, while sustaining a generally high regard for the sexual act, were also aware of the threat it posed, 'through its violence, to the control and mastery that one ought to exercise over oneself', and of its ability to sap 'the strength the individual should conserve and maintain, through the exhaustion it caused' (p. 125). Careful pacing of sexual activity was thus important, 'not simply because excess might lead to an illness [but also] because in sexual activity in general man's mastery, strength, and life were at stake' (p. 125). One classical tradition which influenced Renaissance thinking offered an image of heated liquid overflowing as a model of what happens during sexual intercourse and treated the effusion, the excess, as loss. Clement of Alexandria, quoting Diogenes of Apollonia, suggests that the semen might best be viewed as 'in substance the foam of the blood', and describes a process during which 'the blood, which being by the natural heat of the male agitated and shaken out, in copulation is turned into foam, and deposited in the seminal veins'.[5] 'The sperm of the human male', according to the Hippocratic essay *The Seed*:

> comes from all the fluid in the body: it consists of the most potent part which is secreted from the rest. The evidence that it is the most potent part which is secreted is the fact that even though the actual amount we emit in intercourse is very small, we are weakened by its loss.[6]

---

4. Foucault, *The Use of Pleasure*, p. 125.
5. Clement of Alexandria, *The Instructor*, I, vi, 146.
6. Anon., *The Seed*, p. 317. See Laqueur's *Making Sex* for discussion of this and other (Aristotelian and Galenic) traditions.

The Seed makes it clear throughout that the man is the agent of sexual pleasure and of sexual fulfilment and the woman subject to this male agency. The male act controls and regulates sexual interaction, even ensuring the health of the woman who, in the absence of sexual intercourse with a man, is likely to 'become prone to sickness' (p. 320). At the same time, the act, involving as it does emission of vital fluid, diminishes the man, even if only by a little. In this context, man has a responsibility to avoid indulging in excessive periods of sexual heat that might threaten his control of the sexual act and therefore of his manliness.

This responsibility is succinctly, if obliquely, expressed in Norfolk's attempts to calm Buckingham's fury at Wolsey in the first scene of *Henry VIII*. The focus in this instance is not sexual, but a parallel metaphysical argument is offered which has resonances throughout the play for the king's own particular brand of excessive heat. 'Be advis'd', cautions Norfolk:

> Heat not a furnace for your foe so hot
> That it do singe yourself. We may outrun
> By violent swiftness that which we run at,
> And lose by over-running: know you not
> The fire that mounts the liquor till't run o'er
> In seeming to augment it wastes it? Be advis'd;
> I say again there is no English soul
> More stronger to direct you than yourself,
> If with the sap of reason you would quench,
> Or but allay the fire of passion. (I, i, 139–49)

Norfolk's frustration that Buckingham's inability to contain his rage will lead directly to the 'waste' of his potential neatly conveys the early modern anxiety about emotional (and sexual) expenditure and the paradoxical loss of strength effected through the unmoderated expression of that strength. It also serves to demonstrate the practical, if unacknowledged, equivalence between Buckingham's and the king's modes of immoderate behaviour.

It is heat that is again at issue the first time we directly witness Henry VIII's carnal immoderation. Shortly after the king has appeared in disguise at the Cardinal's party and has first danced with and then kissed Anne Bullen, Wolsey attempts to divert his master. 'Your grace / I fear, with dancing is a little heated', he says to Henry, to which the king replies, 'I fear too much' (I, iv, 99–101), thus appearing to acknowledge the dangers implicit in his excitement. The Cardinal then notes that 'There's fresher air, my lord, / In the next chamber' (I, iv, 101–2), and

47

when Henry orders the dancers to lead their partners into the adjoining room it seems that Wolsey has succeeded in his attempt to remind the king of his manly responsibilities. But Henry immediately follows his order by grabbing Anne once more and insisting on further drinking and another dance, and we find ourselves witnessing Wolsey's first failure to keep the king within the bounds of moderation. 'Sweet heart', Henry says to Anne, 'I were unmannerly to take you out / And not to kiss you' (I, iv, 94–6). The relationship of the (un)manly and the (un)mannerly is at its clearest here, and demonstrates the contradictory position in which Henry finds himself between the two definitions of masculinity. While it might in some cases be considered appropriate to kiss one's chosen partner at the end of the dance, it is of course wholly inappropriate for a married man to choose a young, unattached woman (and one of his wife's immediate subordinates, at that) as that partner. Not to kiss Anne (not to dance with her in the first place) would have been the temperate choice, but might also appear unimpressively coy for someone who makes such claims for complete manhood. Henry's argument is no more than humorous – and, as far as his realm is concerned, dangerous – sophistry.

John Winkler notes that 'at all levels of practical morality and advice-giving' in classical Greek texts, 'we find the undisciplined person described as someone mastered or conquered by something over which he should exert control, usually conceived or conceivable as part of himself'. 'This caution', he notes:

> is premised on the beliefs that male life is warfare, that masculinity is a duty and a hard-won achievement, and that the temptation to desert one's side is very great. This odd belief in the reversibility of the male person, always in peril of slipping into the servile or the feminine, has been noted by Stephen Greenblatt, who observes that for the ancient world the two sexes are not simply opposite but stand at poles of a continuum which can be traversed. Thus, 'woman' is not only the opposite of a man; she is also a potentially threatening 'internal émigré' of masculine identity'.[7]

As the 'great voluptuary', then, Henry is seen to be incapable of the control, the moderation, required of a 'proper' man. His inability to control his lust for Anne Bullen paradoxically undermines the very manliness of the urges that drive him on, both because he ought, as an 'able man', to be capable not only of expressing but also of controlling

7. Winkler, *The Constraints of Desire*, p. 50.

his passions and because his very enthusiasm for unlimited sexual activity threatens the future of the realm by sapping his procreative potential.

As a result, moderation becomes the key issue in the contrast between good and bad that the play sets up, between Wolsey and Buckingham, between Wolsey and Cranmer, between Henry and virtually everyone else (even Wolsey momentarily, at the party, as he attempts to separate the king and Anne), a contrast which is dependent upon what Lorna Hutson calls 'the familiar Protestant / humanist antithesis between the intemperate prodigal whose concern with immediate gratification is expressed as the consumption of wealth ... and the prudent or temperate man concerned with a longer-term calculation of profit'.[8] It is wholly fitting that it should be not, as the nobles assume, Wolsey's letter to the Pope informing him of the progress of the divorce that at last provokes Henry's wrath, but rather the inventory of the secretly hoarded possessions that Wolsey has unwittingly included in the packet he sent to the king. In the overview of the play, Wolsey appears as the personification of excess, of immoderate behaviour – 'no man's pie', we gather, 'is freed / From his ambitious finger' (I, i, 52–3); he is a 'butcher's cur', a 'keech' who 'can with his very bulk / Take up the rays o'th' beneficial sun, / And keep it from the earth' (I, i, 120, 55–7). Cranmer, on the other hand, is characterised by his awareness of the need to take the long view, his sense of the eventual sorting of the wheat and the chaff, a spiritual equivalent of long-term profit (and it is, of course, necessary to note that the 'spiritual' rejection of prodigality is not a rejection of individual profit, but rather a patient building up of interest on the infinitely greater riches stored up in heaven).

This is, in fact, what makes Gardiner, bishop of Winchester, a much more implacable foe for Cranmer than Wolsey ever was, because Gardiner has a strong sense of the need for moderation and restraint, most notably as he lectures a passing pageboy on the obligation to take rest in the hours of darkness even as the king is playing cards by candlelight. 'These should be hours for necessities, / Not for delights', he declares, 'times to repair our nature / With comforting repose, and not for us / To waste these times' (V, i, 2–5). Gardiner's rejection of pleasures, though, marks the opposite boundary of the temperate, tipping him over towards the utter insensitivity that the Greeks held to be the exact (and equally unhelpful) opposite of excess. His 'puritanical' Catholicism (as, in a fine example of the play's time-compression and sectarian eclecticism, the audience would no doubt have seen it) reveals a failure to recognise

8. Hutson, 'Chivalry', p. 45; see also Hutson, *The Usurer's Daughter*, pp. 115–51, 173–4.

Figure 2.1 *Hipocrisy*, from William Marshall's *Goodlye Prymer in Englyshe*, 1535. By courtesy of the British Library.

that leading the temperate life entailed not the outright renunciation of pleasures but rather their proper distribution across the path of life.[9] Paradoxically, then, it is the excess of Gardiner's zeal for and expression of his sense of the moderate and the appropriate that enables the unshakeably temperate Cranmer to escape his plot.

III

Lorna Hutson has recently written about the specific interrelations of the concepts of manliness and of timeliness in early modern discussions of appropriate conduct, an interrelation which pivots on the double connotation of the word 'temperance' as both moderation and the ability to capitalise on the moment. 'For humanists', she observes, '"timing" was an art subordinate to the virtue of temperance, or, to put it another way, the art of good timing was "temperance" in its semiotic aspect', noting that it was 'Cicero's rendering of the Greek *sophrosyne*, or moderation, as the Latin *temperantia* in the *De inventione* and the *De officiis* which first tended to strengthen the temporal associations of "temperance"', and quoting the passage in question as it was translated into English in 1534:

> It is defined of Socrates schole that temperaunce is a syence of those thinges which shall be done or sayde to be set in thyr due place ... They call the place of any dede, opportunitye of tyme. The tyme of dede mete is called in Greke tongue Eukeria, in Latin occasyon. So it is that this temperaunce that we interpretate as I have sayd is a scyence of opportunyte of tyme to do anything.[10]

Thus Hutson observes that '[t]here is good evidence to suggest that the conception of temperance as an art of timing was widely understood in the Renaissance' and that, by the early to mid 1500s, the idea was established among English humanists.[11] Interestingly, she also notes that in 1544 Anthony Cope, who was chamberlain to Queen Katherine Parr, dedicated a translation of Livy to Henry VIII with a prefatory discussion of the brevity of opportunity afforded a man by Time and a consequent injunction that Henry 'tempre dispose and conueigh all his procedynges'

9. See Foucault, *The Use of Pleasure*, pp. 57–8.
10. Hutson, 'Chivalry', p. 46; Whittinton, *Tullyes Offyces*, sig. F3ʳ.
11. Hutson notes that the idea is evident in Machiavelli's work – quoting Martinez, 'Benefit of absence', pp. 129–36 – and that in England a translation of Dominicus Mancinus' *De Quattuor Virtutibus* by George Turberville 'disseminated a similar if simplified version of the Ciceronian version of temperance for the unlearned reader' (Hutson, 'Chivalry', p. 47).

Figure 2.2 Robert Peake's *Portrait of Henry, Prince of Wales* (restored), *c.*1611. By courtesy of the Hamilton Kerr Institute, University of Cambridge

to 'brynge theim to effecte, with prosperous successe', on the grounds that 'as [Occasion] cometh towarde a man, he may take sure holde of her, by hir longe heares[; b]ut in case he mysse to take than his holde, suffrying hir to passe by him: than is there no holde to be taken of hir behynde, but that she runneth awaie without recouerie'.[12] It is thus clear that the idea of temperance as signifying both moderation and timeliness was firmly established by Henry VIII's reign and even perhaps also that it

12. See Hutson, 'Chivalry', p. 48; see also Cope, *Historie*, sig. A2ᵛ. The aim of Cope's translation is to provide exemplary military encouragement prior to the French campaign of 1544.

was possible to suggest politely that the king still had room for improvement in this regard. Certainly, in the Globe play more than half a century later, the king's failure of manhood is represented as a failure of temperance in the combined sense, a failure both to adopt an appropriately moderate lifestyle and a failure, as Gardiner notes to the pageboy, to keep appropriate hours.

This understanding of the relationship of timeliness and manliness provides us with a crucial perspective on Henry's personal, political and dynastic marginalisation at the culmination of the play. The visual image of Time deployed in the debates over temperance, as in Cope's preface, was usually that of Time as Occasion, represented iconographically as a young woman being led by the forelock by an appropriately temperate man. But there was an alternative iconography favoured by militant Protestants in which Time was closely connected with Truth in a manner which foregrounded revelation as the pivot of history, and this alternative tradition is (I would suggest) of some importance to an understanding of the closing moments of *Henry VIII*. This is the image of *veritas filia temporis* ('Truth the daughter of Time'), which focuses on the temporal revelation of Truth in the framework of apocalypse, is based on medieval images of the harrowing of hell, and is depicted typically as the paternal figure of Time stooping over the young female Truth, lifting her up to safety from the jaws of damnation (see Figures 2.1 and 2.2).[13] I have noted elsewhere the status of Truth at this time, claimed as it was by both sides in the course of the sixteenth century, but quite deliberately revived by Elizabeth for the cause of Reformed religion.[14] Soon after her accession, Elizabeth passed through London to be greeted by a figure representing Time who led out Truth in a white dress to hand Elizabeth an English Bible. Happy to confirm her personal

---

13. See woodcut from Marshall's *Goodly Prymer* (Figure 2.1). Cf. references in Fletcher, *The Woman's Prize*, to 'Old father time' (I, iii, 9) and to women who are 'swift to catch occasion / ... by the fore-locks' (II, iv, 51–2). See also Robert Peake's painting of *Henry, Prince of Wales, on Horseback* for a contemporary merging of the image of Time as an old man and of Occasion as a young woman being led by the forelock (Figure 2.2). Cope refers to 'VERITIE' as the 'doughter of tyme' and 'OCCASION' as his sister (sig. A2ᵛ). I am grateful to my colleagues Janet Cowen and Marie Nokes, and to Ron Baxter of the Courtauld Institute, for talking me through the 'harrowing of hell' connection.

14. McMullan, 'Shakespeare', p. 22, for more detailed discussion of the iconography of *veritas filia temporis* and its importance to *Henry VIII*. The present chapter takes further, and in a rather different direction, some of the ideas put forward in the earlier piece.

association with Truth, the queen is said to have stopped and cried out, 'And Time hath brought me hither!'[15]

The final scene of *Henry VIII* depends in part on this iconography and on its particular association with Queen Elizabeth, offering a tableau in which the baby Elizabeth, at the moment of christening, is identified with the Protestant appropriation of Truth within an apocalyptic framework. In order to function visually in this way, however, the scene obviously requires the presence of Time as Truth's father, but that role can equally obviously not be occupied by Henry, the baby Elizabeth's natural father. It will have become abundantly clear by now that the king's immoderation – his lack of temperance – means that his identification with Time would be quite impossible, and I would argue that that role is instead displaced onto Archbishop Cranmer. It is Cranmer who intervenes in the christening process to speak the play's culminating prophecy of Elizabeth and of James, rhetorically generating the eventual male heir whom Henry is incapable of fathering. It is Cranmer who insists on the truth of his words, whose stance – a man standing in a redemptive, authoritative stance over a girl – becomes that of the iconographic representation of Time rescuing Truth from the jaws of hell, and whose prophecy is redolent of this iconography and functions to bridge the years between Henrician and Jacobean England.[16] 'Let me speak, sir', he demands:

> For heaven now bids me; and the words I utter,
> Let none think flattery, for they'll find 'em truth.
> This royal infant (heaven still move about her)
> Though in her cradle, yet now promises
> Upon this land a thousand thousand blessings,
> Which time shall bring to ripeness ....
>   Truth shall nurse her,
> Holy and heavenly thoughts still counsel her;
> She shall be lov'd and fear'd: her own shall bless her;
> Her foes shake like a field of beaten corn,
> And hang their heads with sorrow: good grows with her;
> In her days every man shall eat in safety
> Under his own vine what he plants, and sing

---

15. See Chew, *The Virtues Reconciled*, pp. 70–1.
16. Placing Henry in the role would be particularly inappropriate (and Cranmer, as a martyr, notably more appropriate) since, if the origins of the image in depictions of the harrowing of hell are taken into account, the stooping, saving figure is that of Christ.

The merry songs of peace to all his neighbours ....
Nor shall this peace sleep with her; but as when
The bird of wonder dies, the maiden phoenix,
Her ashes new create another heir
As great in admiration as herself,
So shall she leave her blessedness to one
(When heaven shall call her from this cloud of darkness)
Who from the sacred ashes of her honour
Shall star-like rise, as great in fame as she was,
And so stand fix'd. Peace, plenty, love, truth, terror,
That were the servants to this chosen infant,
Shall then be his, and like a vine grow to him;
Wherever the bright sun of heaven shall shine,
His honour and the greatness of his name
Shall be, and make new nations. He shall flourish,
And like a mountain cedar, reach his branches
To all the plains about him: our children's children
Shall see this, and bless heaven. (V, iv, 14–20, 28–35, 39–55)

In the absence of a properly generative father, Cranmer offers a vision of the future which does not depend upon the physical begetting of a son and which projects the demise of Henry's dynasty even as it promises a glowing future for England. Far from providing a justification of Henry's assertion that his political and personal strength (V, ii, 215) has grown by the end of the play, the final tableau thus reveals a king whose intemperance can only be seen as a failure of true manliness and therefore of political efficacy, and replaces that king as a paternal figure for the nation with a Protestant martyr.

Henry may claim to have been 'made a man' by this girl, or by her birth or her christening, by the 'getting' of Elizabeth, but a Jacobean audience who had just witnessed the whole play would be likely to see things rather differently. Just as, at the Field of Cloth of Gold, a project designed to control the French enemy ended up requiring a public intervention – in the form of the king's proclamation against French fashions – to offset the feminising infiltration of foreign manners into court, so by the end of the play a project premised on excluding a woman in order to promote patriarchal generation – the divorce of Katherine to facilitate the marriage to Anne, that is – concludes with an improvised public mythologising of a baby girl as a vision of England's future. In this context, it is not 'Bluff King Harry' but rather the tear-prone Archbishop Cranmer who is positioned to stand iconographically as the nearest available figurehead for the masculine / paternal principle in the English Reformation and who is obliged, by way of the phoenix metaphor on which his prophecy of the later political situation pivots, to fudge the awkward, ungenerational dynastic transition from Elizabeth Tudor to James Stuart. Cranmer's unexpected centrality in this hastily reworked iconographic tableau sets up Elizabeth and her reign as the offspring not of an intemperate, and therefore finally unmanly, monarch but of an alternative, spiritual paternal figure who is better placed, as a representative of the tribulations and therefore of the triumph (not yet achieved but fully imagined) of the English Reformation, to provide an ideological bridge from Henrician to Jacobean England.

3

'NEAR AKIN':
THE TRIALS OF FRIENDSHIP IN
THE TWO NOBLE KINSMEN

Alan Stewart

Critics have never been happy with *The Two Noble Kinsmen*.[1] It has traditionally been regarded as an unsatisfactory play, compromised, in Ann Thompson's words, by 'many tensions and inconsistencies';[2] to at least one critic, it remains 'that most distressing of plays'.[3] Despite its use of an archetypal story of two male friends brought into conflict over a woman, already tried and tested by Boccaccio (in the *Teseida*) and Chaucer (*Knight's Tale*), its telling here has seemed less than successful. Theodore Spencer went so far as to complain that the story of Palamon and Arcite 'is intrinsically feeble, superficial, and undramatic'.[4] The characters themselves have been 'dismissed as virtually interchangeable emblems of Platonic love and chivalric courtesy – Tweedledum and Tweedledee as Kenneth Muir once called them'.[5] Some have attributed this to the inherent contradictions of the play's genre, tragicomedy.[6] Some have attributed it to its collaborative authorship by Fletcher and

---

1. For the limited critical bibliography to 1990 see Proudfoot, '*Henry VIII*', pp. 391–2. The only monograph devoted to the play is Bertram, *Shakespeare and 'The Two Noble Kinsmen'*.
2. Thompson, *Shakespeare's Chaucer*, p. 166.
3. Donaldson, *The Swan at the Well*, p. 50.
4. Spencer, '*The Two Noble Kinsmen*', p. 256.
5. Wickham, '*The Two Noble Kinsmen*', p. 168.
6. See *The Two Noble Kinsmen*, ed. Potter, 'Introduction', pp. 2–6.

Shakespeare, as if each playwright wrote in solitary ignorance of his partner's work, and the play necessarily betrayed that process.[7] This approach makes possible, for example, the argument that Shakespeare composed the first exchange between Palamon and Arcite, but that Fletcher was responsible for their apparently contradictory quarrel in the prison scene.[8]

In this chapter, I prefer to follow the approach of Richard Hillman, who has argued that 'it is … possible, especially in a post-modern critical climate, to take the play's internal jars, whatever their origin … as integral to the text we have, not as blocking the text that might have been'.[9] I shall argue that, rather than being a failed attempt at a play about idealised male friendship, *The Two Noble Kinsmen* is rather a play about a failed attempt at idealised male friendship. In turn, I shall suggest, this failure derives from the juxtaposition of both classical-humanist and chivalric modes of male friendship with the realities of social relations, and a particular form of kinship, in Jacobean England.

The Two Noble Kinsmen contains a proliferation of variations on that classical and then humanist theme of *amicitia*, the idealised male friendship celebrated in such key Renaissance pedagogical texts as Cicero's *De amicitia* and *De officiis* and Seneca's *De beneficiis*.[10] First, Theseus and Pirithous present an established example of *amicitia*, a legendary male couple revered alongside Orestes and Pylades, Damon and Pythias, and Scipio and Laelius. Pirithous operates to Theseus as *alter ipse*, another himself, to the extent that he stands in as Theseus at his friend's wedding to Hippolyta, because Theseus is honour-bound to avenge the deaths of the husbands of the three queens. In Emilia's words 'The one of th'other may be said to water / Their intertangled roots of love' (I, iii, 58–9).

Second, we encounter the female friendship of Emilia and Flavina. Emilia tells of her love for the innocent 'play-fellow' (I, iii, 50) of her childhood who died young:

> What she liked
> Was then of me approved; what not, condemned –

---

7. Spencer, '*The Two Noble Kinsmen*', p. 255. See also *The Two Noble Kinsmen*, ed. Potter, pp. 24–34. The 'collaboration' argument is also used to explain away the problematic Jailer's Daughter subplot, but my focus here is on the Palamon and Arcite story.

8. Waith, 'Shakespeare and Fletcher', pp. 239–42; Hillman, 'Shakespeare's romantic innocents', p. 73.

9. Hillman, 'Shakespeare's romantic innocents', pp. 70, 71.

10. The classic survey of male friendship in Renaissance English literature remains Mills, *One Soul in Bodies Twain*.

No more arraignment. The flower that I would pluck
And put between my breasts (then but beginning
To swell about the blossom), oh, she would long
Till she had such another, and commit it
To the like innocent cradle, where phoenix-like
They died in perfume. (I, iii, 64–71)

This intense female friendship, located in early pubescence and now irretrievably lost, occupies the same elegiac space as those in earlier Shakespeare plays: Rosalind and Celia in *As You Like It*, and Helena and Hermia in *A Midsummer Night's Dream*, for example.[11]

But the central friendship is that of Palamon and Arcite. As they are imprisoned together, Arcite gives one of the most passionate friendship speeches in English literature:

And here being thus together,
We are an endless mine to one another;
We are one another's wife, ever begetting
New births of love; we are father, friends, acquaintance,
We are, in one another, families;
I am your heir and you are mine. This place
Is our inheritance; no hard oppressor
Dare take this from us; here, with a little patience,
We shall live long and loving. (II, ii, 78–86)

Palamon answers, 'Is there record of any two that loved / Better than we do, Arcite?', to which Arcite affirms, 'Sure there cannot.' 'I do not think it possible', continues Palamon, 'our friendship / Should ever leave us'. 'Till our deaths it cannot', declares Arcite, 'And after death our spirits shall be led / To those that love eternally' (II, ii, 112–17). The tale of Palamon and Arcite as told in this play thus echoes that quintessential humanist fiction of the two male friends, temporarily rent asunder by the intrusion of a woman, who then go on to make up, usually with one of them marrying the woman, and the other marrying his friend's sister. Perhaps the most famous example is the story of Titus and Gisippus, told by Boccaccio in his *Decameron*, and then Englished by Thomas Elyot, and placed centrally in his influential *Boke Named the Gouernour*.[12] The moral of such tales is that, despite the claims of family and marriage,

11. For a discussion of this genre see Miller, *Stages of Desire*, Ch. 5.
12. See Elyot, *Boke Named the Gouernour* (1531); for the importance of this story, see Hutson, *The Usurer's Daughter*, Ch. 2.

male friendship will emerge as the supreme affective force in the lives of the two men.

This superabundance of friendships should, I suggest, raise our suspicions from the start, as couple after couple are introduced displaying apparently textbook adherence to the model. As Theodore Spencer wrote incisively in 1939, '[o]ne of Shakespeare's favourite dramatic devices in his mature work is to establish a set of values and then to show how it is violated by the individual action which follows'.[13] Here, these three instances are introduced precisely to point up the relative failings of two of them. In the case of Emilia and Flavina, the elegiac tone points to the futility of a female version of *amicitia*, always already lost. But more importantly, in Palamon and Arcite something is terribly wrong. From the declaration just quoted, the eternal friendship of Palamon and Arcite lasts exactly two more lines, by which time Palamon has caught sight of Emilia, and Arcite has to urge him (unsuccessfully) to 'forward' with his speech. Their subsequent quarrel over Emilia, leading to an illegal duel, and ultimately to the strange death of Arcite – rather than to the usual double marriage – indicates clearly that all is not well in this telling of their friendship.

The reason for this, I shall suggest, is that in Palamon and Arcite we see a literary, humanist template sitting uncomfortably on a particular Jacobean social reality. The story of Palamon and Arcite is subtly nuanced in each of its retellings. As Eugene Waith notes, in Boccaccio's *Teseida*, it is 'basically a tale of lovers'; in Chaucer's *Knight's Tale*, the relationship is a 'chivalric bond of blood-brotherhood'.[14] In Shakespeare and Fletcher's version, I suggest, Palamon and Arcite are, first and foremost, as the title makes quite clear, *kinsmen*, and as they constantly reiterate, *cousins*. In this chapter, I shall argue that we can make far more sense of *The Two Noble Kinsmen* if we stop thinking of it as a play about friendship, and approach it instead as a play about the problems of kinship, and specifically the problems of cognatic cousinage.[15]

The Two Noble Kinsmen operates, as much of Jacobean England operated, within a culture where women (and figuratively, their virginity) were passed between families in marriage for financial gain; in the upper middling classes and above, these transactions were often complex and lengthy affairs, as befitted such important exchanges of lands, goods and

---

13. Spencer, '*The Two Noble Kinsmen*', p. 270.
14. Waith, 'Shakespeare and Fletcher', p. 236.
15. The importance of kinship rather than friendship in *The Two Noble Kinsmen* is stressed in Mills, *One Soul in Bodies Twain*, pp. 322–3, but he does not address the particular nature of this kinship.

cash. From the first words of the prologue, *The Two Noble Kinsmen* situates itself centrally within such a culture:

> New plays and maidenhead are near akin:
> Much followed both, for both much money gi'en,
> If they stand sound and well. And a good play,
> Whose modest scenes blush on his marriage day
> And shake to lose his honour, is like her
> That after holy tie [the wedding] and first night's stir
> Yet still is Modesty and still retains
> More of the maid, to sight, than husband's pains.
>
> (Prologue, ll. 1–8)

The action of the play is inserted into an interrupted marriage (once again, as in *A Midsummer Night's Dream*, Theseus and Hippolyta have to wait!); the action is concluded when Emilia is exchanged between her new brother-in-law Theseus and the surviving kinsman, Palamon. (Although Arcite appears to give Emilia to Palamon with his dying breath – 'Take her. I die' (V, iv, 95) – in fact it is Theseus who endorses the match). Even the Jailor's Daughter becomes marriageable because Palamon, in gratitude for her actions in springing him from gaol, gives 'a sum of money to her marriage: / A large one' – a gift, of course, not directly to the woman, but to her father, in order that he might marry her to the advantage of both father and daughter (IV, i, 21–4). When Palamon and Arcite are imprisoned, they first bewail the fact that they must remain bachelors; as Arcite puts it:

> here age must find us
> And, which is heaviest, Palamon, unmarried.
> The sweet embraces of a loving wife,
> Loaden with kisses, armed with thousand Cupids,
> Shall never clasp our necks; no issue know us;
> No figures of ourselves shall we e'er see,
> To glad our age, and like young eagles teach 'em
> Boldly to gaze against bright arms and say,
> 'Remember what your fathers were, and conquer!'
>
> (II, ii, 25–36)

Much critical work has been done to illuminate this commodification of women in marriage, most notably Gayle Rubin's reworking of the anthropological work of Claude Lévi-Strauss to uncover the 'traffic in women', and Eve Sedgwick's combining of this with René Girard's triangular formulation to reread male rivalry over women as the prime feature of male homosociality.[16] In her study of quattrocento and cinquecento Florence, Christiane Klapisch-Zuber has shown how these abstract structures operated in practice. 'In Florence', she writes, 'men *were* and *made* the "houses". The word *casa* designates ... the material house, the lodging of a domestic unit ... But it also stands for an entire agnatic kinship group.' These houses, and kinship in general, were 'determined by men, and the male branching of genealogies drawn up by contemporaries shows how little importance was given, after one or two generations, to kinship through women'. She illustrates graphically how, as they married, women moved between houses – both lineage groups and the physical buildings – demonstrating both the stability of the house, and the radical discontinuity of the lives of the women exchanged between them:

> In these *case*, in the sense of both physical and the symbolic house, women were passing guests. To contemporary eyes, their movements in relation to the *case* determined their social personality more truly than the lineage group from which they came. It was by means of their physical 'entrances' and 'exits' into and out of the 'house' that their families of origin or of alliance evaluated the contribution of women to the greatness of the *casa*.[17]

Although the importance of kinship in the English middling classes is thought to have been diminishing during this period, in the upper classes it still held sway. As Keith Wrightson writes, '[i]t is undoubtedly true ... that both the titular aristocracy and the upper gentry were deeply preoccupied with ancestry and lineage and that they tended to recognise a wide range of kinsmen';[18] indeed Anthony Fletcher has asserted that in Sussex county society 'kinship was the dominant principle'.[19] Mervyn James writes that the deepest obligation in any man's life was:

> to the lineage, the family and kinship group. For this, being inherited with the 'blood', did not depend on promise or oath. It could neither be contracted into, nor could the bond be broken. For a man's very being as honourable had been transmitted to him with the blood of his ancestors, themselves honourable men. Honour therefore was not merely an individual possession, but that of the

16. Rubin, 'The traffic in women'; Sedgwick, *Between Men*.
17. Klapisch–Zuber, *Women, Family, and Ritual*, pp. 117–18.
18. Wrightson, *English Society*, pp. 44–51, p. 47.
19. Fletcher, *A County Community*, p. 48.

collectivity, the lineage. Faithfulness to the kinship group arose out of this intimate involvement of personal and collective honour, which meant that both increased or diminished together. Consequently, in critical honour situations where an extremity of conflict arose, or in which dissident positions were taken up involving revolt, treason and rebellion, the ties of blood were liable to assert themselves with a particular power.[20]

Viewed in this English social context, rather than in its humanist literary context, the play reads rather differently. The first words uttered by Arcite put in place a competition between affective and familial links: 'Dear Palamon, dearer in love than blood / And our prime cousin' (I, ii, 1–2). The 'love' that Arcite feels for Palamon is greater than the claim of 'blood', the fact that they are first cousins. Yet they refer to themselves constantly in kinship terms (at least thirty-eight times in the course of the play): 'cousin', 'coz', 'noble cousin' (II, ii, 1), 'gentle cousin' (II, ii, 70 and III, vi, 112), 'fair cousin' (III, vi, 18), 'sweet cousin' (III, vi, 69), 'Clear-spirited cousin' (I, ii, 74), 'My coz, my coz' (III, i, 58), 'kinsman' (III, vi, 21), 'noble kinsman' (II, ii, 193 and III, vi, 17).[21] Even when the two are estranged during their competition for Emilia, they are 'Traitor kinsman' (III, i, 30) and 'base cousin' (III, iii, 44) and Palamon can punningly answer Arcite's 'Dear cousin Palamon' with 'Cozener Arcite' (III, i, 43–4), reminding us that the root of 'cozening' is the cozener's claim to be his victim's long-lost cousin.[22]

'Cousin', like 'kinsman', is a deliberately vague term in early modern English, one that can refer to any loose family connection: Anthony Fletcher writes that in Sussex, 'stress on cousinage in correspondence and account keeping became a mere mark of courtesy. The tight circles of intimate friendship, which were more significant for the dynamics of country affairs, ran within the wider circles of blood'.[23] But these men are not merely 'kinsmen': they share a very particular relationship – to Theseus, they are 'royal german foes' (V, i, 9), implying a close cousin relationship, and in the Herald's words, 'They are sisters' children, nephews to the King' (I, iv, 16). This echoes the Chaucerian source,

20. James, *Society, Politics and Culture*, p. 325.
21. For other uses of 'cousin' and 'coz' see II, ii, 4; II, ii, 63; II, ii, 96; II, ii, 107; II, ii 126; II, ii, 131; III, i, 43; III, i, 69; III, iii, 1; III, iii, 20; III, iii, 23; III, vi, 1; III, vi, 44; III, vi, 47; III, vi, 53; III, vi, 61; III, vi, 73; III, vi, 82; III, vi, 117; III, vi, 262; III, vi, 299; V, i, 23; V, i, 31; V, iv, 93; V, iv, 109.
22. Similarly, 'cousinage' can refer to the writ whereby a legal claim for land is made by one claiming to be a cousin to the deceased.
23. Fletcher, *A County Community*, p. 48.

where they are described as being 'of the blood riall / Of Thebes, and of sistren two yborne' (ll. 1018–19).[24] This point is reiterated strikingly as Palamon and Arcite go through the ritual motions before their attempted duel: Palamon asserts:

> Thou art mine aunt's son
> And that blood we desire to shed is mutual,
> In me thine and in thee mine. (III, vi, 94–6)

In other words, their blood relationship derives from the female line – in Roman or Scottish law terms, their kinship is *cognatic*, rather than *agnatic* (through the male line). Palamon and Arcite are an example, therefore, of what we might call 'cognatic cousinage'.

There is no doubting of course that the kin relationship of cousins german, or first cousins, is extremely close, so close that if one were male and one female, then their right to marry each other would be disputed. However, seen in terms of a culture that exchanges women between patriarchal houses, cousins german whose kinship is cognatic occupy a strangely distant relationship: they are necessarily born into different houses, because their mothers married into different houses. This means, then, that the connection between the two cousins is not necessarily mutually beneficial – what benefits one need not benefit the other.

The peculiarity of this particular kinship relationship – its intense affective claims belied by its signal lack of practical utility – can be glimpsed in the tortuous interactions of two contemporary cousins german: Sir Robert Cecil and Francis Bacon. Cecil was the son of William Cecil, Lord Burghley, by his second wife Mildred Cooke; Bacon was the son of Sir Nicholas Bacon, Lord Keeper, by his second wife Anne Cooke. Mildred and Anne were sisters, two of the renowned and learned daughters of Sir Anthony Cooke, and thus Robert and Francis were first cousins, an instance of cognatic cousinage. But this apparently close family connection was put under great strain after the premature death of Francis's father in February 1579. Left without adequate provision by his father, and unable to call on his estranged elder half-brothers after a dispute about the will, Francis naturally turned to his uncle, Lord Burghley. Throughout his correspondence of the 1580s and early 1590s there are unveiled hints that Burghley might want to become a surrogate parent to his poor nephew. Instead, however, Francis was to be consistently disappointed by his uncle, who put his energies behind his own son, and other protégés. Francis in turn was

24. References are to *The Riverside Chaucer*.

forced to look for support beyond his immediate family, and turned in 1588 to Elizabeth's new young favourite, Robert Devereux, the second earl of Essex.[25]

Essex backed Francis in his bid to become Attorney-General in 1593 and 1594. It soon became clear, however, that Burghley and Cecil were backing another candidate, Edward Coke. This situation produced some highly charged encounters between Bacon's supporters (including Essex and Bacon's mother) and Coke's supporters (Burghley and Cecil). Such an encounter is recorded for us by one of Essex's intelligencers, Anthony Standen, to whom Essex related the anecdote.[26] At the end of January 1593, in the privacy of a shared coach, Sir Robert asked Essex who his candidate was for the vacant post of Attorney-General. Essex affected astonishment, declaring that he 'wondered Sir Robert should ask him that question, seeing it could not be unknown unto him that resolutely against all whosoever for Francis Bacon he stood'.

Sir Robert affected amazement. 'Good Lord', he replied, 'I wonder your Lordship should go about to spend your strength in so unlikely or impossible a matter.' It was out of the question, he continued, that Francis Bacon should be raised to a position of such eminence, since he was simply too young and inexperienced (Francis was thirty-three at the time). Essex readily admitted that he could not think of a precedent for so youthful a candidate for the post of attorney. But he pointed out that youth and inexperience did not seem to be hindering the bid by Sir Robert himself ('[a] younger than Francis, of lesser learning and of no greater experience') to become principal secretary of state, the most influential of all government posts. Cecil retaliated immediately:

> I know your lordship means myself. Although my years and experience are small, yet weighing the school I studied in and the great wisdom and learning of my schoolmaster, and the pains and observations I daily passed, yet I deem my qualifications to be sufficient. The added entitlement of my father's long service will make good the rest.

Unconvinced, Essex passionately reaffirmed his support for Bacon. 'And for your own part Sir Robert', he concluded, 'I think strange both of my Lord Treasurer and you that can have the mind to seek the preferment of a stranger before so near a kinsman as a first cousin.'

25. See Jardine and Stewart, *Hostage to Fortune*.
26. See Anthony Standen to Anthony Bacon, 3 February 1593/4, Lambeth Palace Library MS 650, fols 80–2 (art. 50). This incident is discussed at greater length in Jardine and Stewart, *Hostage to Fortune*, pp. 11–17.

This exchange demonstrates vividly both the symbolic and the practical implications of various relationships between kinsmen. It testifies to the real practical value of the closest kin relationships: Cecil's career is quite explicitly acknowledged as his birthright, because of his father's success. Cognatic cousinage, however, is more complex. On the one hand, we see here the social expectations of the relationship, and of its powerful affective pull ('strange [that] you … can have the mind to seek the preferment of a stranger before so near a kinsman as a first cousin'). On the other, we witness the ineffectiveness of this claim in practical terms: Burghley and Cecil are never swayed to support Bacon (Bacon was not to reach public office for another twelve years, and his career only took off following Cecil's death in 1612). Although the situation was thought unfair by many, Bacon had no legal or moral claim on his cognatic relatives.

The Two Noble Kinsmen is not about either of the cousins' attempting to use the other in any practical sense. As Jeffrey Masten has pointed out, their similarity, a standard trope of *amicitia* literature, is indeed deployed to suggest that they will inevitably enter into competition:

> ARCITE   … am not I
>   Part of your blood, part of your soul? You have told me
>   That I was Palamon, and you were Arcite.
> PALAMON   Yes.
> ARCITE   Am not I liable to those affections,
>   Those joys, griefs, angers, fears, my friend shall suffer?
>
>   (II, ii, 187–91)[27]

However, the futility of their kinship is signalled throughout the play by a skilfully maintained figurative representation. As the chapters in this collection by Helen Hackett and Gordon McMullan amply illustrate, the late plays return insistently to figures of maternity and manliness. These two sisters' sons, who, as we have already seen, describe themselves as their aunts' sons, are constantly referred to in terms of their mothers. When asked what she thinks of Arcite, Emilia answers that 'Believe, / His mother was a wondrous handsome woman; / His face, methinks, goes that way' (II, v, 19–21) (although Hippolyta then contends that 'his body / And fiery mind illustrate a brave father' (II, v, 21–2)). Later Emilia describes Palamon as being 'swart and meagre, of an eye as heavy / As if he had lost his mother' (IV, ii, 27–8). Together, she insists, 'Two greater and two better never yet / Made mothers joy' (IV, ii, 63–4).

---

27. Masten, *Textual Intercourse*, p. 49.

When Palamon berates the kind of men who boast of their sexual conquests, those 'large confessors', he 'hotly ask[s] them / If they had mothers – I had one, a woman, / And women 'twere they wronged' (V, i, 105–7). To Palamon the image of womanhood is his mother.

Firmly established as mothers' boys, the masculinity of both Palamon and Arcite is steadily chipped away throughout the play by a number of analogies, several with Ovidian overtones: as Jonathan Bate argues, '[c]ollaboration with Ovid is one of the marks of Fletcher and Shakespeare's collaboration with each other'.[28] When they are in prison, delineating their *amicitia*, Arcite exclaims that 'We are one another's wife, ever begetting / New births of love' (II, ii, 80–1). Two classical archetypes of passive male sexuality, Narcissus and Ganymede, are reiterated. Immediately after Arcite and Palamon assert their status as wives to each other, Emilia picks some narcissus from the garden, asserting that 'That was a fair boy certain, but a fool / To love himself. Were there not maids enough?' (II, ii, 120–2), referring of course to the myth of Narcissus dying while longing for his own reflection, having rejected the women who loved him. The connection is made explicit when Emilia later compares pictures of her two suitors – Palamon may be to Arcite 'mere dull shadow; / ... swart and meagre, of an eye as heavy':

> As if he had lost his mother; a still temper;
> No stirring in him, no alacrity;
> Of all this sprightly sharpness, not a smile.
> Yet these that we count errors may become him:
> Narcissus was a sad boy, but a heavenly. (IV, ii, 26–32)

As the work of James Saslow, Leonard Barkan and Bruce R. Smith has shown, Ganymede had become by the Renaissance a standard figure for sodomitical, and specifically passive sodomitical, identification.[29] In the same speech, Emilia compares Arcite to Ganymede, one of the 'prettie boyes / That were the darlinges of the gods'. In Golding's words:

> The king of Gods [Jupiter] did burne ere while in loue of *Ganymed*
> The *Phrygian*, and the thing was found which *Iupiter* that sted,
> Had rather be then that he was. Yet could he not beteeme
> The shape of any other bird than Eagle for to seeme:
> And so he soring in the ayre with borrowed wings trust vp

28. Bate, *Shakespeare and Ovid*, p. 265.
29. See Saslow, *Ganymede in the Renaissance*; Barkan, *Transuming Passions*; Smith, *Homosexual Desire*, Ch. 3.

The *Troiane* boy, who stil in heauen euen yet doth beare his cup,
And brings him *Nectar*, though against Dame *Iunos* wil it bee.[30]

Emilia declares:

> What an eye,
> Of what a fiery spark and quick sweetness,
> Has this young prince! Here Love himself sits smiling;
> Just such another wanton Ganymede
> Set Jove afire with, and enforced the god
> Snatch up the goodly boy, and set him by him,
> A shining constellation. What a brow,
> Of what a spacious majesty, he carries,
> Arched like the great-eyed Juno's, but far sweeter,
> Smoother than Pelops' shoulder! (IV, ii, 12–21)

We move from the beautiful shepherd boy Ganymede snatched up to become Jove's cupbearer in the heavens, to Jove's own wife Juno, to the ivory shoulder that replaced the shoulder of Pelops served up by his father Tantalus (and as ever, we are not sure here whether the smooth shoulder is the succulent one eaten, or the ivory replacement).[31] Palamon and Arcite are led through a serious of analogies that cast them as women, or as passive male bodies eaten by men or made love to by men, or as men in love with their own reflection. These images multiply through the play, and no amount of recognition for Arcite's potential prowess as a wrestler is going to shake them off.

What effect might this have on a reading of *The Two Noble Kinsmen*? I return to the speech I quoted earlier, where Palamon and Arcite pledge eternal friendship. It is indeed a remarkable and passionate speech, but we need to see it in context. It comes during the couple's imprisonment: at the beginning of the scene (II, ii), Palamon bewails their situation ('Oh, cousin Arcite, / Where is Thebes now? Where is our noble country? / Where are our friends and kindred?' (II, ii, 6–8)) and Arcite agrees that their 'hopes are prisoners with us' (II, ii, 26), lamenting the fact that they will never marry, nor have children, nor hunt again. It is only then that Arcite exclaims:

> Yet, cousin,
> Even from the bottom of these miseries,
> From all that Fortune can inflict upon us,

---

30. Golding, *The XV Bookes* (1603), sig. Q8ᵛ (Book X, ll.155–61).
31. For Pelops, see Golding, *The XV Bookes*, sig. K8ᵛ (Book VI, ll. 515–25).

> I see two comforts rising, two mere blessings,
> If the gods please: to hold here a brave patience
> And the enjoying of our griefs together.
> While Palamon is with me, let me perish
> If I think this our prison! (II, ii, 55–62)

Palamon replies:

>   Certainly,
> 'Tis a main goodness, cousin, that our fortunes
> Were twined together; 'tis most true, two souls
> Put in two noble bodies, let 'em suffer
> The gall of hazard, so they grow together,
> Will never sink; they must not, say they could.
> A willing man dies sleeping and all's done.
>   (II, ii, 62–8)

It is then that they go on to 'make this prison holy sanctuary / To keep us from corruption of worse men' (II, ii, 71–2), and go into their passionate speech of friendship. As this preamble shows, however, the speech is a set piece, arrived at only after despair has cast them down, and as a pragmatic response to their dire situation. Friendship in the classic Ciceronian mould is only an option once imprisonment takes away their social agency. It does not stand up to comparison with the successful friendship of Theseus and Pirithous, or with the elegaic friendship of Emilia and Flavina, which have been carefully set up before precisely to demonstrate the failings of Palamon and Arcite's friendship; the first oblique comment on their declaration of friendship is Emilia's discussion of Narcissus. And even within the speech just quoted we can sense something awry: these two friends are 'two souls / Put in two noble bodies' (II, ii, 64–5), when the classic formulation of friendship is a single soul in two bodies. The hyperbole of being each other's wife, family, heir is merely a response to the deprivation of social agency; the minute that a way back into the real world is spied (in the form of Emilia, marriage to whom will ensure not only freedom but social success in Athens) the eternal friendship is shelved.

While the influence of Ciceronian *amicitia* is evident throughout, the play's immediate source requires that the authors also deal with the male friendship associated with chivalric codes. Here again, all is not as it might be. Chaucer's *Knight's Tale* has an ending which can still been seen as happy within the expectations of its genre: one knight wins his lady in honourable chivalric contest, but dies in an accident; after a suitable period, the lady is granted to the honourable loser. Much has been written about the chivalric elements of *The Two Noble Kinsmen*: it has been seen as linked to a neo-chivalric movement associated with Prince Henry;[32] it has even been read as a *roman à clef* of international politics, with Arcite as Henry, who has to die before his sister Elizabeth (Emilia) can marry her betrothed Frederick (Palamon).[33] In *The Two Noble Kinsmen*, the elements are similar to Chaucer's, but their treatment is noticeably different, and the end result unsettling: as Philip Finkelpearl has written, '[a]lthough the knightly code may originally have been designed to curb uncivilized instincts, here it sanctions and dignifies the urge of revenge, murder, and suicide'.[34]

Richard Hillman sees the fundamental contradictions as suggestive of an unbridgeable gap between medieval and Jacobean notions of chivalry: '[p]recisely by endlessly trying and failing to measure up to the inherited images of romance perfection, these pale Jacobean imitations deconstruct the very business of image-making. They are trapped by their own attempted appropriation of a medieval past'.[35] The kinsmen's 'failure to measure up' is, moreover, treated harshly, even callously. The chivalric contest now carries a death penalty for the loser, and there is virtually no time lost between the winner's death and the loser's marriage. The death of one knight, an incidental detail in Chaucer (since it does not matter who marries the lady), here becomes essential to the happy ending. Significantly, a successful conclusion can only come at what Palamon calls the 'miserable end of our alliance' (V, iv, 86), the accident in which Arcite is fatally injured. Even here, the nature of his death – Arcite is left hanging upside down from his mount, after the horse rears away from a spark from the cobbles ('Arcite's legs, being higher than his head, / Seemed with strange art to hang' (V, iv, 78–9)) – suggests something less than chivalric. As Richard Abrams notes, '[b]y the play's end, disabused of *The Knight's Tale*'s heroic mystique, we recognise the strangeness of a world where a question of love-rights is automatically referred to a determination of which kinsman is the stronger fighter'.[36]

Arcite must die for Palamon to win: as Palamon laments, 'That we should things desire, which do cost us / The loss of our desire! That nought could buy / Dear love, but loss of dear love' (V, iv, 110–12). *The*

32. See for example Hillman, 'Shakespeare's romantic innocents', p. 79; Finkelpearl, 'Two distincts, division none', pp. 184–99.
33. Wickham, '*The Two Noble Kinsmen*', *passim*.
34. Finkelpearl, 'Two distincts, division none', p. 191.
35. Hillman, 'Shakespeare's romantic innocents', p. 71.
36. Abrams, 'Gender confusion', p. 75.

Two Noble Kinsmen demonstrates, and demands, highly developed under-standing of concepts of friendship and kinship, developed enough to accommodate both parody and sincerity about such concepts. The friendship of Palamon and Arcite is no more than a game to while away long hours of incarceration; their constantly reiterated claims to kinship dissolve in the face of a prize (Emilia) that might benefit them as individuals and their immediate family groups; the play's happy ending necessitates the dissolution of their 'alliance'. Fletcher and Shakespeare indulge their audience in the comfortable humanist myth of *amicitia*, and the reliable codes of chivalric courtship, only to force that audience to accept the fact that ultimately these are no more than myths and codes, and that they cannot thrive together. We are faced with the sobering fact that artistic closure is not always compatible with social reality: to secure our desired happy ending, there may be fatalities.

PART II
ART, AESTHETICS AND SOCIETY

4

SOCIAL DECORUM IN
THE WINTER'S TALE

Jennifer Richards

One of the most difficult problems facing critics of *The Winter's Tale* is the source of Leontes' jealousy. At one moment in I, ii, Leontes is encouraging his wife, Hermione, to persuade Polixenes to extend his visit ('Tongue-tied, our queen? Speak you', I, ii, 28); a few minutes later, he is plunged into passionate doubts ('To mingle friendship far is mingling bloods', I, ii, 108). So unexpected is his rage that the search for motivation becomes tempting, even preoccupying. Critics alert to the dangers of character criticism either ignore this temptation, advising us to read his jealousy as a theatrical effect, or avoid the pitfalls of a psychological reading by focusing on the play's interest in the mediacy of language, and the ambiguity of Hermione's words and gestures.[1] In a contribution to this debate, I would like to use the *search* for motivation as a means to address a more recently identified area of neglect in current criticism: the play's concern with social distinction.[2] Leontes' rage is motivated by a sensitivity not just to the mediacy of language but to its inability to represent adequately distinctions in rank; and from the

---

1. *The Winter's Tale*, ed. J. H. P. Pafford, p. lxxii; Felperin, '"Tongue-tied",' p. 9. See also the discussion of motivation in *The Winter's Tale*, ed. Orgel, pp. 22–8; cf. Sokol, who argues that Leontes' 'breakdown closely resembles a real psychological development', *Art and Illusion*, p. 32.
2. Orkin, 'A sad tale', p. 5.

moment at which he descends into passionate tyranny, the play forces us to confront his unwavering belief that social distinction exists 'in nature'.

Leontes' concern with social, as well as sexual, transgression is indicated in his depiction of Hermione as 'As rank as any flax-wench that puts to / Before her troth-plight' (I, i, 274–5). As Leontes' pun on 'rank' suggests, Hermione's imagined infidelity is socially demeaning. She has forgotten her place in the social order, and has behaved little better than an undisciplined country-girl. But Leontes is not just concerned with Hermione's manners. He also calls attention to the dangers of linguistic familiarity. 'O thou thing', he scornfully addresses Hermione:

> Which I'll not call a creature of thy place
> Lest barbarism, making me the precedent,
> Should a like language use to all degrees,
> And mannerly distinguishment leave out
> Betwixt the prince and beggar. (II, i, 82–7)

Leontes' sensitivity to linguistic familiarity is twofold. On the one hand, he intuits his own contribution to the collapse of 'mannerly distinguishment' through a careless use of language. To name Hermione a 'whore', to attribute to her the 'bold'st titles' proffered by 'vulgars', is to commit *cacemphaton* or *Scurra*, the rhetorical figure which George Puttenham translates in *The Arte of English Poesie* (1589) as 'foule speache' and advises the 'courtly maker' to 'shunne' at all costs if he is to speak decorously, that is, in keeping with his social station.[3] On the other hand, though, Leontes is alert to the ambivalence of one linguistic marker of social distinction: he cannot call Hermione a 'creature of [her] place' – or queen – because to do so is to acknowledge immediately that she is indeed a 'quean' or whore.[4] In this respect, he identifies a new problem, that a term designating high status, rather than confidently denoting its social exclusiveness, alludes to its demeaned opposite. And he prompts a different kind of question in a play often too narrowly defined as 'courtly' or 'aristocratic': not 'how can one secure "mannerly distinguishment"?', but rather, 'can it be secured at all?'.[5]

Leontes' suppressed punning on the term 'queen', and his paranoid

---

3. Puttenham, *Arte*, pp. 253–4.
4. See also *Henry VIII*, II, iii, 24, and Foakes's discussion in his introduction to this edition, pp. xlviii–xlix. Commented on by Briggs in this collection, p. 217.
5. *The Winter's Tale* dramatises a question posed in its source, Robert Greene's *Pandosto*: when does 'familiar courtesy' become a 'too private familiarity' (*Pandosto*, ed. Stanley Wells, in *The Winter's Tale*, ed. Orgel, Appendix B, pp. 235–6)? For a discussion of this see Holderness *et al.*, *Shakespeare Out of Court*, pp. 205–6.

interpretation of Hermione's 'entertainment' of Polixenes, will probably strike us as evidence first and foremost of the self-feeding and obsessive character of his anxiety. After all, it is Leontes, not Hermione, who is ultimately 'guilty' of speaking vulgarly.[6] Yet, Leontes' rantings, I suggest, should be taken seriously, because they draw attention to the linguistic transgression so characteristic of this and other late plays. Indeed, it is perhaps useful to think of Leontes as a character who has been cast into the wrong play. His commitment to neoclassical standards of decorum – to the suiting of speech to character and status – and to the related 'moralisation of status terms' seem curiously out of place in *The Winter's Tale*, which displays its disrespect for the kind of 'mannerly distinguishment' he craves.[7] 'Never a man who paid much attention to the requirements of neoclassical decorum when constructing character', writes Anne Barton, 'the Shakespeare of the late plays seems to have abandoned even the basic convention by which, earlier, his servants and lower-class characters generally expressed themselves in homely, colloquial, if vivid, prose.' In *The Winter's Tale* itself, the rustic characters of its pastoral world 'dodge in and out of their status-defined, comic roles in ways for which there are no real parallels in earlier plays'.[8] From the other side, Autolycus, a demoted court malcontent, slips as easily into beggar's weeds and words as he does into the aristocratic costume and 'court-contempt' of his erstwhile master, Prince Florizel (IV, iv, 729). Leontes' anxiety may seem to come from nowhere, but it can be explained through Hermione's ambiguous 'courtly' display, and even through the action of the play, which consistently confounds his neoclassical tastes.

Of course, to observe merely that Shakespeare transgresses neoclassical standards of decorum in one of his late plays is hardly new, as Anne Barton's work suggests. In fact, Shakespeare's indecorum is a topic well covered in two book-length studies: T. McAlindon's *Shakespeare and Decorum* (1973) and John D. Cox's *Shakespeare and the Dramaturgy of Power* (1989). These critics may disagree over the intentions of Shakespeare's distaste for decorous hierarchies, but they share a belief that

---

6. On Leontes' vulgar language see Smith, 'The language of Leontes'; Barton, 'Leontes and the spider'; cf. Neely, '*The Winter's Tale*'. See also Evans, 'Elizabethan spoken English', and Crane on *As You Like It* in 'Linguistic change'.

7. On the 'moralisation of status terms' see Lewis, *Studies in Words*, pp. 21–3. Hall's description of 'decorum' as 'a class concept' is useful here: 'a king should speak as a king is expected to, while a commoner should use idioms common to the people.' (Hall, *Renaissance Literary Criticism*, pp. 181–2).

8. Barton, 'Leontes and the spider', pp. 140–1. (For instances of social mobility see IV, ii, 38–40; IV, iii, 13–14; IV, iv, 9–10; IV, iv, 21–2, 415–17.)

Shakespeare departs from the neoclassical standards set up in the six-teenth- and early seventeenth-century courtesy handbooks.[9] As I will argue, though, these texts are helpful in interpreting the play's sensitivity to the *limits* of linguistic and social decorum, and also for accounting for its courtly tone. Usually understood to offer a defence of the privileges of the established aristocracy, these 'elitist' texts also appeal to a broader audience, and engage in a search not just for a narrow definition of nobility, but for an understanding of a shared 'humanity'.[10] Courtesy treatises understand that courtly display is already potentially transgres-sive, indebted as it is to the low, not the high, style of classical decorum. Against these texts, we will be able to see more clearly that *The Winter's Tale* affirms a dialectical, rather than a fixed, relationship between the 'low' and the 'high': it explores how the 'low' is implicated in the 'high' (just as Hermione's courteous actions can simultaneously be read as 'common' and 'queanish'), and also how the 'low' and the 'high' can grow into one another (just as a 'queen' can become a 'quean', or conversely, a 'queen of curds and cream' can be noble indeed (IV, iv, 161).

I

Such a claim for *The Winter's Tale* might seem odd in view of the fact that, for many of its critics, it aims only to restore the natural superiority of the aristocracy, and to 'replicate seventeenth-century notions of hier-archy'. Leontes' refusal to call Hermione 'a creature of [her] place', Martin Orkin suggests, depends 'on a series of implied inscriptions about normative courtly behaviour that distinguishes the courtier from any "barbarous" disregard of hierarchy', and which are dramatised in the play itself. For example, Perdita's desire 'to tell' the snobbish Polixenes 'plainly' that 'The selfsame sun that shines upon his court / Hides not his visage from our cotage' (IV, iv, 440–2) is received by an audience 'secure in the knowledge … that she is an aristocrat'. For Rosalie Colie, this 'conspicuously ill-made' play never fulfils its offered questioning of the concept of 'nobility'. In the famous art / nature debate at its heart, we catch a glimpse of a levelling perspective in the argument put

9. McAlindon, *Shakespeare and Decorum*, p. 16; Cox, *Dramaturgy of Power*, esp. preface, Ch. 3, and Ch. 10. Cox has an excellent discussion of the 'popular dramaturgy' of *The Winter's Tale*, pp. 207–21. For more recent attention to Shakespeare's indecorum see Palfrey, *Late Shakespeare*, esp. pp. 14ff.
10. See Whigham, *Ambition and Privilege*, esp. Ch. 1. For Whigham, courtesy treatises are intended for an elite audience, but are often appropriated by the upwardly mobile. See also Javitch, *Poetry and Courtliness*.

forward by Polixenes (and challenged by Perdita) that 'we marry / A gentler scion to the wildest stock, / And make conceive a bark of baser kind / By bud of nobler race' (IV, iv, 92–5). But, because 'Perdita is in fact royal', Colie insists, 'Polixenes' views about grafting are not in fact relevant to his own son's union; and Perdita's hierarchical conception of rank ... is confirmed, not challenged, by the ultimate arrangement of the plot'. In the course of the play, Andrew McRae adds, Perdita merely 'demonstrates in her growth to maturity' a motif integral to aristocratic pastoral romance – 'the predominance of regal nature over rustic nurture' – which is intended unambiguously to suppress the social aspirations of the 'middling' ranks.[11]

It is difficult to argue against such a perspective when the play so insistently voices the prejudices of its noble characters, and even allows that the demand for 'mannerly distinguishment' should be interpreted as a mark of an aristocratic nature, a naturally refined sensibility. Leontes may figure himself as a betrayed 'everyman' once he is convinced of Hermione's infidelity ('And many a man there is, even at this present, / Now, while I speak this, holds his wife by th'arm, / That little thinks she has been sluiced in's absence' (I, ii, 190–2)), yet he also imagines his discernment as an example of his own aristocratic temper. In the same scene, Leontes perceives that Camillo shares his suspicions, and praises his conceit as above that of 'common blocks': 'Not noted, is't', he remarks, 'But of finer natures? By some severals / Of headpiece extraordinary? Lower messes / Perchance are to this business purblind?' (I, ii, 222–5). Quite simply, men of lower rank do not share his superior insight. For Leontes, Mamillius' illness is itself a sign of the 'nobleness' of his nature, a physical recoiling from 'the dishonour of his mother' (II, iii, 13–14).

Of course, Leontes' aristocratic insightfulness may be discredited quite early in the play – after all, what he perceives as Camillo's insight turns out to be merely an expression of bewilderment. Even so, a more sympathetic outlet for such views is offered with the character of Polixenes, king of Bohemia. Sensitive to Leontes' mood swings in Act I, Polixenes seeks insight from Camillo with an appeal to his gentility and education: 'As you are certainly a gentleman, thereto / Clerk-like experienced, which no less adorns / Our gentry than our parents' noble names' (I, ii, 386–8). In the later pastoral scenes Polixenes' sensibilities will be (credibly) offended at the sight of his son, 'a sceptre's heir', courting a mere 'knack', the shepherdess Perdita (IV, iv, 416, 425).

11. Orkin, 'A sad tale', p. 9; Colie, *Shakespeare's Living Art*, pp. 266, 277; McRae, *God Speed*, p. 269.

Polixenes' and Leontes' shared belief in the simple-mindedness, undis-criminating taste and sexual naiveté of the 'Lower messes', moreover, is apparently proven by the court malcontent and disguised peddler, Autolycus: 'My clown, who wants but something to be a reasonable man', he reflects on his profitable sale of trifles, 'grew so in love with the wenches' song that he would not stir his pettittoes till he had both tune and words, which so drew the rest of the herd to me that all their other senses stuck in ears – you might have pinched a placket, it was senseless' (IV, iv, 601–6). So 'senseless' are the rustic 'herd', he suggests, that they are susceptible to his (and other disguised courtiers') commercial and sexual exploitation.

Perdita's recovery, discussed in V, ii, seems not only to affirm an essentialist conception of 'nobility' but to offer a correct interpretation of gentle manners. In contrast to Leontes, who misreads Hermione's courtly 'entertainment' as common and unqueenlike, the Third Gentle-man accepts Perdita's 'affection of nobleness' as a sign of her innate gentility in spite of her rural appearance (l. 36). Such a reading seems to be reinforced a moment later, through the reference of the newly ennobled Clown to his 'preposterous estate' (l. 142), to his new status as a 'gentleman 'born' (l. 130).[12] We laugh at his naive assumption that his clothes make him a gentleman: 'See you these clothes? Say you see them not, and think me still no gentleman born – you were best say these robes are not gentlemen born?' (ll. 126–9). His short-sightedness appears as a poor and revealing imitation of the displayed 'court-contempt' of Autolycus, disguised as Florizel, when he confronts the Shepherd and Clown earlier in the play: 'I am a courtier. Seest thou not the air of the court in these enfoldings? Hath not my gait in it the measure of the court? Receives not thy nose court odour from me?' (IV, iv, 725–9).

The Winter's Tale, then, seems to insist on 'mannerly distinguishment' in aesthetic terms; it appeals to the 'bifurcation' of audience – which Eduardo Saccone describes as integral to aristocratic culture – into those who 'belong' to a courtly 'club' because they know how to read its signs, and those who are merely its admiring 'victims'.[13] Shakespeare's sensitiv-ity to the refined tastes of an aristocratic audience is arguably present in earlier comedies, most notably *A Midsummer Night's Dream* and *Love's Labours Lost*.[14] Such rank-consciousness is marked spatially in the

12. See Parker, 'Preposterous estates', for discussion of the 'preposterous' in Shakespeare.
13. Saccone, '*Grazia, sprezzatura*', p. 60; see also Stallybrass and White, *The Politics and Poetics of Transgression*, and Schmidgall, *Shakespeare and the Courtly Aesthetic*.
14. See esp. the play-within-the-play in *Midsummer Night's Dream*, V, i, and *Love's Labours Lost*, V, ii.

conclusion of *The Winter's Tale*. As Orkin observes, in V, ii, the newly ennobled Clown and Shepherd, and demoted Autolycus, significantly 'are left *outside*, when, in the final scene, the courtiers go *inside*, to the home of Paulina'. '[W]hatever the "discoveries" or assertions of maturity attained in the home,' he adds, 'these are also hereby presented as implicitly possible only for the aristocratic body', that is, the appreciation of Hermione's living 'statue' as 'aristocratic, "high", classical' art (p. 16). In a world in which courtly status is defined partly by proximity to the body of the monarch, the Clown's and Shepherd's exclusion provocatively undermines their new kinship to Leontes. But they are also 'outsiders' in a different sense, for they are too simple-minded to appreciate genteel culture. Their attempt to define themselves as 'insiders', as 'gentlemen-born', is revealed to be a 'preposterous' miscomprehension of the natural order which insinuates their distance from the real nobility.

Even so, it is still important to consider the extent to which Shakespeare presents a glib defence of 'natural' nobility in this play. For alongside the self-confidence of the aristocrats, it invites us to question the quality of their insights, and the ease with which they interpret the world around them, suggesting that Alison Thorne's argument in this collection, concerning the hermeneutic complexity of *Cymbeline*, applies equally to *The Winter's Tale*. We are asked, for example, not only to discredit Leontes' superior perspicuity, but to observe the dramatised mistaken readings of other characters (for example, Antigonus' misinterpretation of Hermione in his dream in III, i). The play also cultivates in its audience an awareness of its own susceptibility to misreading. We may be puzzled by Leontes' sudden jealous passion and by the ambiguity of Hermione's playful engagement with Polixenes, and we will probably find ourselves uncomfortably uncertain of the motives of Perdita's suitor, Prince Florizel. In view of such interpretative anxieties, is it not significant that we, like Autolycus (and unlike the Shepherd and Clown), are also excluded from Perdita's discovery towards the play's conclusion? And that though in contrast to the Shepherd, Clown and Autolycus we do make our way into Paulina's home at the end, we find ourselves, like the humiliated Leontes, to be the admiring victims of Paulina's 'trick'? The only knowledge we do possess with any certainty is that Perdita is nobly born, but this does not mean that she is innately noble. It *is* significant, as Orkin suggests, that the discovery of Perdita's royal identity takes place off-stage, but not for the reasons he offers. Rather than having the satisfaction of seeing the characters realise what we already know, we are invited instead to consider their responses to this revelation. How it is possible, for instance, that so self-evident a 'queen' could have been earlier dismissed as an ignoble, although beautiful, 'queen of curds and cream'?

Shakespeare's invocation in *The Winter's Tale* of the experience of being 'outside' and 'inside' invites us to reflect more carefully on its presumed courtly elitism or exclusivity. Aristocratic culture is usually understood to be 'exclusive' in its dependence on 'mannerly distinguishment' between courtiers and clowns, and the gentle and the ungentle. It is also often presumed to be uncritically bound to the 'hegemonic coherence of the ideology of social rank' integral to the Elizabethan and Jacobean courts.[15] The task of the modern critic, who is historically 'outside' its cultural discourse, then, is to expose a text's elitism, and its concomitant appropriation of theories of natural right. Derek Attridge begins his subtle reading of Puttenham's *Arte*, for example, with a recognition of his own critical short-sightedness and the relinquishment of the 'illusion' of 'standing outside the field that provides the structures to [his] thought and writing'.[16] At the same time, though, he recognises the possibility of reading between the lines – of discovering 'much more than the writer's conscious intentions' – in an earlier text. In relation to the *Arte*, historical distance allows Attridge to explore the text's contradictions and to expose Puttenham's restricted and unthinking application of the adjective 'natural' to aristocratic taste. As he argues, in the *Arte* 'Decorum is what comes "naturally" not to all humanity but to an elite; and members of that elite can be identified by their "natural" sense of decorum. What comes naturally to the majority, who are ignorant and inexperienced, is not *truly* natural' (p. 269). Yet such an approach *in general* does not adequately recognise the critical capacity of early modern texts.[17] In the case of the courtesy treatises which are seen to disseminate standards of decorum it is insufficiently attentive to the ways in which they qualify such stock notions as 'natural' nobility and 'mannerly distinguishment', or to the way in which they recognise how the outsider to aristocratic culture – the rustic clown – is, in some sense, already inside. In the case of *The Winter's Tale*, it is insensitive to the way in which it confounds decorous tastes and explores the gap between the

15. Wrightson, 'Estates, degrees, and sorts', p. 20. On social mobility see Wrightson, *English Society*, and on changing perceptions of 'nobility', James, *Society, Politics and Culture*.
16. Attridge, 'Puttenham's perplexity', p. 257.
17. Patterson, *Reading Between the Lines*, p. 6; cf. Morse, 'Metacriticism and materiality'. Shakespeare was himself an 'outsider'. On his aspirations to gentle status see Schoenbaum, *William Shakespeare*, Ch. 13, and on his low status as a 'player' see Barroll, *Politics, Plague*, Ch. 1.

language of status and the social mobility which characterised the reality of early modern England. It is also insensitive to the fact that the play already contains its own distancing tactic in its allusion to off-stage action.

II

To understand Shakespeare's exploration of the limits of 'mannerly distinguishment', it is helpful to turn, as McAlindon has suggested, to the 'so-called courtesy books', and especially to Castiglione's *The Book of the Courtier* (trans. 1561), Stefano Guazzo's *Civile Conversation* (trans. 1581) and James Cleland's *The Institution of a Young Nobleman* (1607) (p. 4). These courtesy treatises, McAlindon argues, inculcate in their readers a sensitivity to 'class or office', and to the decorous conception of 'the relationship between man and name or title' as it is expressed in speech and dress (p. 9). In Book V of the *Institution*, for example, Cleland advises the young nobleman to ensure that his 'speech' is not 'popular' since his 'qualitie [is] above the common', and he also urges him 'to put a distinction betweene [his] discourses and a *Scythians*, a *Barbarians* or a *Gothes*', adding that 'it is a pitty when a Noble Man is better distinguished from a Clowne by his golden laces, then by his good language'.[18] Treatises such as Cleland's, John D. Cox notes, display a revived taste for the stratification of styles according to classical decorum, and also 'the emergence of a confident English high style' (p. 57). Alongside the development of English to accommodate Cicero's 'magnificent, opulent, stately and ornate' grand style,[19] we find the 'eloquent dismissal' of medieval and Protestant plain speech or *sermo humilis* (p. 52). In contrast to Hugh Latimer, who, writing in the 1550s, could proudly identify himself as the son of a 'yeoman', and compare preaching to husbandry, humanist writers in the 1560s such as Thomas Wilson, associated more closely with the centralised Tudor court, distance themselves from their humble backgrounds. In *The Arte of Rhetorique*, for example, Thomas Wilson – the son of a yeoman farmer – places 'linguistic solecisms … in the mouths of anonymous "country fellows" who blunder about awkwardly in his anecdotes before their social betters' (p. 52).

But what exactly is 'courtly speech'? The examples just given imply that it is spoken by members of the aristocracy, and that it is 'ornate' and 'stately'. Such an account, however, is hardly adequate. For instance,

18. Cleland, *The Institution*, sig. Aa[v].
19. Cicero, *Orator*, xxviii, 97.

Cleland may insist that '[s]peech is the image of the minde, and messenger of the heart', and invite us to imagine that a gentleman's language reflects his innate gentility (sig. Z4ᵛ). Yet, in the same treatise, he insists that nobility is a virtue which is 'husbanded' through education rather than inherited, so that it is not clear whether courtly speech is spoken naturally by the well born, or whether it is a standard of English acquired artificially, alongside gentility itself, through study and practice. Any decorous understanding of courtly speech, which takes into consideration the rank of the speaker, then, is undermined by the disputed definition of 'nobility' in such treatises. In addition, we might note that courtiers were expected to use the full range of available styles, and were restricted partly by context and intent.[20]

More confusingly, though, courtesy writers are unexpectedly united in their *formal* description of 'courtly' speech in the terms of the classical 'low' style.[21] Cleland's description of a gentleman's language stresses its prosaic rather than stately qualities: it should be 'plaine and perspicuous, as flowing from a natural fountaine of eloquence', he explains, so that it can be 'understood as wel as the common talke of the village, and pearceth and perswadeth the heart of the hearer besides' (sig. Aaʳ⁻ᵛ). He echoes the advice of Castiglione in his preface to the *Courtier* to choose words from 'commune speach',[22] and of Guazzo's Annibale in *Civile Conversation*, 'to proceede in common talke simply and plainly, according as the truth of the matter shall require'.[23] The model for gentlemen, I suggest, is not Cicero's grand, but rather his 'restrained and plain', orator who follows 'ordinary usage [consuetudo]' (*Orator*, xxiii. 76), and who differs from untrained speakers only to the extent that his 'natural' style is premeditated, and aims at a 'careful negligence [neglegentia diligens]' (*Orator*, xxiii. 78).

Attridge's comments on the aristocratic appropriation of 'naturalness' are best understood in this context. For upwardly mobile Elizabethan and early Jacobean writers were committed to creating in English a classical plain *courtly* style which would replace the native *sermo humilis*, and provide an elite form of discourse. There is a great difference, for instance, between the native idiom of the mid-Tudor preacher Hugh Latimer and the cultivated plain style of the courtier-poet Philip Sidney. Sidney himself wanted to ensure that we do not forget this distinction.

20. I am grateful to Alison Thorne for reminding me of this point. See Puttenham's discussion of Andrew Flamock's experiments in decorum, *Arte*, pp. 268–9.
21. See also Trimpi, *Ben Jonson's Poems*, p. 281 n.18.
22. Castiglione, *Courtier*, p. 15.
23. Guazzo, *Civile Conversation*, sig. G8ʳ.

In his pastoral romance *Arcadia* he roughly dismisses the rustic character Dametas, a 'most arrant doltish clown', who wins the admiration of the foolish King Basilius because he expresses himself 'with such rudeness, which he interpreted plainness – though there be a great difference between them'.[24] Sidney might well concur with Attridge's wry comment on Elizabethan decorum that '[w]hat comes naturally to the majority, who are ignorant and inexperienced, is not *truly* natural' (p. 269), and he might also see the relationship between courtly speech and *sermo humilis* as constitutive of a natural order, led by a hereditary nobility. And yet, that same relationship between courtly speech and the low style also threatens any attempt at 'mannerly distinguishment' and the concomitant creation of a natural order, because it evokes the quite distinct search for a general conception of 'humanity' which finds its roots in natural law. After all, *sermo humilis*, as the idiom of ordinary people, betokens not simply 'their' low social degree, but 'our' shared innate possession of the 'seeds of virtue', the capacity for speech, reason *and* judgement which distinguishes us from animals, not one another.[25] Even Sidney's *Arcadia* includes two 'cultivated' shepherds, Strephon and Claius, who are 'beyond the rest by so much as learning doth add to nature' (p. 83).

The connection between *sermo humilis*, courtly speech and natural law is apparent, for instance, in Guazzo's *Civile Conversation*. It is true that Annibale, its main speaker, insists on the observation of decorum; he recognises, for example, that a gentleman is 'so much the more esteemed of, by howe muche our Civilitie differeth from the nature and fashions

---

24. Sidney, *Arcadia*, pp. 77–8.
25. See Cicero, *Tusculan Disputations*, III, i, 2: 'The seeds of virtue are inborn in our dispositions and, if they were allowed to ripen, nature's own hand would lead us to happiness of life [Sunt enim ingeniis nostris semina innata virtutum …]'. This idea governs Cicero's attitude to rhetoric and civil society: see esp. *De Re Publica*, *De Legibus*, I, xxv, 40; II, iii, 8; II, xlii 69. See White, *Natural Law*, and McCabe, *Incest, Drama and Nature's Law*.

I am aware that such an emphasis might be seen by post-structuralist and new historicist critics to imply an essentialist conception of human 'nature' (see esp. Dollimore, *Radical Tragedy*). In response, I would suggest that this criticism springs from a misguided perception of the close association between a nineteenth-century Christian idealism and early modern humanism. For an alternative perspective see Norbrook on 'the strong critical element' of 'rationalistic theories of natural law': '[a] sceptical relativism about claims to an unproblematic "human nature" is placed against a searching, universalizing quest for a more general notion of humanity' (Norbrook, '"What cares these roarers for the name of king?"', pp. 124–5). The place of natural law in the courtesy tradition is discussed in my forthcoming monograph, 'Courtliness and Rhetoric in Early Modern Writing'.

of the vulgar sorte'. Yet, a moment later, when prompted by Guazzo to explain how a gentleman can speak sincerely and eloquently, he advises that 'a man ought to proceede in common talke simply and plainly', and proceeds to offer a rather unexpected model:

> if you consider how in Villages, Hamlets, and fields, you shall find many men, who though they leade they life farre distant from the graces and the Muses (as the proverbe is) and come stamping in with their high clouted shooes, yet are of good understanding, whereof they give sufficient testimonie by their wise and discreet talke. (sig. G8^{r-v})

'[Y]ou cannot denie', he adds, 'but that nature hath given and sowed in us certaine seedes of Rhetorique and Philosophie', which we need to develop with the help of art or study (sig. G8^r). Civility depends on the cultivation of this native gift, just as the tool of the civilised – the art of rhetoric – is a development of effects found in ordinary, unstudied and 'natural' speech. Annibale returns to this point a little later, when he recognises that the 'ornaments and flowers of speache growe by chiefly in the learned, yet you see that nature maketh some of them to flourish even amongst the common sort, unknowing unto them'; 'you shall see artificers, and others of low estate, to apply fitly to their purpose in due time and place, Sentences, pleasant Jestes, Fables, Allegories, Similitudes, Proverbes, Comptes, and other delightful Speache' (sig. H3^r).

The contribution of the notion of the democratically distributed 'seeds of virtue' to the courtesy tradition has long been neglected, no doubt partly out of the need to establish a quotable and certain source for an elitist aesthetics. Its presence, though, often serves to qualify claims of aristocratic natural right, and to anticipate a more inclusive conception of 'nobility'. In Castiglione's *Courtier*, for example, one interlocutor's commitment to this notion will undermine Count Lewis's carefully constructed defence of the innate nobility of the well born. In response to Lewis's insistence that noble men are predisposed to virtue, Gaspar Pallavicino sharply notes that 'nature hath not these so subtle distinctions … we se many times in persons of most base degree, most high giftes of nature' (p. 40). Lewis's response in turn is revealing, for he admits that 'in men of base degree may reigne the very same vertues that are in gentlemen', but explains that what really matters is the *perception* of their social status, and presumed superior virtue: '[f]or where there are two in a noble mans house which at the first have geven no proofe of themselves with woorkes good or bad, assoone as it is knowen that the one is a gentleman borne, and the other is not, the unnoble shall be muche lesse estemed with everye manne, then the gentleman'. The difficult discussion in Book I of the *Courtier*, I suggest, is designed to bring us to an acceptance not so much of the importance of heredity *per se*, as of its continued impact on the popular imagination. As Lewis explains, 'howe waightye these imprintinges are every man may easily judge' (p. 41).

The emphasis on *sermo humilis* will also help us to recognise a second gesture of 'inclusiveness', though, by reminding us that courtesy treatises are indebted not just to neoclassical standards of decorum, but to alternative Christian rhetorical tastes, in which the 'low' is valued more than the 'high'. As Erich Auerbach reminds us in a commentary on Augustine's *De doctrina christiana*, 'in the Christian context the highest mysteries of the faith may be set forth in the simple words of the lowly style which everyone can understand', while Christ 'the King' chose 'voluntary humiliation' by living 'on earth in the lowest social class'.[26] Christian humility may appear to have little in common with courtly modesty, and the kind of disguised artfulness or *sprezzatura* (aptly translated by Thomas Hoby as 'disgracing') promoted by Castiglione, but its influence is felt more readily in other treatises which are indebted to the *Courtier*. '[T]ruely I knowe many men of meane calling', offers Guazzo's Annibale, 'who in Gentlemanlike and curteous conditions, in good bringing up, and in all their talke and behaviour excell many Gentlemen. And contrariwise, I am sure you know many Gentlemen more uncivill than are Clownes themselves' (Book. I, sig. B5ᵛ). Such a doctrine informs Guazzo's insistence on courtly familiarity, or civil behaviour towards others. The second interlocutor, William, may insist that 'everyone [should] keepe that maiestie and state whiche is due to his estate', but he simultaneously insists that contempt for others is 'intollerable':

> for that there is no man that thinketh so vilely and abjectly of himselfe, that he deserveth to be scorned ... And if it be a fault to floute such as one knoweth, it is a greater fault to deride those he knoweth not, whiche some rash and insolent fellowes use to doe, who (as the saying is) judging the horses by the stables and furnitures, consider not that oft times under a clownishe coate is hidden a noble and lively understanding. (Book II, sigs. K2ᵛ–K4ᵛ)

Similar advice can be found in Cleland's treatise, in which biblical echoes are glossed in the margins. Noblemen should be 'lowly and humble to al men', he declares in a chapter in Book V entitled 'Of

26. Auerbach, *Mimesis*, pp. 37, 41.

common behaviour towards all sortes of men' (sigs Y^v–Y2^r). It 'is great wisdom for a man to accommodate himselfe and to frame his manners apt and meete for al honest companie, and societie of men', he explains, and 'a most rare quality in a Noble man to be common, that maketh him imitate Gods goodnes' (sigs X4^v–Y^r). Such advice accords with the early modern law of hospitality, 'a clearly formulated series of conventions', Felicity Heal explains, 'that dictated particular behaviour towards outsiders', and which derives from the Roman *ius hospitii* and the Stoic tradition of natural law.[27]

III

Rosalie Colie's somewhat harsh judgement of *The Winter's Tale*, that it is a play 'conspicuously ill-made', is fuelled partly by what she sees as its 'contradictions and ambivalences', and partly too by its refusal to pry into motivation (pp. 266, 275). In particular, she observes that in the gillyvor dispute Perdita and Polixenes take views *against* their own interests: the socially aspiring Perdita argues against intermarriage while the narrow-minded and snobbish Polixenes identifies its virtues. As she adds, no matter how enlightening this debate seems to be, its questioning of social hierarchy 'is not pursued to its final conclusion' and it is 'Perdita's hierarchical conception of rank' which 'is confirmed … by the ultimate arrangement of the plot' (p. 277). I want to suggest, however, that the play does continue its early exploration of social decorum, and that it endorses the very 'familiar courtesy'[28] which Leontes found so disturbing when practised by Hermione, and on two different accounts.

First, the play presents us with one compelling – and easily recognisable – example of 'familiar courtesy' in its *low* pastoral world. 'Fie daughter,' the Shepherd reprimands the tardy Perdita, 'queen' of the feast, 'when my old wife lived, upon / This day she was both pantler, butler, cook; / Both dame and servant; welcomed all, served all', and then in a gesture which makes clear that 'mannerly distinguishment' has no place in the practice of proper hospitality, he bids her cease her blushing and introduce their uninvited guests, the disguised Polixenes and Camillo: 'Pray you bid / These unknown friends to's welcome, for it is / A way to make us better friends, more known' (IV, iv, 55–66). Secondly, it invites us to pry into motivation, questioning the gap between what we expect

---

27. Heal, *Hospitality*, p. 4.
28. I have borrowed the term 'familiar courtesy' from Greene's *Pandosto*; see n. 5 above.

from characters, given their social status, and their self-expression, and to inquire into the ideological basis of their assumptions. Rather than affirming the 'naturalness' (and rightness) of aristocratic tastes, the play encourages us to explore the impact of perceived status on judgement, and leads us to understand just 'how waightye [are] these imprintinges' of social status.

The weight of these 'imprintinges' is unexpectedly apparent, I suggest, in *The Winter's Tale's* troublesome penultimate scene, in which we learn from the conversation of three gentlemen of the Sicilian court that Perdita has been rightly identified as Leontes' lost daughter. 'That which you hear you'll swear you see, there is such unity in the proofs', the Third Gentleman begins:

> The mantle of Queen Hermione's; her jewel about her neck of it; the letters of Antigonus found with it, which they know to be his character; the majesty of the creature in resemblance of the mother; the affection of nobleness which nature shows above her breeding; and many other evidences proclaim her with all certainty to be the King's daughter. (V, ii, 31–9)

Most critics seem to 'see' what they 'hear', concurring in the 'unity' of these proofs which confirm not just Perdita's identity, but the natural right of the nobly born. Thus, in this scene we seem to share the characters' attainment of the knowledge we already possess: that Perdita is a princess. But, in contrast to both *Pericles* and *Cymbeline*, the long-awaited family reunion takes places off-stage, so that what we are actually experiencing is not the moment of acknowledgement itself, but only its telling. In fact, we do not 'see' at all, and this distance from the action should prompt us to reflect on the attitudes of the gentlemen, and, indeed, on our own unwavering perception of Perdita's nobility. The question I want to raise here is not whether Perdita is nobly born, but rather whether she is always *apparently* innately noble, or whether her innate nobility only becomes apparent once her true status is known. Quite simply, I want to question the basis on which the Third Gentleman is convinced of Perdita's status. For there is something undiscriminating in the parity he assumes between quite distinct kinds of proof, the external witnesses – the mantle, the jewels and the letters – and his impression of her disposition to nobleness. Perdita's 'nobility', I suggest, is only fully apparent (or fully registered) once the fact of her royal birth has been uncovered. In effect, the Third Gentleman is akin to the blinkered nobleman Belarius in *Cymbeline*, whose recognition of the 'invisible instinct' which 'frame[s]' the two 'lost' princes 'To royalty unlearn'd' is juxtaposed to his respect for the vicious but high ranking Cloten (IV, ii, 177–9).[29]

The elevation of Perdita, a 'queen of curds and cream', to the status of a queen, should recall, rather than resolve, the problems of decorum we first associated with Leontes' suppressed pun on queen / quean. In I, ii, Leontes' fastidiousness alerts us to the threat posed to 'mannerly distinguishment', and to the integrity of noble families, by Hermione's familiar bearing. In a sense, though, Leontes misunderstands the nature of 'courtly' entertainment, which, as the Shepherd demonstrates, depends on a degree of 'familiar courtesy'. In V, ii, his misreading appears to be set right when Perdita is made 'familiar', and reintegrated into the royal family. In this instance, her native nobility is recognised in spite of her lowly appearance. Such a reading, however, assumes that Perdita's birth-right is consonant with an innate nobility when the play does not clearly affirm this relationship. It may be possible to establish that Perdita is Leontes' daughter from the external witnesses, and even – at a push – from her physical traits, which recall those of Hermione (V, i, 225–6), but this does not establish her *innate* nobility. As the example of the courteous Shepherd suggests, Perdita may seem noble to the Third Gentleman because of – not in spite of – her lowly demeanour. I suggest that the Third Gentleman is no less prejudiced than Leontes; it is just that the consequences of his 'reading' contribute to the comic resolution of the play.

Ultimately, it is the courtly 'outsiders', the preposterous Clown and Shepherd, who are the real insiders at the end of the play. Their exclusion from Paulina's home in V, iii, has been seen to imply their outsider status. But it is possible, too, that they do not need to share in 'our' final humiliation at the hands of Paulina. Rather than being excluded from an appreciation of Hermione's living statue as 'aristocratic, "high", classical' art, they leave us with an insight into the unreadability of the 'artificial' signs of nobleness. In V, ii, when asked by Autolycus to act as his patron at court, and to give a 'good report' of him 'to the prince my master' (l. 145), the Clown promises to 'swear ... thou art as honest a true fellow as any is in Bohemia' (l. 152). And then in response to the insistence of his father, who now understands Autolycus' dishonesty, that 'You may say it, but not swear it', the Clown offers his newly acquired insight into courtly speech: 'If it be ne'er so false, a true gentleman may swear it in the behalf of his friend.' 'I'll swear to the prince thou art a tall fellow of thy hands, and that thou wilt not be

29. See also *Cymbeline*, IV, ii, 245–52.

drunk – but I know thou art no tall fellow of thy hands, and that thou wilt be drunk' (V, ii, 153–61). In contrast to their first, awe-inspired response to Autolycus, their final naiveté indicates rather that they have become 'insiders'. For they understand that a courtier is also a natural 'outsider', one whose outward show is unlikely to be (in Cleland's words) the 'messenger' of his 'heart'.

5

PERICLES AND THE POX

Margaret Healy

Louis MacNeice's poem *Autolycus* (1944–7) gives aptly magical expression to the dominant apprehension of Shakespeare's late plays in our century. *Autolycus* evokes a picture of the Bard at the sunset of his career mysteriously moving away from the 'taut plots and complex characters' of the major tragedies, conjuring instead 'tapestried romances ... / With rainbow names and handfuls of sea-spray', and from them turning out 'happy Ever-afters' (ll. 3–6). MacNeice's words capture a certain ambivalence towards this Shakespearean sea change: indeed, the romances, with their emphasis on the production of wonder, their tendency towards straggling plots and emblematic representation, and their preponderance of 'childish horrors' and 'old gags' (*Autolycus* ll. 14, 15), are often experienced as charming but enigmatic and not altogether satisfying puzzles – even as regressive aberrations. The latter is most true of the 'unwanted child' *Pericles*, a play of suspect parentage, excluded from the First Folio, and only available to us through what most editors agree is a particularly bastardised quarto and its numerous offspring (it was printed six times to 1635, including twice in one year, 1609 – an unusual occurrence).[1]

Frequently vilified and rarely performed today, *Pericles* has been the

---

1. Shakespeare probably collaborated with at least one other playwright in writing *Pericles* – the second writer remains a matter for speculation. I can see no justification for the designation of Q1 as a particularly corrupt, 'bad' quarto.

focus of considerable bewilderment: why, critics repeatedly ponder, was this play so acclaimed and popular in the Jacobean age when it has proven so relatively unappealing in ours?[2] The title page of the first quarto of 1609 describes it as 'The Late, and much admired Play ... As it hath been divers and sundry times acted by his Majesties Servants, at the Globe'; and contemporary references suggest that it was a huge box-office success in London playhouses, a favourite for private house production, and for court performance, too.[3] It was, moreover, one of two Shakespearean plays – the other being *King Lear* – put on by a professional company with recusant sympathies (Sir Richard Cholmeley's Players), which toured Yorkshire in 1609.[4]

When *Pericles* was performed by the RSC in 1990, however, one theatre critic, dismissing the play 'as just a far-fetched fairy tale', could only explain its early seventeenth-century appeal in the following derogatory terms:

> It is fanciful to think that business had been flat at the Globe, and Burbage suggested that something with more sex and violence would pull audiences in. 'Incest and brothels will,' he might have said, 'do the box-office a power of good.'[5]

Steven Mullaney reached much the same conclusion in his important book, *The Place of the Stage*. Contesting the popular thesis that this is an experimental play which evolved to suit the new context of the Blackfriars theatre, Mullaney argues that *Pericles* rather 'represents a radical effort to dissociate the popular stage from its cultural contexts', a shift into 'pure' aestheticism, and that its subsequent literary fortunes testify to 'the limits of any work that seeks to obscure or escape its historical conditions of possibility'.[6] For Mullaney then, this was an experiment of a different kind which went badly wrong. For him, *Pericles* is unalloyed aestheticism pandering to the tastes of emergent liberal humanism – any quest for dissonant voices will get short shrift here.

Sandra Billington's *Mock Kings in Medieval and Renaissance Drama* obliquely reinforces this perspective. In her view the character of Pericles represents kingly perfection; he is 'an ideal courtly lord and effective prince, whose virtue does not waver despite the effects of the

---

2. For a taste of this 'vilification' see theatre reviews for April 1990 (Royal Shakespeare Company) and May 1994 (Royal National Theatre) in *London Theatre Record*.
3. Hoeniger, 'Gower and Shakespeare', p. 461.
4. Sisson, 'Shakespeare quartos', pp. 136–7.
5. Shulman, 'Review of *Pericles* (RSC)', *Evening Standard*, 17 April 1990.
6. Mullaney, *The Place of the Stage*, pp. 147–51.

plot on it'. She finds *Pericles* an 'exception' in the world of plays from this period dominated by depictions of dubious and tyrannical monarchs, possibly, she suspects, because 'the devil has the most dramatic plots'.[7] Frances Yates and Glynne Wickham, and more recently Jonathan Goldberg and David Bergeron, also forestall a more questioning reading of the play when they argue that *Pericles* contains a thinly veiled likeness to James VI and I in the figure of its hero.[8] Indeed the majority of commentators are admiring of 'patient' king Pericles and if they read James, his family, and the events of his reign into the play, it is almost inevitably viewed as a eulogy to James and a celebration of his rule.[9] Such readings appear to be endorsed by the fact that the text of *Pericles* resonates with James's own aphorisms in his voluminous writings about kingship, a prime example from the beginning of the play being its hero's utterance, 'kings are earth's gods' (i, 146) – arguably the monarch's favourite tenet. Thus, once again, Shakespearean drama is construed as shoring up royal absolutism. This play's undisputed 'happy ending' bears witness to this: the royal marriage which allies two kingdoms is understood as a particularly fortuitous and positive outcome, the topical analogy being the projected peaceful Union of England and Scotland through James's mediation. The latter was a highly topical matter in 1607, and one which had achieved extravagant courtly representation in January of that year in *The Lord Hay's Masque* to celebrate the betrothal of a Scottish favourite and the daughter of an English lord. The masque opens with a fulsome address to 'Gracious James, King of Great Britain':

> O then, great Monarch, with how wise a care
> Do you these bloods divided mix in one,
> And with like consanguinities prepare
> The high and everliving Union
>   'Tween Scots and English. Who can wonder then
>   If he that marries kingdoms, marries men.[10]

The 'marriage' of kingdoms was certainly a subject close to the king's heart throughout this decade.

The English–Scottish 'marriage' was not, however, the only one preoccupying James and exercising his patience *c.*1606–7 when *Pericles* was

---

7. Billington, *Mock Kings*, p. 238.
8. Wickham, 'From tragedy to tragi-comedy', p. 44; Goldberg, *James I*; Bergeron, *Shakespeare's Romances*, p. 23; see also Tennenhouse, *Power on Display*, pp. 182–3.
9. Two notable exceptions are Dickey, 'Language and role', and Relihan, 'Liminal geography'.
10. Campion, *The Lord Hay's Masque*, ll. 15–20.

probably written. The king was simultaneously engaged in plans to ally Britain with Spain, and this projected 'marriage', for the majority of his subjects, was undoubtedly more pressing and more controversial. In fact, 'the Spanish Match' was unlikely to have won widespread public approval: James's repeated attempts to marry his son Henry to the Spanish Infanta and his daughter Elizabeth to the Duke of Savoy would hardly have been construed by the bulk of the populace (for whom Spain was the epitome of the Antichrist) as desirable, or as the stuff of happy endings and fairy-tale romance.[11] Building on this perspective, this chapter will argue that *Pericles'* ending, in particular the betrothal of Marina to Lysimachus, is far from suggestive of uncomplicated 'happy Ever-afters', and that analysis of this play's representations of early modern syphilis (the Pox), and its medico-moral politics, provides new contexts and substantial support for more dissonant readings.

My focus will be on the last two acts of *Pericles*, and in particular on the brothel scenes where discussion of the Pox and its consequences are rife and nauseatingly explicit. I should point out that there are no references to syphilis or its consequences in either of the play's two reputed sources: John Gower's *Confessio Amantis* (Book 8) and Lawrence Twine's *The Patterne of Painfull Adventures* (a translation of the 153rd story of the *Gesta Romanorum*). Interestingly, too, George Wilkins' novel of the play, *The Painfull Adventures of Pericles Prince of Tyre* (1608), erases all references to the Pox, recuperates Lysimachus as a healthful and virtuous governor, and concludes by assuring its readers of the fruitfulness and happiness of this union.[12]

I will begin, though, by reminding you where we are at this stage in the action. The first three Acts of *Pericles* portray its hero being tossed

11. See Gardiner, *History of England*, vol. I, p. 343; in July 1605 Spain suggested that if Prince Henry married the eldest daughter of the King of Spain, Spain would surrender to the young couple its claims to a large portion of the Netherlands. Spain later retracted the offer, raising objections to the Infanta marrying a Protestant. Also Gardiner, *History of England*, vol. II, pp. 22–3; in 1607 the abortive scheme for the marriage was renewed, together with a demand for the conversion of Prince Henry to Catholicism. The offer was refused because of the latter demand. However, in October of the same year James suggested an alternative plan: that his daughter Elizabeth be married to the son of Philip's brother-in-law, the Duke of Savoy. See also *Calendar of State Papers: Venetian, Vol. XI*, 15 August 1607: 'the Ambassadors of Spain are putting it about that by a matrimonial alliance and the death of the Archdukes the States might well come under the dominion of the King of England' (p. 23).

12. Gower's, Twine's and Wilkins' texts are in Bullough, *Narrative and Dramatic Sources*, vol. VI.

impotently around the exotic world of the eastern Mediterranean, a prey to forces greater than himself, yet – in the manner of romance – managing to fall in love, marry and beget a child, Marina, in the process. Life is cruel but virtue flourishes in hardship: Marina, for all intents and purposes an orphan, grows up to be a paragon princess – beautiful, talented and saintly. Her tragic destiny, however, catches up with her, and her wicked guardian Dionyza threatens her with murder at the hands of a servant just at the point she is mourning the death of her beloved nurse. Marina's suffering seems unremitting; she escapes murder through being captured by pirates, only to be sold by them to a brothel and to a fate – in her opinion – worse than violent and sudden death ('Alack that Leonine was so slack, so slow. / He should have struck, not spoke' (xvi, 61–2)).

Meanwhile the audience is introduced to Pander, Bawd and Bolt bewailing the poor state of their trade, caused not through a lack of customers ('gallants'), but rather through the 'pitifully sodden' condition of their prostitute wares (xvi, 18). The comic potential of this scene is undermined by the tragic import of the discussion, which would not have been lost on a Jacobean audience. For early modern playgoers child prostitution and syphilis were very real and allied diseases. The audience learns how the Pox is the inevitable fate of the Bawd's poor 'bastards', but in this subterranean world of inverted moral values the sympathy expressed is solely for an adult lecher (the 'poor Transylvanian' (xvi, 20–1)) who has lain with a 'little baggage' – an exhausted commodity grown 'rotten' with 'continual action' (xvi, 8–9). Is this to be the Princess Marina's fate?

Installed in the Mytilene brothel Marina bewails her plight, only to be consoled by Bawd with the knowledge that she will 'taste gentlemen of all fashions' – a far from edifying prospect (xvi, 75). Whilst Boult, Bawd and Pander banter about the Spaniard's mouth watering at Marina's description, at Monsieur Veroles (the French word for syphilis) cowering 'i' the hams' (xvi, 101) – in other words Jacobean society's foppish foreigner stereotypes of the diseased – it is native 'gentlemen' and 'the governor of this country' (xix, 58) who actually arrive at the brothel to threaten Marina's well-being. One by one Jacobean society's comforting stereotypes of the disease's victims and polluters are being undermined, 'safe boundaries' for the representation of the Pox are being trangressed: young children and an innocent woman are at risk from 'gentlemen' in this murky play world.[13]

13. On safe boundaries for the representation of syphilis see Helms, 'The saint in the brothel', and Gilman, *Disease and Representation*.

But Marina's eloquent powers of persuasion prove more than a match for Mytilene's lecherous gentlemen, whose wayward morals she reforms in the very brothel.[14] The dramatic climax of the brothel scenes is undoubtedly the arrival and conversion of none other than the 'Lord Lysimachus', governor of Mytilene. Bawd announces that there's no way to be 'rid on't' (Marina's maidenhead) but, as she puts it,

> by the way to the pox.
> *Enter Lysimachus, disguised*
> Here comes the Lord Lysimachus disguised. (xix, 23–5)

Whilst it is never directly stated or implied by any of the characters that Lysimachus has the Pox, the language of the scene conspires to sow strong seeds of suspicion that he does. The proximity of the words 'pox' to 'it' (Marina's virginity) and the foregrounding of Lysimachus' disguise – disguise being intimately associated in early modern discourse with the Pox, which was also known as the great 'masquerader', the 'secret' disease – begin the process.[15] Lysimachus requests Boult find him some 'wholesome iniquity' (xix, 32) with which to do 'the deed of darkness' (xix, 37). He hides his dishonourable intentions in a cloak of euphemistic language, but the audience is not to be hoodwinked, for Bawd replies 'Your honour knows what 'tis to say well enough' (xix, 39). Furthermore the brothel's mistress is 'bound' (xix, 60), as she says, to this governor; by implication Lysimachus is a regular customer, all too familiar with the iniquitous business in hand. This established, Bawd's words serve to highlight Lysimachus' supreme status in Mytilene society; finally she declares 'Come, we will leave his honour and hers together' (xix, 69). There is, of course, a pun on 'honour' here. Marina later appropriates Bawd's terms and upbraids Lysimachus with them. She challenges:

> And do you know this house to be a place
> Of such resort and will come into it?
> I hear say you're of honourable blood,
> And are the governor of this whole province. (xix, 81–4)

Thus Lysimachus' honour is thrown seriously into question, and he increasingly resembles one of the hypocritical types, like Iniquity and Infidelity, who would have been familiar to many amongst the original audiences as stock vices from the morality plays. Tail between legs, the governor leaves the brothel claiming that Marina's speech has altered his

14. On syphilis and declamation, see Helms, 'The saint in the brothel'.
15. See Davenport-Hines, *Sex, Death and Punishment*, p. 21.

'corrupted mind' (xix, 128). Lysimachus' mask may have been temporarily lifted, his vice exposed, but he appears to go quite unpunished for his misdeeds; indeed, he even seems to be rewarded, for Marina's princely father eventually betroths her to this nobleman of dubious honour and health.

But is this not taking the stuff of romance, emerging from a make-believe world, rather too seriously? What may seem just good bawdy and fun to a modern audience, however, is fraught with serious implications for contemporary playgoers familiar with other stage representations of fornication and disease.[16] This play, it has been repeatedly observed, returns to an emblematic form of theatre which invites spectators to search critically for understanding. The audience witnesses a series of emblematic tableaux, is called upon to make sense of the wooing knights' 'devices' on their shields, and listens to riddles, mottoes and endless aphorisms, especially ones about the abusive operations of power and kingship. Frequently there is a disparity between the morals the characters tritely recite and the action the audience observes on the stage. Thus sham morality, hypocrisy, is repeatedly exposed. Through these theatrical structures the audience is encouraged to observe the action with a heightened sceptical consciousness, and to be especially alert to emblematic representations.

Pericles is particularly partial to trotting out mottoes and adages about kingship (much like King James himself), but there is one that he omits which educated Jacobean playgoers may well have been thinking about when witnessing Pericles' rather casual consignment of his daughter to Lysimachus' care. As Gower relates, Lysimachus entertains the king with 'pageantry', 'feats', 'shows', 'minstrelsy and pretty din', which so impresses Pericles that he rewards the governor of Mytilene with a wife – his daughter, the heir to the throne of Tyre (xxii, 6–12). It is my contention that many among the original audiences of *Pericles* would have responded with horror to this marriage outcome, to this 'unequal match', because of their familiarity with the horrors of contracting syphilis and the intense and prolonged suffering associated with the most dreaded chronic disease of the Renaissance. Those with at least a grammar-school education would have been familiar, too, with widely disseminated Erasmian views on such hazardous 'matches', and some spectators would undoubtedly have seen a popular emblem which illustrated a 'Nupta contagioso' (see Figure 5.1).

16. The topic of my forthcoming monograph, 'Fictions of Disease: Bodies, Plagues and Politics in Early Modern Writings'.

Nupta contagioſo.

EMBLEMA CXCVII.

Dii *meliora piis*, Mezenti. *cur age ſic me*
Compellas : emptus quòd tibi dote gener;
Gallica quem ſcabies, dira & mentagra peruſit:
Hoc eſt quidnam aliud, dic mihi ſæue pater,
Corpora corporibus quàm iungere mortua viuis,
Efferáq₃ Etruſci faſta nouare ducis?

Cupreſ-

Figure 5.1 *Nupta contagioso*, from Andrea Alciato's *Emblemata*, 1608.
By courtesy of Edinburgh University Library.

This emblem first appeared in a collection by Andrea Alciato (*Emblemata*) published in 1550; it was subsequently adapted, translated and distributed widely throughout Europe. It depicts a king on a dais overseeing a man and woman being bound together on the floor with a rope. As the accompanying poem describes, this is a savage deed comparable to that committed by a cruel Etruscan king who was in the habit of punishing his victims by tying them to a corpse. It reveals that for a dowry this king has purchased a son-in-law seared by the Gallic scab, apparent in the dreaded sore on his face: through self-interest he has committed his daughter to a living death, a 'Nupta contagioso'. This horrific emblem about the Pox was undoubtedly influenced by an Erasmian colloquy published in 1529 entitled *The Unequal Match* or *A Marriage in Name Only*, which was among the dramatic dialogues that English pedagogues recommended all boys should read.[17] Erasmus' colloquies were a tool to teach schoolboys colloquial Latin but they were also intended, in Erasmus' own words, to impress on 'young people … [the] safeguarding of their chastity'.[18]

The two participants in *The Unequal Match*, Gabriel and Petronius, discuss, with horror, how a beautiful, talented girl with winning manners has just been married off by her father to a rotting corpse – unmistakably a chronic syphilitic – because of his title. This wayward nobleman's dicing, drinking, lies and whoring have apparently earned him this 'living death' which will now be inflicted upon his young wife. Gabriel's words are hard-hitting. He exclaims:

> But this outrage – than which you could find nothing more barbarous, more cruel, more unrighteous – is even a laughing matter with the governing class nowadays, despite the fact that those born to rule ought to have as robust health as possible. And in fact, the condition of the body has its effect on mental power. Undeniably this disease usually depletes whatever brains a man has. So it comes about that rulers of states may be men who are healthy neither in body nor mind. (p. 407)

This colloquy thus functions as a powerful rebuke to parental, and especially princely parental, selfishness, greed and folly.

Pericles, I wish to argue, is a satirical play with the same cautionary message as *The Unequal Match*. The potential polluter of a beautiful young woman is a luxurious gentleman who abuses the privileges that

17. See Watson, *English Grammar Schools*, pp. 328–9, and Clarke, *Classical Education*, p. 47.
18. Erasmus, 'De Utilitate Colloquiorum', *Colloquies*, p. 629, quoted by Thompson in the same edition, p. 154.

his nobility favours him with. Through marriage, an innocent young woman will be placed at his disposal by the very person who should most seek to protect her – her father. Marina's response to the intended match is articulate silence. It is informative to read this outcome in relation to Petronius' condemnation of the 'unequal match' in Erasmus' dialogue: 'Enemies scarcely do this to girls captured in war, pirates to those they kidnap; and yet parents do it to an only daughter, and there's no police official with power to stop them!' (p. 408). Marina has escaped rape and murder at the hands of her enemies, has survived her passage with her pirate-captors intact, and then just when the audience is relaxing, thinking her safely delivered to the protection of her family, her father subjects her to an 'unequal match'. As Gabriel declares in the dialogue, such dubious matches reflect badly on the parents and have important implications for the commonwealth and its government: '[a]s private individuals, they're disloyal to their family; as citizens, to the state' (p. 408). Irresponsible father-rulers are putting both the health of their offspring and the state in jeopardy through this 'madness'.

The medico-moral politics of *Pericles* depend to some extent on the audience's experience of this tragic and widespread disease of the Renaissance – its unsightly, disfiguring, disabling and painful progress – and on their knowledge of popular humanist texts surrounding it. The Pox was in fact the most widely written-about disease in the Renaissance. These contexts are clearly not readily available to modern audiences and consequently the potential serious import and impact of *Pericles'* late scenes have been considerably watered down, even erased.

However, yet further Renaissance contexts require amplification before modern readers can appreciate the range and density of meanings and resonances circulating, often in partially submerged form, in this richly layered play. Whilst reforming intellectuals like Erasmus worried and wrote about the savage effects of this disease and called for preventive health measures to combat it, they were also not averse to utilising knowledge about its painful and horrific effects for propaganda purposes. Intent on foregrounding what he viewed as the corruption and decay of the Catholic Church, Erasmus began to disperse images of syphilitic priests throughout his writings. His message was that the clergy had grown so corrupt their fornication was spreading the new disease among them, to their innocent victims, and throughout the globe. Lutheran reformers seized upon Erasmus' powerful metaphor of church corruption, and English polemicists like John Bale, John Foxe, Lewis Wager and William Turner quickly appropriated the emblematic syphilitic body for the Protestant cause.

The mid sixteenth-century Edwardian stage displayed spotted, decaying and disabled 'Pocky' bodies lamenting their disease and proclaiming it to be the consequence of fornication encouraged by Catholic Vices such as Infidelity and Iniquity, who inevitably disguise their corruption and hypocrisy under their religious vestments. The early Protestant dramatists clearly recognised and exploited the compelling theatrical value, the tantalising erotic and comic possibilities, of sin: 'godly myrth' was extremely bawdy. As John King has argued, in the Protestant interlude fornication tends to become 'a composite symbol for the seven deadly sins'.[19] He cites as the main reason for this John Bale's development and popularisation for the English context of the Lutheran identification of the Whore of Babylon of Revelation with the Church of Rome: dramatic bawdry thus came to symbolise 'the spiritual fornication' of Roman ritualism.

When, therefore, the audience witnessed the seduction and fall of young virgins in the Protestant interludes, they were simultaneously engaging with the plays' allegorical levels of meaning, in which, according to the Protestant reformers' version of history, the True, undefiled Church was sullied and temporarily superseded by the corrupt False Church of Antichrist. Naturally the harlot Church, like her lascivious priests, had a special imagined affinity with venereal disease. In his propaganda pamphlet, provocatively entitled *A New Booke of Spirituall Physik for Dyverse Diseases of the Nobilitie and Gentlemen of Englande* (1555), the Marian exile William Turner reconstrues the origins of the 'pokkes' in a 'noble hore' of Italy: 'Ther was a certeyne hore in Italy, whych had a perillus disease called false religion ... all the kynges and nobilitie of the earth ... they committed fornication wyth her ... and caught the Romishe pokkes.'[20]

This symbolism and allegorising surrounding the Pox, fornication and the Romish church was alive and flourishing in the first decade of the seventeenth century. Thomas Dekker's play *The Whore of Babylon*, staged by Prince Henry's Men probably about a year before the first production of *Pericles*, bears strong witness to this. Indeed *The Whore of Babylon* provides an important additional context to illuminate some of the fading emblematic resonances in *Pericles*. As the preface to the text explains, *The Whore of Babylon* is designed to lay bare the 'blody stratagems, of that Purple whore of Roome' in the reign of Elizabeth I.[21]

19. King, *English Reformation Literature*, p. 283.
20. Turner, *A New Booke*, fol. 74ʳ.
21. Dekker, *The Whore of Babylon*, p. 497.

However, its real thrust was undoubtedly to persuade Jacobean spectators that the iniquitous forces of Antichrist continued to pose a substantial threat to England and the Reformed Church, and to encourage a
more militant stance against Rome. It features the lustful harlot the
Empresse of Babylon, alias Rome, strumpet to her slaves, the kings of
Spain, France and the Holy Roman Empire, and her Cardinal entourage.
She is also served by her Bawd, Falsehood, who wears the garb of Truth
(a gown of sanctity) but whose hypocrisy is evidenced by her red
pimples – she, like her mistress, as Plain Dealing informs us, has a bad
case of the Pox. Babylon's design is none other than to 'swallow up the
kingdome of Faiery' (IV, iii, 37), whose queen is Titania (Elizabeth I),
served by spotless Truth and her fairy lords.

The Empress's first stratagem is to send her kings off to woo Titania/
Elizabeth. When they arrive at her court Titania asks them if they've
come to 'strike off a poore maiden-head' (I.ii.85), that is to rape her. The
sexual manoeuvres and language of this play have the political meanings
common to sixteenth-century Protestant discourse: raping a virgin sig-
nified a state adhering to the Reformed, true faith being engulfed
forcibly by a Romish power. Rome is a rapist as well as a harlot in
Protestant polemics. However, the kings reassure Titania that marriage
rather than ravishment is their aim, but it does not matter which of the
three Titania chooses because their desire is simply to please the Empress
by wedding the forces of Babylon to those of Fairyland. Thankfully,
Titania is not fooled by this suspect marriage proposal. She declares (and
I think these words will throw a very important light on the marriage
proposal in *Pericles*):

> When kingdoms marrie, heaven it selfe stands by
> To give the bride: Princes in tying such bands,
> Should use a thousand heads, ten thousand hands:
> For that one Acte gives like an enginous wheele
> Motion to all. (I, ii,162–6)

The marriage alliance rejected, Babylon and her followers turn grisly:
the Spanish Armada is sent into action and a plot is hatched to murder
Titania with the aid of recusant spies. At the close of the play the forces
of Truth triumph but, importantly, Babylon is not eradicated, just temporarily subdued: the Poxy threat persists.

Many among the original London audiences would probably have
shared Dekker's perspective on the threat posed by Popishness and
Spanish ambitions; and the Shakespearean play, as represented by the
virtually identical 1609 quartos, is undoubtedly engaging in a more

subtle way with the same concerns. This is how Pericles addresses Marina in the recognition scene:

> Prithee speak.
> Falseness cannot come from thee, for thou look'st
> Modest as justice, and thou seem'st a palace
> For the crowned truth to dwell in. (xxi, 108–11)

Pericles' words identify his daughter as an embodiment of Truth: Truth which the audience has observed being captured by a pirate with the same name, Valdes, as one of the Spanish Armada captains in *The Whore of Babylon*; whom they have seen threatened with but fending off rape; and who is about to be betrothed to a probably Poxy spouse by her negligent father. Pericles certainly does not use 'a thousand heads' in choosing his son-in-law.

All of this has important negative implications for how we read the character of Pericles in the Jacobean context. Pericles is a prince who is seldom in his own state (Tyre is a troubled kingdom 'without a head' (viii, 34));[22] who flees from danger rather than confronting it; who readily commits his young daughter to the care of rather dubious others; whose wallowing in self-pity comes dangerously close to incurring a charge of effeminacy ('thou art a man, and I / Have suffered like a girl' (xxi, 125–6)); and who, through betrothing Marina to a potentially diseased son-in-law, is putting both her health and his future princely heirs' at stake. He may, unwittingly, through neglect and poor government, be introducing 'corruption' into the virgin body of his daughter and his kingdom.

Indeed, on the latter points King James himself had been nothing if not voluble in his treatise of advice to his son Henry, *Basilikon Doron* (1599), which specifically warns about the dangers of bodily pollution:

> First of all consider, that Mariage is the greatest earthly felicitie or miserie ... By your preparation yee must keepe your bodie cleane and unpolluted, till yee give it to your wife ... For how can ye justly crave to bee joyned with a pure virgine, if your bodie be polluted? Why should the one halfe bee cleane, and the other defiled?[23]

---

22. On this matter one of Erasmus' adages famously declared: 'Sheep are no use, if the shepherd is not there ... the common people are useless unless they have the prince's authority to guide them', *Adages*, II, vii, 26.

23. James VI and I, *Basilikon Doron*, p. 34.

The *Basilikon Doron*'s constructions resonate with Erasmian maxims, and the above illustration suggests that James may well have been familiar with one of the numerous reproductions of Alciato's emblem. The treatise proceeds to rail against lust and fornication, reminding the young prince that the right end of sexual appetite is 'procreation of children', and stressing monarchical duty: 'Especially a King must tymously Marie for the weale of his people … in a King that were a double fault, as well against his owne weale, as against the weale of his people [to] … Marie one of knowne evill conditions' (p. 35). Crucially, there then follows a protracted discussion about religion, marriage and monarchy, in which James advises Henry, 'I would rathest have you to Marie one that were fully of your owne Religion', and warns about the hazards of 'disagreement in Religion'. The betrothal of two princely 'members of two opposite Churches' can only 'breed and foster a dissention among your subjects, taking their example from your family' (p. 35).

If the neglectful manner of rule of Pericles' royal protagonist bore resemblances to James VI and I's style of administration *c.*1607–9, some pointed comments about Jacobean power politics are thinly concealed in this play. James's management of the country was being heavily criticised in this period; not least because his instinct and drive was to make peace with Spain, exercise a policy of leniency towards recusants, and seek Catholic Spanish marriages for his devoutly Protestant children, Henry and Elizabeth. The Venetian ambassador to London confided to the Doge and Senate in 1607, that: 'His majesty … loves quiet and repose, has no inclination to war … a fact that little pleases many of his subjects … The result is he is despised and almost hated.' Furthermore, throughout 1607 the Venetian ambassador (Zorzi Giustinian) sent anxious reports to his masters about the unsettled British populace, who 'would clearly like to, on the excuse of this rumour of a Spanish Armada', disturb 'the calm'. His dispatches repeatedly lamented: 'They [the populace] long for a rupture with Spain.'[24] Meanwhile their monarch was negotiating marital alliances with the enemy, which could well lead to 'dissention' (see above quotation from *Basilikon Doron*) among his subjects. It seems that James, like Pericles, was an expert purveyor of adages about kingship, but for many of his subjects he too seldom put them into action. He would have done well to take note of the emblem and motto of the fifth knight in *Pericles*: 'an hand environèd with clouds, / Holding out gold that's by the touchstone tried' and '*Sic spectanda fides*'

---

24. *Calendar of State Papers: Venetian, Vol. X*, p. 513; and *State Papers: Venetian, Vol. XI*, pp. 17, 27, 39.

(vi, 41–3), which might be rendered as, 'the trial of godliness and faith is to be made not of words only, but also by the action and performance of the deeds'.[25]

But all this begs the question of why a Yorkshire company of players with recusant sympathies should choose to stage *Pericles* in 1609. Perhaps it was for counter-propaganda purposes? The very fact that an Erasmian text is glanced at in this play would make it a prime target for appropriation by both sides of the religious divide. The preface to William Burton's translations of seven of the *Colloquies* (1606) is illuminating in this respect, for it reveals a religio-political intent partly motivating his project: readers will readily perceive, he declares in his preface, 'how little cause the Papists have to boast of Erasmus as a man of their side'. Ownership of Erasmus (with all the authority that implied) was hotly contested by English Catholics and Protestants in this period. Furthermore, Cholmeley was accused in 1609 of staging anti-Protestant plays, and the Star Chamber trial documents lend strong support to the view put forward by Sissons in 1942, that the company interpolated and omitted scenes, and improvised, according to 'the religious colour of their audience'.[26] This should perhaps serve as a timely reminder that plays are highly slippery art forms, and that ultimately their meanings reside with their equally unstable audiences. There is no way of knowing, for example, how closely a version of *Pericles* played at the Globe resembled the Yorkshire version(s) or, indeed, a production at Whitehall before distinguished guests: but it is easy to see how with a little fine tuning *Pericles* in performance could be construed as a pro-Jamesian play.

What can be said with certainty is that with its roots deep in the Jacobean cultural context, and engaging critically but obliquely with its power politics, *Pericles* – as represented by the 1609 quartos – has been wrongly consigned to the scrapheap of unalloyed aestheticism and 'happy Ever-afters'. *Pericles* is not a bastion of royal absolutism, though to discern its heterodox perspectives we need to penetrate its mirror-like surface, which appears to be reflecting Jamesian orthodoxy. As *Pericles* reminds its audiences, this was an age in which kings were 'earth's gods' (i, 146), one in which saying 'Jove doth ill' (i, 147) was fraught with danger. Indeed, as Philip Finkelpearl reminds us in an important essay on

---

25. *Pericles*, ed. Hoeniger, II, ii, 38n. (p. 56), citing Claude Paradin, *Devises Héroiques*, trans. P. S. (London, 1591), sig. O3 (p. 213).
26. See *Star Chamber Proceedings*, PRO, STAC 19/10; 12/11. Sisson, 'Shakespeare quartos', p. 142.

stage censorship, 'from 1606 it became a crime to speak against dignitaries even if the libel were true'.[27] Criticism of the reigning monarch was certainly best kept partially occluded, and, in skilful hands, the emblematic characterisation, straggling plots, exotic locations and make-believe worlds of romance were perfect structures for 'artistic cunning' and veiled comment.[28] Pocky bodies, medico-moral politics and dubious marriages were, I have argued in this chapter, powerful stage vehicles for coded dissent: *c*.1607–9 men could not say the king 'doth ill' but they could seek to reveal it, or at least gesture towards it, through dramatic representation.

27. Finkelpearl, ' "The comedians' liberty" ', p. 123. Finkelpearl suggests that 'the employment of arcane codes mastered by the cognoscenti' may have operated in Jacobean England, p. 138. See also Annabel Patterson, *Censorship and Interpretation*. Indeed satire against the king had led to Jonson, Chapman and Marston being imprisoned in 1605 for their parts in *Eastward Ho!*; and in 1606 'sundry were committed to Bridewell' for producing *The Isle of Gulls*.
28. The expression is Finkelpearl's, ' "The comedians' liberty" ', p. 138.

6

INSUBSTANTIAL PAGEANTS: *THE TEMPEST* AND MASQUING CULTURE

James Knowles

There is no better index of the transformation of critical approaches towards *The Tempest* over the twentieth century than the different attitudes displayed towards Prospero's 'masque' in IV, i. In 1953 Frank Kermode devoted considerable space to defending the integrity of the text against arguments that the masque was interpolated as a topical compliment for the marriage of Princess Elizabeth and the Elector Palatine largely irrelevant to the rest of the play.[1] In contrast, Stephen Orgel's 1987 edition places the masque as integral to the whole play, not only Act IV.[2] In the intervening thirty years scholarship has ceased to regard masques as ephemeral 'toys' rooted in nothing but empty flattery and hollow spectacle, recognising the complexity of the form, its tropes, structure and hermeneutics. Although few critics would now accept Glynne Wickham's view that Shakespeare 'incorporated the fully developed Jonsonian masque, complete with anti-masque, into the fabric of the play', the argument that it was less the masque effects and more its iconography, hermeneutics and underlying political ideology which shaped *The Tempest* continues to be highly influential. While Wickham's essay belongs to the 'sentimental' school of *Tempest* criticism, which

1. Shakespeare, *The Tempest*, ed. F. Kermode, pp. xx–xxiv.
2. *The Tempest*, ed. Orgel, pp. 1–2. Arguments about interpolation are relegated to a single footnote (p. 44 n. 1).

embeds Prospero's 'vision' in the reconciliatory and harmonising patterns of the play, envisaging him as an ideal, Platonic monarch-magus, even Orgel's outstanding edition, which traces the fissures and tensions of the play, still installs the masque as a central, if more ambiguous, symbol of the play's interconnection of art and power.[3] Few critics, however, have considered what *kind* of masque is played in IV, i, of *The Tempest*.

This chapter starts with that question, showing how Prospero's masque diverges from Jonsonian court masques. Second, by reconsidering the nature of the masque and the masquing tradition, this chapter outlines how the Jonsonian masque represents only one strand of a broader, aristocratic masquing culture and suggests a different interpretation of Prospero's masque, which does not align the play with the Jonsonian masque or with royal ideology. In particular, I shall suggest that we need to pay greater attention to the chronology of the development of masque form, looking at *The Tempest* in the context of masques written before 1613, showing that, especially in its staging (an issue at the heart of many critical arguments which tie both this and other late plays to a growing coterie tradition), the play should be read not only in the light of public theatre conventions, but also in relation to the tradition of non-court, aristocratic masques. Part of the purpose of this chapter is to resituate *The Tempest* within a much more diverse and polyvalent conception of aristocratic rather than court or royal culture. This pluralist culture encompasses a more questioning, sceptical political and intellectual vision than the conservative Shakespearean political dramaturgy, connected to the court through patronage, the propagandisation of Stuart policies or the adoption of court styles, offered by many interpretations of the relations between the masque and this play.

I

Prospero's masque in IV, i, of *The Tempest* presents the most substantive evidence for the influence of masques and court staging techniques on the late plays. Critics have cited a wide range of possible cross-influences, noting that the scenery conjured up in the play (rocks, seascapes, islands, caves and clouds) recalls masquing properties, while more sophisticated approaches have stressed the use of symbolic persons and esoteric mythology, the deployment of courtly pastoral modes, the epithalamic

3. *The Tempest*, ed. Orgel, p. 13 (citing Harry Berger).

and panegyric elements (which echo *Hymenaei* (1606) and other early Jacobean masques), and, most of all, the introduction of stage machines for Juno's descent (IV, i, 102.1).[4] Such interpretations argue Shakespeare absorbed the esoteric and exclusive iconographics of the masque and that *The Tempest* participates in the new masque hermeneutic. Yet Prospero presents not a 'court masque' but rather 'a dramatic allusion to one' and its elements and effects cannot be straightforwardly linked to the court masque, combining heterogeneous elements which, although used by Jonson and other masque writers, derive from the broader discourses of the public theatre and the Elizabethan entertainment tradition.[5]

For instance, in contrast to the erudition demanded by *Hymenaei* or the *Masque of Queens* (1609), Prospero's masque deploys a simple mythology. In those masques the extensive rehearsal periods seem to have been used to coach the participants in the meanings of their roles, while for the audience, who may have received pamphlets detailing the action, understanding the allegory demonstrated intimacy with the court elite and, literally, with the *arcana imperii*.[6] The printed texts which later broadcast the masques are peppered with footnotes to establish the authority of both poet and court. The esoteric, erudite iconography deliberately excluded some, creating a privileged textual community whose insider knowledge manifested their insider status.

The Tempest's deities are familiar. Two of the goddesses are carefully named (Ceres, IV, i, 60; Juno, IV, i, 102) and their functions are explained to the audience. Iris addresses Ceres as 'most bounteous lady' (l. 60), Iris is described as 'many-coloured messenger' (l. 76), and Juno's role as 'wife of Jupiter' (l. 77) and 'Highest Queen of state' (l. 101) is spelled out, to such an extent that the description of Iris actually repeats her self-characterisation (ll. 70–1). Moreover, the dancer-spirits present familiar and rather sober reapers and nymphs, rather than intellectually exclusive references such as the classical queens found in Jonson's *Masque of Queens*. Even the basic fiction of the masque, the opposition of married love which produces fertility and Venusian desire which engenders

---

4. Gilman, "'All eyes'", p. 216; Wickham, 'Masque and anti-masque'. More recently: Norbrook, "'What cares these roarers for the name of king?'", pp. 21–54, esp. pp. 36–8, and Lindley, 'Music, masque and meaning', pp. 47–59.
5. *The Tempest*, ed. Orgel, p. 44.
6. BL MS Harley 6947 (fol. 143) contains a summary which may have been circulated before the performance; see Jonson, *The Masque of Queens*, Appendix XIV, in *Ben Jonson*, vol. VII, pp. 318–19. All subsequent references to Jonson's masques are to this edition.

nothing but scandal and wantonness (ll. 86–101), is carefully explicated, right down to the precise relations of Venus and Cupid.

This emphatic *openness* contrasts with the exclusivity of masques, recalling the mythological pageants of late Elizabethan public theatre (such as the appearance of Peace, Plenty, Plutus, Ceres, Bacchus and 'harvest-folkes' in *Histriomastix*, *c*.1599), as well as the older-style masked entries performed at the Elizabethan court, ditched by Queen Anne after Daniel's *Vision of Twelve Goddesses* (1604).[7] Both *Histriomastix* and Daniel's *Vision* explicate the mythology and attributes of their central figures, and *The Tempest* follows this, even introducing Prospero as a presenter, echoing *Pericles* rather than court masques. In fact, in terms of the court masque the interposition of Prospero echoes the role of Night in Daniel's *Vision*, while the employment of spirits (rather than goddesses descended to earth or courtiers) accentuates our distantiation from the masque (IV, i, 120). Prospero's interventions constantly shape the audience perception of his 'present fancies' (l. 122) and 'vision' (l. 151), emphasising fictitiousness in a way which resembles Daniel's *Vision* conjured by Night and Somnus, or his later evocation of 'pleasures [which] vanish fast, / ... by shadows expressed' (*Tethys' Festival* (1610), ll. 349–50), rather than Jonson's rationalist 'high and heartie *inuentions*' which 'furnish the inward parts, ... grounded vpon *antiquitie* and solid *learnings*' (*Hymenaei*, ll. 14–16).[8] Indeed, while the IV, i masque recalls the court masque, it echoes Daniel's *Vision* rather than the Jonsonian masque, deploying an older style of iconography, narrative and presentational style.[9]

Much critical discussion has centred upon the antimasque elements (the harpies' banquet, Caliban and the conspirators' entry, the glittery transvestism, and the hunting dogs have all been nominated).[10] Such approaches misconstrue the nature and function of antimasques before 1613, for, while the antimasque appears post-1608, it was less differentiated from the main masque (Jonson uses 'foil' as a metaphor for the

7. Marston, *Histriomastix*, I, i, in *Plays*, vol. III, p. 254.
8. Daniel's Night and Somnus (Sleep) offer 'strange sightes / Strange visions' and 'bright visions': *The Vision of the Twelve Goddesses*, ll. 222–3, in *A Book of Masques*; see *Tethys' Festival*.
9. Jonson and Daniel had radically different conceptions of the masque and its politics: see Lowenstein, 'Printing and the "multitudinous presse"', pp. 169–70, and Norbrook, 'The reformation of the masque', pp. 94–110, 96.
10. Wickham proposes the banquet ('Masque and anti-masque', p. 5) but the act-break would have been filled by music (see Gurr, 'The *Tempest*'s tempest at the Blackfriars', p. 93). Gilman, Lindley and Norbrook all argue for a reversal of generic expectations, and Norbrook sees anti-masque features dispersed throughout the play.

relation),[11] and not as oppositional as in later examples.[12] Early anti-masques were more often 'antic' or 'antique' than antithetic, as in the *Haddington Masque* (1608) where Cupid and twelve boys 'antickly attyr'd', representing the 'sports, and prettie lightnesses that accompanie *Loue*, vnder the titles of *Ioci*, and *Risvs*', performed a 'subtle and *capriccious Daunce*, to as odde a *Musique* ... with other varietie of other ridiculous gesture, which gaue much occasion of mirth, and delight, to the specta-tors' (*Haddington*, ll. 158–61, 171–5).[13] Whereas all these masques empha-sise scenic transformation to symbolise moral metamorphosis, in both *Haddington* and *Oberon* (1611) Cupid and the satyrs are transformed to be reincorporated into the masque world, unlike *Queens*, which follows the pattern of expulsion seen as more typically Jonsonian.[14] Perhaps these very 'antic' qualities are found in the 'properly habited' 'sunburned sickle-men' performing a 'country-footing' which is still 'a *graceful* dance' (my italics) and who are not expelled as part of the masque action, but absorbed into an image of temperance, as the hot reapers combine with the 'temperate nymphs' (IV, i, 132–138.1–2).

In this use of the 'antic' Prospero's masque does converge with the court masque, although not in the way most critics have argued, and there is little which conforms to the Jonsonian structure of transforma-tions or expulsions. Orgel cites 'barren hate, / Sour-eyed disdain, and discord' (IV, i, 19–20) as the textual traces of antimasque figures (they can be read as Hate, Discord and Disdain), but unlike the Jonsonian masque where the dramatic transformations or expulsions are enacted, here the marginalisation of desire is achieved without the agency of either the deities or the other masquers. Indeed, it is simply accidental (IV, i, 88–101), rather than relying upon the inherent improbability of

11. Jonson, *Masque of Queens*, l. 14 (p. 282). Foil is the gold leaf used to offset a jewel, suggesting the interplay of equally precious materials, rather than base substance which must be removed.

12. As Orgel argues, a fundamental structural dichotomy of courtly virtue against 'whatever opposes or threatens it' (*The Tempest*, p. 45) existed right from the genre's inception, but only in the 1620s are more realistic, plebeian and contemporary figures introduced to heighten the opposition (and, incidentally, raise the political stakes).

13. In *Oberon*, the lustful satyrs sing and dance in a decorously grotesque fashion as Needham and Johnson's music for the satyrs' songs, 'Buzz, quoth the blue fly' and 'Now my cunning lady, moon', shows: see Jonson and others, in *The Masqve of Oberon*, tracks 9–10.

14. *Queens* stands out as unusual here, with the Hags confined to the antimasque and vanishing at the loud music heralding Fame (ll. 354–63), but in *Haddington* and *Oberon*, the antic figures remain on-stage, mixing with the masque visions of global sphere and Oberon's Palace, transformed to new grace.

vice or danger submitting merely to the revelation of courtly virtue. The apparent harmoniousness of the vision, without 'foil' or 'antimasque', heightens the shock at its abrupt termination, making it significant that Caliban and the conspirators are *not* like antimasque figures of the period (boys, witches, satyrs, Robin Goodfellow).[15] They may *act* like antimasquers from the later Jacobean masque, but their disruptive effect increases as the masque vision is punctured by a reality clearly outside its bounds and imaginings.[16]

Equally, the very factors which made the masque significant within early modern culture are absent in this dramatic evocation of the masque. There is no monarch present either to watch, gain proximity to, or be seen by in *The Tempest*, which means that although Prospero's masque may *allude* to the magical qualities of the court masque it simply cannot bear the quasi-religious significance which has led some commentators to see these occasions as 'liturgies of state'.[17] Moreover, with spirit-actors not courtiers, the masque lacks the important interplay between masque role and the identity of specific individuals, removing the political meanings of participation. This immateriality has great significance if we consider a contemporary masque description such as the Venetian ambassador's of the *Masque of Beauty* (1608):

> I must just touch on the splendour of the spectacle, which was worthy of her Majesty's greatness. The apparatus and the cunning of the stage machinery was a miracle, the abundance and beauty of the lights immense, the music and dance most sumptuous. But what beggared all else and possibly exceeded the public expectation was the wealth of pearls and jewels that adorned the Queen and her ladies, so abundant and splendid that in everyone's opinion no other court could have displayed such pomp and riches.[18]

This description, with its emphasis upon splendour, magnificence and conspicuous material consumption, embodies all that Prospero's masque shuns. Unlike contemporary masques, Prospero's 'vanity of mine art' (IV, i, 41) eschews architectural features (the House of Fame, Oberon's

---

15. In *Haddington, Queens, Oberon* and *Love Restored* respectively. It might be objected that the witches in *Queens* are clearly malevolent, but they are highly ambiguous figures deriving from the king's own witchcraft pamphlets. *Queens* has been read as a critique of James's views of women or of Anne's overly masculine pretensions to power.
16. Grundin, 'Prospero's masque', pp. 405–6.
17. Strong's phrase, cited in J. Limon, 'The masque of Stuart culture', p. 215.
18. *Ben Jonson*, vol. X, p. 457, citing from State Papers, *Calendar of State Papers: Venetian, Vol. XI: 1607–10*, p. 86.

Palace, or the Prison of the Night), or magical transformations based on the architectural vision. Indeed, from Prospero's invocation of his 'vanity' to his valedictory 'baseless fabric of this vision' (l. 151) the etheriality of the masque is emphasised, as spirit-actors rather than 'cloud-capped towers, the gorgeous palaces, / The solemn temples, the great globe itself' melt 'into air, into thin air' (ll. 152–3, 150). This illusoriness contrasts markedly with the Stuart masque, where performers crossed between the illusionistic space of the scene into the dancing space, and where fictions became actual individuals.[19]

For many critics, however, the 'majesty of Juno in the clouds' and the 'peering-forth of Iris in the shrouds' clinches the connection of *The Tempest* to the masque.[20] Yet this single spectacular 'flying' effect cannot be attributed to court masques as the staging devices in the play, especially the use of descent or flight machinery, derive from the *public* playhouse.[21] As early as 1592 Henslowe may have sought to provide descent machinery from his new Heavens for the Rose (a technological advance presumably designed to compete with other companies and their machines),[22] and the most elaborate Jacobean descents were mounted at the Red Bull, the most downmarket of the amphitheatres.[23]

The current consensus amongst *Tempest* editors interprets Juno's entry as an example of the convention of the 'floating deity', so that Juno enters at line 74.1, hovering above the stage, only descending at line 102.1.[24] This convention appears to have been particularly common-

19. Limon, 'Masque of Stuart culture', pp. 213–15.
20. *An Expostulation with Inigo Jones*, ll. 33–4, in *Ben Jonson*, vol. VIII.
21. *The Tempest*, ed. Orgel, pp. 2–4. Orgel notes that the masque staging techniques themselves did not derive from Jones's Italian trips (see Orgel and Strong, *Inigo Jones and the Theatre of the Stuart Court*, vol. I, p. 23).
22. Wickham, '"Heavens", machinery, and pillars in the theatre', argues strongly against the presumption of heavens, pillars or any machinery before the construction of the Rose (pp. 10–12).
23. Such descents, associated with the public stage, are ridiculed as the 'creaking throne [that] comes down the boys to please': Prologue (l. 16), *Every Man In*, probably revised for Blackfriars performances c.1611–13: *Ben Jonson*, vol. III, p. 303.
24. The solution proposed by Jowett, 'New created creatures'. The Oxford *Complete Works*, eds Wells and Taylor, elaborates the stage direction as 'Juno [appears in the air]' and '[Music. Juno descends to the stage]' (IV, i, 72.1, 102.1). Wells and Taylor, *Textual Companion*, p. 615, give '*Iuno [appears in the ayre] Iuno descends*'. Indeed, the Oxford editors attack previous relocations of the stage direction (usually to IV, i, 102), arguing it is not an anticipatory stage direction to prepare the stage hands for the descent. They conclude that 'descends' often used to 'signify an appearance in the air rather than descent to the stage'. Unfortunately, consideration of the staging of IV, i, is complicated by the inconsistency and unworkability of the stage directions as they survive in the First Folio (1623) (see Roberts, 'Ralph Crane', and Jowett, 'New

place in the private hall theatres, such as the Blackfriars, where, for instance, Chapman's *The Widow's Tears* (1604) presents a masque in which 'Hymen descends, and six Sylvans enter beneath, with torches.'[25] At court, however, such stagings were rare and only two masques used machine descents before 1613: *Hymenaei* and *The Somerset Masque* (1613). Both Daniel's *Vision* and Jonson's *Blackness* (1605) used shutters or a traverse on the upper stage, which 'discovered' the moon 'in the upper part of the house' surrounded by clouds and a starry vault (*Blackness*, ll. 212–20).[26] Indeed, court stagings in this period employed a split-level stage as their most common, if not characteristic, device along with the *machina ductilis* (the shutters which could be withdrawn to effect scenic transformation).[27] A surviving design for *Love Freed* (1611) (Figure 6.1) shows how such arrangements might operate, with an upper stage topped with a *machina versitalis* and two stage-level doors,[28] a layout which corresponds to the Second Banqueting House, which had a gallery on at least three sides accessed by two staircases at the northern (stage) end.[29] These masque stagings (unfortunately no designs survive for stage performances) may help us to understand common uses of the

---

created creatures'). Most critics agree that these directions originate with the copyist for the underlying manuscript, Ralph Crane, who consistently augmented the stage directions in the light of performances he had seen or was possibly influenced by other masques he had copied. These difficulties are compounded by our uncertainty as to what kind of text Crane himself was copying, although, given the lack of practical directions in this scene, it seems probable he followed an authorial rather than a theatrical manuscript. As Crane worked predominantly after 1619 and the Folio transcripts were probably assembled *c.*1621–2, there remains a strong likelihood that Crane's directions embody staging practices of a considerably later date rather than deriving from the original staging.

25. After Hymen has addressed the audience one character comments 'O, would himself descend and me command!' (III, ii, 107), which in conjunction with the 'beneath' implies that Hymen hovers above the masquers: Chapman, *The Widow's Tears*, ed. Yamada. The exit of Hecate and the Cat-spirit in *Macbeth* III, v, illustrates the convention more clearly: the two figures ascend, hover above the stage and eventually 'disappear above' (l. 64.1): see *Macbeth*, ed. Brooke). 'The other three spirits appear above' (47.2) suggests that this scene also combines upper stage and machines, as in *The Golden Age* (see below, n. 31).

26. In *Vision* Iris descends from a mountain where the deities were assembled (ll. 144–50), an arrangement which also suggests a discovery and pedestrian descent. This was performed in the Hall at Hampton Court.

27. Campion's *Lord's Masque* (1613) also used a two-level stage, with an upper stage of clouds containing the star-masquers discovered by a falling traverse.

28. Orgel and Strong, *Inigo Jones*, vol. I, no. 74 and fig. 30.

29. Colvin, Ransome and Summerson, *The History of the King's Works*, vol. III, p. 322. See also Wickham, *Early English Stages*, vol. II, part II, p. 164, fig. 19, for a reconstruction of this staging based on Robert Smythson's (1618) plan.

Figure 6.1 Inigo Jones, design for *The Release of the Daughters of the Morn,* from *Love Freed from Ignorance and Folly,* 1611. By courtesy of the Devonshire Collection, Chatsworth. Reproduced by permission of the Chatsworth Settlement Trustees: photograph Courtauld Institute of Art.

available architecture of the Banqueting Hall, and may suggest how play-stagings might have been approached. Indeed, if we consider the spatial resources of the Banqueting House, an upper-stage discovery and pedestrian descent become the most likely way to stage IV, i, at court.[30] 'Juno descends' precedes her actual entry (ll. 101–2) by some thirty lines, allowing the upper stage to open at 'Her peacocks fly amain' (l. 74) and her physical descent to occur during the dialogue of Ceres and Iris (perhaps during ll. 76–101), with adequate time for movement between the upper stage on the balcony and the lower stage.[31]

The machine-powered descents for *Hymenaei* and *The Somerset Masque* were only achieved after considerable, expensive effort (*Blackness* required the construction of a huge pageant car within the Banqueting Hall which carried all the machinery).[32] Regular descents were not commonplace until after 1615 and were only achieved with ease after the construction of a fly gallery in 1631.[33] Jacobean court *dramatic* performances were not even afforded the luxury of a single playing

30. Jowett, 'New created creatures', p. 115, admits the possibility of an upper stage, but sees free flight as the more effective staging, noting 'the stage directions themselves are neutral and could be adapted'. The current editorial consensus leaves unresolved the contradiction between the stage directions and the text, as at l. 102 (TLN 1763) Ceres comments 'Great Juno comes; I know her by her gait.' In order to dovetail this description, which appears to require Juno to walk on stage, editors have to regard 'gait' (l. 102) as metaphorical, meaning 'bearing, carriage – not necessarily implying that she walks on to the stage': *The Tempest*, ed. Orgel, IV, i, 102n. (p. 177). However, both literary allusion and stage convention might support 'gait' meaning step. Kermode in his 1953 edition annotated 'I know her by her gait' as a reference to Virgil's description of Venus in *Aeneid*, Book I, revealed to Aeneas simply by her tread (*The Tempest*, ed. Kermode, IV, i, 102, and note). In *Aeneid*, Book I, ll. 404–5, 'down to her feet fell her raiment, and in her step she was revealed a very goddess' ('pedes vestis defluxit ad imos, / et vera incessu patuit dea'), as translated in Virgil, *Eclogues, Georgics, Aeneid I–VI*, while in *Pericles* (*c*.1608) Diana enters on foot, an entry which, although it may have been prompted by staging resources (or the lack of them: Wickham, '"Heavens", machinery and pillars", p. 9, points out that it was quite possible for gods and goddesses to enter on foot), may also derive from a mythological point, as this foot-borne entry may represent Diana's appearance in earthly guise. I owe this point Dr Michael Pincombe.

31. This staging pattern also derives from the public stage and shutters were regularly used at the Red Bull; see Reynolds, *Staging*, p. 101. Heywood's *The Golden Age* shows the spectacular effects the public stage might attain: 'Sound a dumbe shew. Enter the three fatall sisters, with a rocke, a threed, and a paire of sheeres; bringing in a Gloabe, in which they put three lots. Iupiter drawes heauen: at which Iris descends and presents him with his Eagle, Crowne and Scepter, and his thunder-bolt. Iupiter first ascends vpon the Eagle, and after him Ganimed.' See *The Dramatic Works of Thomas Heywood*, ed. Shepherd, vol. III, p. 78, and Reynolds, *Staging*, pp. 106–7.

32. PRO AO 1/37/2418, cited in *Ben Jonson*, vol. X, p. 445.

33. Orgel and Strong, *Inigo Jones*, vol. I, pp. 18–20.

place, moving with the court to wherever it was located (Wilton, Greenwich, Whitehall and so on), adapting previously existing spaces, such as the hall, great chamber and cockpit.[34] The limited surviving evidence about the costs of theatrical playing, even for the Banqueting House, shows considerably less effort and expense were expended.[35]

Court dramatic performances were very much the poor relations of both commercial theatrical performances and the court masques. Until the Cockpit at Court's conversion (1629) there was no permanent playing place for theatrical performances and, until that point, it seems highly unlikely that complicated descents could have been mounted.[36] It is possible that in the early 1620s (and presumably after 1629), it may have been possible to mount elaborate performances at court using masque-like descents and the full panoply of mechanised staging but, in general, large-scale stagings are reserved for plays which originate with the court (such as *Hymen's Triumph* (1614) or *The Shepherd's Paradise* (1633)) rather than commercial stage-plays. It is even possible that the sophisticated descent similar to that envisaged for Townshend's *Tempe Restored* (1632), which closely resembles the descent of Jupiter in *Cymbeline* (V, iii, 186.1–3), may have been introduced into pre-existing texts such as *The Tempest*.[37] However, it is interesting to note, for a play with such supposedly court-like and masque-derived effects, that amongst the late plays *The Tempest* fell out of fashion (while both *Cymbeline* and *The Winter's Tale* were revived in the Caroline period), and that Charles I, the masque's keenest exponent, did not express any particular interest in the play.[38]

II

The implications of the discriminations I have outlined above, especially in the way Prospero's masque borrows its 'glistering apparel' (IV, i, 193.1) of stage effects and mythological figures from the commercial London stage, and its masquing style from Daniel's masque rather than Jonson's, can be pursued further if we consider how IV, i, relates to the wider tradition of aristocratic masquing in this period. This relocation of Prospero's masque in this aristocratic masquing culture has a profound impact on the way we might then consider the political aesthetics of the late plays.

34. Bentley, *The Jacobean and Caroline Stage*, vol. VI, *Theatres* (1968), pp. 269–70.
35. Orrell, *The Theatres of Inigo Jones*, p. 10.
36. Orrell, *The Theatres of Inigo Jones*, Ch. 5, *passim*.
37. Orgel and Strong, *Inigo Jones*, vol. II, no. 218.
38. His copy of Shakespeare's *Works* (1632) contains no annotations for *The Tempest*. I am grateful to the Royal Library, Windsor Castle, for this information.

Few discussions of the interconnection of the court masque and *The Tempest* recognise how problematic the concept of *the* court masque might be, or how the form evolved over the Jacobean period.[39] Most discussions concentrate on the narrow tradition embodied by the Jonsonian Twelfth Night masques, excluding the extensive and varied masquing culture which embodies a much more contested and factional aristocratic culture, with an often ambiguous or oblique relationship either to the court or to Jacobean royal ideology. Historians of Jacobean (rather than Elizabethan or Caroline) court culture now emphasise its diversity, its lack of cohesiveness and its polycentricity, with major grandees and dynasties espousing differing aesthetic and political styles, not in opposition to the court, but as alternative models of court culture.[40] This interplay of different *courts* even shapes the Twelfth Night masques, as in the period 1603–1613 *Hymenaei*, *Lord Hay's Masque* and the *Haddington Masque* were all sponsored by aristocratic families, and many of the masques associated with Queen Anne and Prince Henry (notably *Oberon*) can be read as providing alternative models of royal politics and culture.[41]

Most interpretations relating *The Tempest* to the masque draw upon the canon of Twelfth Night masques, usually by Jonson, because these are the occasions for which texts and documentation survive.[42] This, however, ignores both the important sequence of royal and aristocratic entertainments (Althorp (1603), Highgate (1604), Theobalds (1606 and 1607), Salisbury House, London (1608), Woodstock (1612) and Caversham (1613)) mounted to entertain the monarchs and their guests, and the country-house masques, (*The Entertainment at Ashby* (1607), the *Wedding Masque* for Lord de Walden and Lady Home (*c.*1612), and the *Shepherd's Song* (1613)). These masques, produced by at least five authors (Campion, Chapman, Daniel, Jonson, Marston) plus unknown others, undermine Jonson's apparent dominance of the form and accentuate the variety inherent within the genre.[43] Many of these entertainments raise matters which could not be articulated in the controlled and decorous Twelfth Night masques, and some grandees used such occasions to

---

39. *The Tempest*, ed. Orgel, pp. 43–6, is an exception.
40. Smuts, 'Cultural diversity', pp. 104–5, and Elton, 'Tudor government'.
41. Smuts, 'Cultural diversity', p. 104. For opposed readings of these masques see Lewalski, *Writing Women*, pp. 15–43, and Orgel, 'Jonson and the Amazons', pp. 119–39.
42. It is tempting to wonder what influences might have accrued from the *Masque of Indian and Chinese Knights* (1604), *Juno and Hymenaeus* (1605), mounted for the Pembroke/Vere marriage, and the unknown Shrovetide masque (1608).
43. Norbrook, 'The reformation of the masque' surveys this tradition.

influence royal policy (notably Robert Cecil, Lord Salisbury) or to establish a dynastic policy at a discreet distance form the court (for example, the Hastings family, earls of Huntingdon).[44] Although these were *entertainments*, they formed an important channel of political communication, participating in the networks of exchange of influence, favours, gifts, people and ideas which cemented the Jacobean politico-cultural elite together.

In many ways Prospero's masque in its scale, style and even subject matter resembles aristocratic household masques or entertainments. These diverse, often fragmentary texts were usually designed to entertain important arriving guests at the home of an aristocratic family, although in the seventeenth century they less frequently celebrated royal entries, being used for intra- or inter-family occasions, often celebrating special anniversaries or events (betrothals, marriages, christenings or birthdays), or Christmas. Key moments of the progress of the guest could be marked, such as the arrival, the presentation of gifts, the first night, the departure, while the exact topics and forms might vary according to the identity of recipient, guest, host, location or practical exigencies. Usually, such entertainments invoke pastoral conventions, perhaps seeing the banishment of winter or witchcraft and their replacement with spring / summer or by joy at the arrival of the guest. Although a masque might form the centrepiece of these multi-sectional entertainments, the scale is usually smaller and more intimate, and the qualities of family position and honour filtered through hospitality and gift-giving rather than through outright magnificence.[45]

Generically, Prospero's masque is closer to the hybridity of Marston's *Entertainment at Ashby*, the only other known example of a betrothal masque (see below, p. 124).[46] Marston's text combines Elizabethan entry-entertainment conventions with elements from the Jacobean court marriage-masques (notably *Hymenaei* and *Blackness*) to encompass the arrival of a dynastic matriarch, the extension of the dynastic connection through betrothal, and the consolidation of familial position and power. Here the arriving dignitary, the Countess of Derby, was prevented from entry by a sorceress who had frozen the household in winter until the Countess's identity was declared, the spell broken and the sorceress

44. Knowles, 'Shopping with Cecil'.
45. Brown, 'Milton's *Arcades*', delineates many of these elements as the conventions of the form.
46. All references are to *The Poems of John Marston*. See also, Knowles, 'Marston, Skipwith and *The Entertainment at Ashby*'.

transformed, outfaced by aristocratic virtue. 'Magical' gifts were then bestowed by the reformed sorceress, and later that night an elaborate masque featuring Ariadne, Cynthia and stellar knights, which celebrated the lineage of the family and, especially, the chastity and virtue of its women, was performed. These entertainments were staged over several days, involving not only the Ashby household but surrounding gentry families, in semi-dramatic amusements, concluding with a farewell eclogue by a despairing shepherd and a mourning nymph, who offered parting gifts as the Countess left.

Prospero's masque resembles this text using more transparent mythology than the court masques (see p. 110 above), its central conceit centring upon the transformed seasonal cycle and the welcome offered honoured guests in a numinous place. So the entertainment in *The Tempest* centres upon welcome ('Approach, rich Ceres, her to entertain' (l. 75)), place ('the short-grassed green' (l. 83)), magical fecundity and translated seasons:

> Earth's increase, foison plenty,
> Barns and garners never empty,
> Vines with clust'ring bunches growing,
> Plants with goodly burden bowing;
> Spring come to you at the farthest,
> In the very end of harvest! (IV, i, 110–15).

Even the purpose of this visitation ('some donation freely to estate' (l. 85)) recalls the gift-givings central to the country-house masques, as the holiday mood (l. 136) transforms from simple pleasure into a magical and quasi-religious occasion (literally, a holy day).

Although these country-house masques might be quite elaborate (Ashby required a falling traverse, a mount and heraldic tree decorated with imprese shields, and no fewer than two flying cloud-borne goddesses) the pivotal moment depends less on the revelation of an architectural wonder than on the fiction, or on the symbolic meanings attached to the presence of the guests. Where the court masques centre upon elaborate architectural revelations, such as the Palace of Oberon appearing to a chorus of 'Melt earth to sea, sea flow to air' (*Oberon*, ll. 300–13), as the audience are subdued into wonder, architectural spectacle is rejected in Prospero's entertainment (esp. IV, i, 149–56, cited above). As with the country-house entertainments, in Prospero's masque the presence of the goddesses signals the significance of the occasion, while the relative simplicity of the setting, mythology and fiction emphasises ideas, notably chastity and fecundity, above wonder. 'All eyes' may evoke wonder, but not simply for its own sake, rather as a provocation to virtue. Like the country-house masque, the magical location (Ferdinand calls it 'paradise' (IV, i, 124), reinforces the dynastic connection, so that Ferdinand salutes his 'so rare a wondered father and a wife'.

The use of pastoral in Prospero's masque, which is often seen to echo or even prefigure the court masque, can also be linked to these country-house entertainments. In this respect, perhaps the closest analogue to Prospero's masque lies in Jonson's *Entertainment at Highgate* (1604), which accompanied Anne and James's May Day visit. This *Entertainment* consisted of a welcome and tour of the house, guided by the Penates, speeches in the garden from Mercury, and songs from Aurora, Zephyrus and Flora, culminating in Maia's appearance enthroned in a bower. In the after-dinner entertainment Mercury offers a 'new, and strange spectacle' (*Highgate*, l. 179) of Bacchus' magic fountain of laughter with nymphs fleeing from a Pan determined to offer them refreshment from the spring. Pan then offers the drink to the assembled company (who presumably duly laughed at his antics), although Mercury eventually closes the action, begging the monarchs' forgiveness for Pan's rudeness and offering his 'divinations' of the future longevity, prosperity and fecundity of the royal couple and household.

The culmination of the first part of the *Entertainment* occurs in the blessing offered to the monarchs by Maia, which combines a huge range of classical allusions, bringing all together in a vision of decorous plenty:

> If all the pleasures were distill'd
> Of eu'ry flower, in eu'ry field,
> And all that *Hybla* hiues do yield
> Were into one broad mazor fild;
> If, therto, added all the gummes,
> And spice, that from *Panchaia* comes,
> The odour, that *Hydaspes* lends,
> Or *Phœnix* proues, before she ends;
> If all the Ayre, my *Flora* drew,
> Or spirit, that *Zephyre* euer blew;
> Were put therein; and all the dew
> That euer rosy *Morning* knew;
> Yet, all diffus'd vpon this bower,
> To make one sweet detayning houre,
> Were much too little for the grace,
> And honor, you vouchsafe the place.
>
> (*Highgate*, ll. 116–31).

The image of the 'broad mazor' not only suggests the hospitable drinking of (here magical) healths, but the blending together to produce the superlative 'one sweet detayning hour'. The decorousness of Maia at this point, a figure who herself combines classical and vernacular traditions, prefigures precisely the balance of fertility and temperance, classicism and homespun, which characterises Prospero's 'present fancies'.

Perhaps, however, the most interesting feature of the Highgate *Entertainment* lies in its structure and how that may relate to Prospero's masque. Whereas, as discussed earlier (p. 111), later Jacobean court masques employ an anthithetical structure of antimasque and masque, the *Entertainment* includes Pan and his 'rusticke impudence' (*Highgate*, l. 185) as part of the fauna of the place. Indeed, Maia in her speech even offers both satyrs and nymphs as a possible future entertainment to cheer the monarchs:

> ... we will haue the wanton fawnes,
> That frisking skip, about the lawnes,
> The *Paniskes*, and the *Siluanes* rude,
> *Satyres*, and all that multitude,
> To daunce their wilder rounds about.
> (*Highgate*, ll. 136–40).

This emphasis upon the rustic and antic as part of the landscape echoes not only the variety of landscapes evoked in *The Tempest*, but also the 'sunburned sickle-men' who are joined and cooled by the 'fresh', 'temperate nymphs' in 'country-footing' (IV, i, 137, 132, 134). As at Highgate, the classical and decorous and the rustic and vernacular are brought together and reconciled in *The Tempest* in the image of the 'graceful dance' (138.2).

The significance of this realignment of Prospero's masque with the aristocratic rather than the court masque is to allow the possibility of greater freedom from the decorum demanded in the Twelfth Night masques (tellingly Highgate is a 'Private Entertainment'), but also to allow a more critical stance towards court culture. At Ashby, Ariadne's and Cynthia's ('chaste queen') appearances voice a critical distance from the court and its mores:

> Lasciuous youth not dare to speake
>   the language of loose Cytty,
> He that Dyanas bondes doth breake,
>   is held most rudely witty
> Now meete, now breake, then fayne a warlike salley

> So Cinthea sports and so the Godes may dalley
> Disgratious dullnes yett much marrs
> the shape of courtly talking
> He yt can scilent touch such starrs
> his soule lyes in his walking.
>
> (*Entertainment at Ashby*, ll. 364–72)

The prominent role of the women, and the charm spoken here which praises those who 'court chaster pleasure' (l. 354), a neat ironic reversal, not only celebrated Alice Egerton, the Dowager Countess of Derby, and her daughters through an appropriation of Elizabethan images, it articulated one aristocratic faction's ideological location, emphasising chastity, chivalry and, ultimately, Protestant militancy, in ways outside the court norm. The implicit criticisms of such texts are vocalised through nuance rather than outright statement, but their presence suggests some aristocratic unease with the Jacobean court, highlighting the manner in which *The Tempest* may also constructively but critically engage with court culture, and with an aristocratic culture which overlaps with, but is by no means coterminous with, the court.

The importance attached to chastity in Prospero's *betrothal* masque echoes *The Entertainment at Ashby*, and counterpoints the court weddings and epithalamia which dominated the first decade of the Jacobean masque. Whereas in court epithalamic masques Juno and Venus operate in concert (as in *Haddington*), the careful separation of Venus and Juno in *The Tempest* places a subtly different emphasis, while although this masque is a dynastic alliance, it is celebrated in an entirely different manner from Claribel's match (II, i, 69–74),[47] rooted in personal affection as much as policy. Again, as by 1610 some of the Jacobean political matches were clearly unravelling and the political union they sought to embody still remained uncomfortable, the implication may be critical. Particularly telling, then, is the invocation of Ferdinand and Miranda's 'vows … that no bed-right shall be paid / Till Hymen's torch be lighted' (IV, i, 96–7), because it stresses not the magical powers of monarchy, but the necessity of human labour towards virtue, supported by the benison of the gods. Here *The Tempest* prefigures *The Masque at Ludlow* with its rather ambiguous emphasis on chastity and virtue as achieved states rather than instantly granted or inherited gifts.

If we return to this chapter's initial question, we can see that the *kind* of masque Prospero presents has considerable implications. Not only

---

47. Wilson, 'Voyage to Tunis', p. 336, on the connections of this match and the Barbary piracy and slave-trading.

should we recognise the much more complex interaction of court and public theatre in this period, with the commercial shaping the courtly as much as vice versa, but also that within the court, within the idea of the 'courtly', different inflections and articulations are possible. The heterogeneity of the country-house masques and entertainments might be symbolic of the diversity which we should seek in early modern culture. Equally, the relocation of these 'insubstantial pageants' within a various tradition opens the way for a far more critical reading of the masque and its ideologies, both in the play and in the masquing culture itself. Prospero's masque, in its figures, tropes, mythologies and even the exact details of its presentation, suggests a Shakespeare whose art is far from 'tied to rules / Of flattery'.[48]

48. Fletcher, *The Maid's Tragedy*, I, i, 10–11.

7

'AN ART LAWFUL AS EATING'?
MAGIC IN *THE TEMPEST* AND
THE WINTER'S TALE

Gareth Roberts

In imitation of those frequent moments of recollection in both *The Winter's Tale* and *The Tempest*, this chapter starts with a moment of retrospection to the middle of Shakespeare's dramatic career, in order to look at a magician in a pastoral comedy written by Shakespeare some twelve years before his two last pastorals. In the figure of this magician we can find some of the origins of the representation of magic in both the later romances. This magician is the non-existent relative of a non-existent Shakespearean character: he is Ganymede's uncle in *As You Like It*.

Ganymede's uncle is first heard of when Rosalind – disguised as Ganymede – tells Orlando 'an old religious uncle of mine taught me to speak' (III, ii, 333–4) and in the same scene cites his authority on matters of love (III, ii, 335–59). Then in Act IV, when the love-entanglements of the play reach an extremity of impossible complication, Ganymede again invokes his uncle's authority, declares it to be magical, appropriates its power and undertakes with its aid a resolution of the play's love entanglements. In this undertaking we sense the promise of a final wonderful turn towards the play's happy ending:

> Believe then, if you please, that I can do strange things. I have since I was three year old conversed with a magician, most profound in his art, and yet not damnable. If you do love Rosalind ... it is not impossible to me, if it appear not inconvenient to you, to set her

before your eyes tomorrow, human as she is, and without any danger. (V, ii, 56–65)

I have identified Ganymede's 'old religious uncle' with this magician because it is what Orlando does, apparently on Ganymede's authority, when he and Duke Senior ponder the similarity between Ganymede and Rosalind, as the play turns towards its end:

> My lord, the first time that ever I saw him,
> Methought he was a brother to your daughter.
> But, my good lord, this boy is forest-born,
> And hath been tutored in the rudiments[1]
> Of many desperate studies by his uncle,
> Whom he reports to be a great magician,
> Obscurèd in the circle of this forest. (V, iv, 28–34)

Ganymede's uncle is now an old religious man, expert on speaking, a great yet licit magician who is capable of doing the impossible, and is apparently still active somewhere in Arden, which is here figured as a magic circle inside which he operates. Then in a final development in V, iv, he unnervingly seems to assume a life outside what we have assumed was Rosalind's fiction, when he is reported to be the author of the play's last unlikely coincidence and happy resolution. In *As You Like It*'s final crescendo of unlikelinesses the play exuberantly manages the only appearance of the third de Boys brother. His one speech (V, iii, 153–64) provides the play's final romance narrative, in which attention is drawn to the unlikely fictiveness of its contents by Jacques de Boys' aggressive assertion of their veracity, 'This to be true, / I do engage my life' (V, iv,163–4). In his speech, with its delight in unlikely symmetry typical of

---

1. Modern editions of *As You Like It* (e.g. Penguin, Arden, Oxford) offer no gloss of this use of 'rudiments', which makes magic a quasi-educational process, as rudiments are 'the first principles or elements of a subject' (OED *sb.* 1a). Shakespeare uses the word only twice elsewhere, when Hortensio promises to teach 'the rudiments of art' of the lute to Bianca (*The Taming of the Shrew*, III, i, 64) and when a schoolmaster berates his country pupils (*The Two Noble Kinsmen*, III, v, 3). In *As You Like It*, Shakespeare is often thinking of Marlowe (as when Rosalind quotes *Hero and Leander* at III, v, 82–3) and so may have had in mind Valdes' promise to teach Faustus magic: 'First I'll instruct thee in the rudiments, / And then thou wilt be perfecter than I' (*Doctor Faustus*, A-text, I, i, 163–4). King James too in his *Dæmonologie*, I, iii, speaks of the male art of magic as a quasi-educational process with its scholars, school and 'rudiments'. Given the argument of this paper, it is noticeable that these contexts for the uses of 'rudiments' are all those of 'art', and of processes of instruction by (male) masters of their pupils.

the play, it is surely Ganymede's uncle who converts Rosalind's uncle and diverts him from his destructive invasion of Arden:

> Duke Frederick …
> … to the skirts of this wild wood he came
> Where, meeting with an old religious man,
> After some question with him, was converted
> Both from his enterprise and from the world,
> His crown bequeathing to his banished brother,
> And all their lands restored to them again
> That were with him exiled. This to be true
> I do engage my life. (V, iv, 152–64)

In this essay I want to take Rosalind's relation to Ganymede's uncle as a template to lay on *The Winter's Tale* and *The Tempest*, two plays with which it has much in common, and see what that exercise may reveal about magic in those late plays, and about its operation by Paulina and Prospero. The nature of Rosalind's relation to Ganymede's uncle is, at least simply understood, that of a woman to an older male figure of authority, an authority which is in part a religious one, and who seems first fictitious and then perhaps becomes real. However, in the play's complicated fiction, questions about Rosalind's gender are as teasing as those about the ontological status of Ganymede's uncle, or for that matter, and especially in the play's epilogue, reality itself. Three areas of investigation emerge from this curious relationship. (Of course it has to be three for the magic of this chapter to work: Renaissance writers on magic never tire of quoting Virgil on triple repetition, 'the gods like uneven numbers'.)[2] These are magic, gender and authority; magic and religion; and finally magic, miracles and the creation of fictions. All three are connected, I think, with the authorship of wonders.

Rosalind's construction of her old authoritative uncle expresses the traditional assumption that magic, as opposed to witchcraft, is a male art. Orthodox theological opinion, including the writings of demonologists, consistently claimed that there was no difference between magic and witchcraft and both were ultimately diabolical and utterly unlawful. But an understanding that was a popular one, and was also that of practising magicians themselves and assumed in the many surviving manuscript clavicules, 'keys' and other conjuring books (and, for that matter, some representations in demonological treatises), was that magic was a male

---

2 'numero deus impare gaudet [in an uneven number heaven delights]', Virgil, *Eclogues*, Book VIII, 75.

art which commands supernatural power, and was quite unlike witch-craft, which was a female practice which supplicates it. Magic, so these views went, was a learned art which worked either by the manipulation of occult virtues of creation, or by the compulsion of spirits through the virtues of the operator, or by the accessing of heavenly power of various sorts. Witchcraft was overwhelmingly practised by women and operated through submission to or compact with spirits of various kinds. In King James's dialogue, *Dæmonologie*, Epistemon comments on the popular distinction to his pupil Philomathes, and also allows some limited truth to it:

> PHILOMATHES What difference is there betwixt this arte [magic] and Witch-craft?
>
> EPISTOMON Surelie, the difference vulgare put betwixt them is very merrie, and in a maner true; for they say, that the Witches ar servantes onlie, and slaves to the Devil; but the Necro-manciers are his maisters and commanders.[3]

Although the gender roles in *As You Like It*, especially Rosalind's, are extremely complicated, in Rosalind we have a female figure appropriating the authority of a male magician. What Rosalind fashions in Ganymede's uncle is the figure of a magical 'author' (or perhaps Foucault's author-function) in most of the senses one can find for that word or indeed for the Latin *auctor*: originator, constructor, ancestor, expert; many of which are of course historically gendered male.[4]

A line of descent from *As You Like It*, and Rosalind's appropriation of the authority of Ganymede's uncle, to *The Tempest* and to Prospero is clear enough. In Ganymede's uncle we can see *in potentia*, as Jonson's Surly would say, the eremetical magician of *The Tempest* who, like Rosalind with the aid of the fiction of the useful uncle, authors a betrothal masque, manages the delightful restoration of a 'lost' daughter to her father, magically manipulates the happy ending, and speaks an epilogue in the persona of a magician half-out of role. In the epilogue Rosalind, anticipating Prospero, takes up again her role as magician to conjure the audience in that strange half-way house that exists at the very end of *As You Like It*, and which is the same equivocal space which Prospero occupies for *The Tempest*'s epilogue. In it we experience an elision of the play's fictions with the theatrical reality of an address to the audience. When Rosalind again takes up the power of the male magician ('My

---

3. James VI and I, *Dæmonologie*, I, iii, p. 9.
4. An author is 'He who gives rise to an action' (OED *sb.* 1c) or 'One who begets; a father, an ancestor' (OED *sb.* 2a).

way is to conjure you' (Epilogue)), we can hear an authorial voice introject itself into the play's text. Sidney uses the same voice and the persona of magician when he addresses his readers at the end of the *Apology*, 'I conjure you all … in the name of the nine Muses.'[5]

In Ganymede's magician-uncle too, especially in his appearance in Jaques de Boys' speech, we see the brief appearance of the author, in *As You Like It*'s equivalent to Alfred Hitchcock's appearance in his own films, for example carrying a double-bass in *North by North-West*. In Ganymede's uncle we can detect the play's author's projection of himself, or perhaps his function, into his work. Hitchcock's appearances in his own works was anticipated in various ways by many Renaissance and baroque artists' self-insertions into theirs: Dufay, Michelangelo, Donne, Botticelli, Bach. In particular Spenser's appearance as Colin Clout in *The Faerie Queene* (Book VI, x, 1–29), in a supernatural moment of vision, surely influenced Prospero's creation of a masque of an ideal world and its sudden disappearance, which causes both sadness in its fashioner and a breaking of the frame of fiction. We have, of course, since the nineteenth century had interpretations of *The Tempest*, of which Thomas Campbell's in 1838 was apparently the first, which see Prospero in some way as Shakespeare.[6]

The genealogy is less clear to Paulina in *The Winter's Tale*, but we can see in *The Winter's Tale* an analogy to Rosalind's relationship with Ganymede's uncle in another female character's pretence to magical power and her relation to a male author, in the sense of originator or constructor. This is the joint authorship of Hermione's statue by Paulina with 'that rare Italian master Giulio Romano' (V, ii, 95).[7] Julio Romano has the same odd ontological status as Ganymede's uncle: he is cited as equivocal authority for a feat of art which seems to become magical, but that does not actually exist. When we are first led to believe in the statue's existence, we are told by the Third Gentleman of Perdita's intention to visit it:

> The princess hearing of her mother's statue, which is in the keeping of Paulina – a piece many years in doing, and now newly performed by that rare Italian master Giulio Romano, who, had he himself eternity and could breath into his work, would beguile nature of her custom, so perfectly he is her ape. (V, ii, 92–8)

5. Sidney, *Apology*, p. 141.
6. See Nuttall, *Two Concepts of Allegory*, pp. 5–6.
7. On Julio Romano see Barkan, '"Living sculptures"', and Baughan, 'Shakespeare's confusion'.

The Third Gentleman's tribute to Julio Romano's art is that in imitating nature he goes beyond it, and, anticipating Paulina's apparent later feat, that he might (in a daring imitation of God's breathing life into Adam in Genesis 2.7) even animate his work and bring it to life. There is an antecedent in an earlier play by Shakespeare for this co-operation of Paulina and Julio Romano in their art, in the almost miraculous skill shared in *All's Well* by Helena and her father, Gerard de Narbon, another skilful master of his art we never see. Helena inherits from her father an art that rivals and surpasses nature and which puts life into the lifeless. According to Lafew, Helena is herself a medicine which could 'breathe life into a stone' and her touch could 'araise King Pépin' (II, i, 72, 75). The Countess tells us that Gerard de Narbon had near miraculous powers which brought him close to cheating death, for his 'skill was almost as great as his honesty; had it stretched so far, would have made nature immortal, and death should have play for lack of work' (I, i, 17–20). Rosalind, Helena and Paulina produce their wonderful effects by accessing the skill of an absent male artist with almost miraculous powers, and in the two later plays this is manifested as the raising of the dead, a sort of necromancy. In Prospero's most powerful evocation of his art in *The Tempest* (V, i, 33–57) the situation is interestingly the opposite. The 'Ye elves of hills' speech is of course a sustained remodelling of the words of a female enchantress, Medea in Ovid's *Metamorphoses* (Book VII, 192–219), often cited in demonologies as evidence for the powers of witches and magicians. The very self-conscious act of imitation here is that of a male author, accessing another male author, through a female medium. Stephen Orgel has a very interesting discussion about male and female power and magic in his edition of the play.[8]

Paulina practises a male magical art at the end of the play when she apparently animates Hermione's statue. At the end of *The Winter's Tale*, Paulina and her magic are quite different from cunning women such as Mother Bombie in Lyly's play, or the wise woman in Heywood's *The wise-woman of Hogsdon*, both of whom also attempt to bring about the comedic resolutions of the plays they inhabit by a pretence of magic: 'Well, trust to me, and I will set all things straight' (*The wise-woman of Hogsdon*, IV, ii, 28–9). Heywood's wise woman is an illiterate fraud who pretends to be a cunning-woman and has a thriving practice. She is also a bawd and procuress, those things that Leontes accuses Paulina of being in the first half of the play (II, iii, 67–8). Heywood's Second Luce points

---

8. *The Tempest*, ed. Orgel, pp. 18–23.

out the difference between what the wise woman pretends to and the art of magic as practised by the learned and educated:

> What can this witch, this wizard, or old trot
> Do by enchantment or by magic spell?
> Such as profess that art should be deep scholars.
> What reading can this simple woman have?
> 'Tis palpable gross foolery. (I, ii, 34–8)

At the end of *The Winter's Tale* Shakespeare wants in Paulina's art that which apparently animates Hermione's statue, a magic distanced from any suggestions of illicitness, an art, to quote Rosalind, of 'a magician, most profound in his art, and yet not damnable'. This entails constructing it at the end of the play as a male art. Paulina had been accused of wicked magical practices, specifically gendered female, earlier in the play in Leontes' furious outbursts, explicitly in 'A mankind witch! ... A most intelligencing bawd!' (II, iii, 67–8), and perhaps implicitly in 'A gross hag!' (II, iii,107). These characterisations place her in a long tradition of witch-bawds, and in a context of grotesque and unruly female practices associated with the supernatural and female sexuality: 'hag' here perhaps has the additional sense of witch or even succubus.[9] The end of the play carefully distinguishes its magic from any illicit practices. It raises the spectre of wicked practices, and then later dismisses it, as when Leontes expresses his and Perdita's initial reaction to the statue:

> O royal piece!
> There's magic in thy majesty, which has
> My evils conjured to remembrance, and
> From thy admiring daughter took the spirits,
> Standing like stone with thee. (V, iii, 38–42)

In this scene Paulina is careful to distance herself from accusations of diabolic practices and from witchcraft, and the rest of the play then works hard to dispel the notion of 'unlawful business' (V, iii, 96)[10] and turn Paulina's magic into something like Nicholas Rowe's description of Shakespeare's own magic, 'very solemn and very poetical'.[11]

What Paulina practises at the end of the play is a male art whose details often recall the operations of Cerimon in resurrecting Thaisa in

---

9. See Pearson, 'Witchcraft in *The Winter's Tale*', p. 201; Baroja, *World of the Witches*, pp. 100–2; Kiessling, '*The Winter's Tale*', pp. 93–5.
10. For stories of moving statues involving practitioners of the black arts see Baum, 'The young man'.
11. Rowe in *The Works of Shakespear*, ed. Hanmer, vol. I, p. xxxviii.

Pericles, for example in the use of music and the gradual sense of the statue warming into life. Although we may not want to go as far as Frances Yates and claim that Paulina was practising Hermetic magic,[12] the animation of statues is usually described as a feat of male priests or male magical technicians,[13] and the archetype for this scene is of course Ovid's account of the male artist Pygmalion (*Metamorphoses*, Book X, ll. 243–97), with its famous statement about art's concealments: 'so does his art conceal art'.[14] And in Paulina's application of music, which we may want to relate in some way to the magical experiments of Florentine academicians,[15] looks forward to its accompaniment of Prospero's magic in *The Tempest*. Female witchcraft is always bad, but there is a chance that male magical art might just be allowable, and it is as an 'art' that the king legitimises Paulina's magic (V, iii, 38–42).

Ganymede's uncle is a learned, religious man removed from the world, a benevolent hermit-magician living in a romance wood, and the very thing that Spenser's Archimago pretends to be in *The Faerie Queene*, Book I. This comparison, with Spenser's Protestant representation of a duplicitous Catholic hermit-magician, clearly points up that an important model for the early modern magician in all sorts of ways was the Roman Catholic cleric. Keith Thomas showed us the way that early modern magical beliefs and practices were bound up with Catholicism and what happened to them after the Reformation, and Stuart Clark the ways that magic was at the very heart of reforming processes.[16] Magic and its representation in the early modern period necessarily negotiated with Catholicism.[17] In this context I would like briefly to think about

12. Yates, *Shakespeare's Last Plays*, pp. 89–91.

13. The archetype is the famous passage in Trismegistus, *Hermetica*, pp. 80–1. See also Yates, *Theatre of the World*, pp. 29–30; Yates, *Giordano Bruno*, pp. 147–9; French, *John Dee*, pp. 108–9.

14. 'ars adeo latet arte sua'; Ovid, *Metamorphoses*, Book X, l. 252. I am grateful to two friends for providing me with examples of female statue-makers. Robert Maslen reminded me that in Lyly's *The Woman in the Moon* a female figure, Nature, makes a statue. Lancaster, 'Hermione's statue', p. 233, notes that F. W. Moorman, *The Works of Shakespeare, The Winter's Tale* (London, Methuen, 1912), p. xxxi, suggested *The Woman in the Moon* as a source for *The Winter's Tale*. Susan Wiseman tells me that Aphra Behn has a poem in which a female Pygmalion fashions a male statue.

15. For the experiments of humanists with magical music see Walker, *Spiritual and Demonic Magic*.

16. Thomas, *Religion*, especially pp. 27–89, 301–32; Clark, *Thinking with Demons*, pp. 435–545.

17. For a subtle account of the relationship of magic and religion after the Reformation, which sees the continuing attraction of certain 'magical' beliefs, see Scribner, 'Reformation, popular magic'.

the male magician in *The Tempest* and about superstition in *The Winter's Tale*.

In the Renaissance magic is the male art *par excellence*, as many of its practices and theories model themselves upon those of an exclusively male coterie, Roman Catholic priests. High magic attempted to distinguish itself from witchcraft by insistence on learning, purity and male ideals of sacerdotal purity and chastity. Agrippa's magician in Book III of his *De Occulta Philosophia* (1533) is clearly modelled on an ideal of priesthood. In Agrippa and in magical manuscripts we can see that the practices of high magic modelled themselves on ideas of the powerful purity of the priesthood and of the sacraments and sacramentalia the priest consecrated and administered. The figure of the male Catholic priest lurks behind many representations of magical practice, and not only in England. The sorcerous Roman Catholic priest is a figure of importance to some Continental demonologists: in Henri Boguet's *Discours des Sorciers* (Lyons, 1602) and Francesco Maria Guazzo's *Compendium Maleficarum* (Milan, 1608) he is the priest who celebrates a parody mass at the sabbat. Thanks to the work of Ruth Martin, Guido Ruggiero and others[18] we know of the particular magical efficacy attributed in Continental Europe to the priest's person and that the demonologists' accounts had some basis in fact, for some Catholic priests did indeed have sidelines as sorcerers. In some English pamphlet accounts of witchcraft accusations we can detect, either implicitly or explicitly, a Protestant search for the Catholic priest as the male originator of magical practices.[19] And Protestant propaganda is of course littered with tales of necromantic popes. According to John Bale all the popes between Sylvester II and Gregory VII were magicians,[20] and similar lists are catalogued by English Protestant demonologists. In Protestant writings generally, popery was seen as idolatrous, magical, a religion of false miracles.[21]

It is something of this magical power of the old religion that Shakespeare is carefully negotiating in the two late plays. Prospero's cell and Paulina's chapel are sites of magical operation which suggest, but not too

18. Martin, *Witchcraft;* Ruggiero, *Binding Passions*, esp. pp. 175–222; Gentilcore, *From Bishop to Witch;* O'Neil, 'Sacerdote overro strione', pp. 53–83.
19. The priest Robert of Drayton was the preceptor of the cunning-man John Walsh's examination at Exeter (1566), Father Rosimond was involved in the Windsor case of 1579, and Jesuits were involved in the Salmesbury case of 1612. See Rosen, *Witchcraft in England*, pp. 64–71, 83–91, and Ewen, *Witchcraft and Demonianism*, p. 216.
20. Bale, *Pageant of Popes*, sig. K^{r–v}.
21. See Lake, 'Anti-popery', pp. 72–106.

specifically, Catholic locations. Prospero, like Greene's Friar Bacon, has a cell. He is the last in a succession of manipulative clerical figures, like the friars in *Romeo and Juliet* and *Much Ado About Nothing*, who scheme to bring about happy endings, and most like that meddling duke disguised as friar, Vincentio in *Measure for Measure*. His mistake, to neglect his dukedom for his library, suggests ideals of contemplation and retreat rather than Renaissance ideals of civic humanism and a life of action. Paulina's chapel is presumably the one Leontes resolves to visit in penance at III, ii, 236–8. It has no equivalent origin in *Pandosto*, where Pandosto merely resolves to visit Bellaria's tomb. At the end of the play the characters pass through Paulina's gallery (V, iii, 10–120) to her chapel (V, iii, 86). There seems some evidence that 'chapel' might have conjured up a Catholic location.[22] Shakespeare may be deliberately sailing close to the wind in making Paulina's chapel the location for the apparent magic of the animation of Hermione's statue, and so of superstitious beliefs and practices. This is not the only place in *The Winter's Tale* where this happens and two other moments, both related to an image of Hermione, signal an awareness of a possible accusation of 'superstition' in the sense of a false religion.

When Perdita sees her mother's statue she says 'And give me leave, / And do not say 'tis superstition, that / I kneel' (V, iii, 42–4). Kneeling to a statue could constitute 'idol worship, with Roman Catholic overtones', as Orgel's edition notes. And a wonderful statue, to which a character kneels and which will shortly in an apparent miracle move, must have invoked Catholic stories of miraculous statues, which Protestants were keen to ridicule, and to expose as frauds of diabolical wonders.[23] Among John Bale's stories of cunning and necromantic priests is one about St Dunstan, who made the Rood speak on his behalf. In this he 'sought out a practise of the old Idolatrous Pryestes, which wer wont to make theyr idolles to speake, by the Art of Necromnacy, wherein the Monkes were in those dais expert'.[24] Earlier, after Antigonus' account of the apparition of Hermione, he comments, 'Dreams are toys; / Yet for this once, yea superstitiously, / I will be squared by this' (III, iii, 38–40). Both moments

---

22. It has the sense of a place of private worship, an oratory, especially in a mausoleum where masses are said for the dead (OED *sb*. 2b). Archimago has 'an holy Chappell edifyde' (*Faerie Queene*, Book I, i, 34.5) and a pamphlet of 1558 describes 'chappelles of idolatrie' (Traheron, *A Warning to England*, sigs B5^v–B6).

23. See Walker, 'La cessazione dei miracoli'. Female moving statues in various sorts of amatory context are often to be found among stories of miracles; see Baum, 'The young man'.

24. Bale, *The First Partes of the Actes*, sig. O3^r.

are close to some Protestant accounts of Catholic superstition. Antigonus'
account of Hermione's apparition presents us with a story like that often
ridiculed by Protestant writers as a trick, a diabolical delusion, the sort of
story and perhaps even event that was common in bygone popish days,
when false apparitions and strange sights flourished in what were indeed
the times of winter's tales.[25] Again, Bale gives a typical account of popish
times when spirits walked:

> For from the foresaid *Sylvester* till to *Gregorie* the seventh (a notori-
> ous parson) all the Popes were famous enchanters: by theyr charm-
> ing they sturred up walking spirits, bugs, goblins, fierye sightes, and
> divers terrible goastes and shapes of thinges, with howlinges and
> groaninges aboute deade mens graves, perswadinge the simple
> people that they were deade mens soules. And those spirites beinge
> conjured up by priestes, deluded men, dessemblinge that they were
> the soules of the dead, complaynynge theyr untollerable paynes in
> Purgatorye fyre, and craved to be released by the meritorious
> deedes of theyr frendes and kindred, bestowinge dirges, masses, and
> trentalles on them.[26]

Antigonus' account begins 'I have heard, but not believed, the spirits
o'th' dead / May walk again' (III, iii, 15–16), and Hermione's apparition
in its white robes, sanctity and ritualistic gestures ('she ... thrice bowed
before me' (III, iii, 22–3)) suggests these stories. In anticipation of the
later spectacle of the moving statue, the apparition is rather like an
automaton: Hermione is 'a vessel of like sorrow', her eyes 'Became two
spouts' (III, iii, 20, 25). In these moments Shakespeare is carefully and
delicately accessing ideas of the supernatural powers of the old religion,
to produce effects of ambiguous wonder.

Rosalind promises, through the operation of her uncle's magic, the
impossibly happy conclusion and resolution of *As You Like It*. This
chapter now turns to those moments in the late plays, especially their
endings, where magic aspires to become miracle.

Shakespeare often expressed the delightfully happy and unexpected
endings of his comedies in supernatural terms. As well as the explicit talk
of magic at the end of *As You Like It* and *A Midsummer Night's Dream*,
moments of unlooked-for revelation and their consequent effect of

25. Lavater, *Of Ghostes and Spirits*, Translator to Reader, pp. 28–44, 65–7; James VI and I,
    Dæmonologie, II, vii; Harsnet, *A Declaration*, p. 134; Holland, *A Treatise against Witchcraft*,
    fol. 14ᵛ; Perkins, *A Discourse*, I, iv, p. 25.
26. Bale, *Pageant of Popes*, sigs Kᵛ–K2ʳ.

wonder are often associated with the apparition of spirits in early, middle and problem comedies:

> DUKE   One of these men is *genius* to the other:
>   And so of these, which is the natural man,
>   And which the spirit? Who deciphers them?
>   (*The Comedy of Errors*, V, i, 334–6)

> VIOLA   If spirits can assume both form and suit
>   You come to fright us.
> SEBASTIAN   A spirit I am indeed.
>   (*Twelfth Night*, V, i, 233–4)

> *Enter Helen and the Widow*
> KING   Is there no exorcist[27]
>   Beguiles the truer office of mine eyes?
>   Is't real that I see?
>   (*All's Well*, V, iii, 306–8)

In the late plays the production of the happy ending is expressed in terms not just of the appearance of spirits, but as the operations of a magic which often seems to produce events so wonderful that they are beyond nature and seem miracles. The late plays come after Shakespeare's most painful tragedy and his most demon-inspired play which ends when a last-minute miracle fails to happen, and a dead child is not raised. *King Lear*, which has a profound debt to Samuel Harsnett's treatise on fraudulent miracles, *A Declaration of Egregious Popish Impostures* (1603), is a play in which, after a fictitious account of non-existent demons and after their equally unnecessary exorcism, Edgar tells his father (after a non-fall from a non-cliff) 'Thy life's a miracle' (*The Tragedy of King Lear*, IV, v, 55). It is that most sensational and divine miracle that fails to happen at the end of *Lear*, the raising of the dead, that the various sorts of magic in the late plays aspire to. The wish of the magical operators in these plays is not Stephen Greenblatt's to speak with the dead, but to raise them. Cerimon's revival of Thaisa and Paulina's of Hermione both appear as operations which transcend nature. In *The Tempest* Prospero seems often to the other characters to have brought the dead back to life: Ferdinand and Alonso thought each other dead, and Prospero tells

---

27. Although 'conjuror' is a common meaning for 'exorcist' in the sixteenth century, the word's use in *All's Well* is intriguing, as the play was probably written between *Twelfth Night* and *King Lear*, which both draw extensively on pamphlets and books dealing with possession and exorcism.

Alonso he too lost his daughter in 'this last tempest' (V, i, 153). But then, in a scene of multiple reunions, Ferdinand and Miranda are discovered playing at chess, and in another of Prospero's *coups de theatre* the 'dead' are delightfully restored in a tableau which presumably in its original staging duplicated Paulina's discovery of the statue, and which Sebastian (of all people) greets with the cry 'A most high miracle!' (V, i, 177). Before Prospero's speech (V, i, 33–57) turns to renunciation of magic he evokes the extreme potency of his art as the raising of the dead:

> Graves at my command
> Have waked their sleepers, oped, and let 'em forth
> By my so potent art. But this rough magic
> I here abjure. (V, i, 48–51)

What Ovid, and perhaps Golding's translation, described is necromancy, divination by the spirits of the dead:[28] what Prospero practises is the resurrection of the dead, those who 'sleep', in the language of the Bible.

The boundary between a miracle (*miraculum*) and a wonder (*mirum*), often in some way a false event, had always been an important one in theological and particularly demonological discourse and had been rigorously policed.[29] In fact in discussions of the distinction demonological works often quote the tag *Mira non miracula* (wonders, not miracles). Augustine drew a clear and influential distinction between God's miracles and the devil's production of false wonders in magic.[30] The former are acts above nature which may change it through a new creation and therefore are only possible to God, the latter apparent wonders which spirits actually effect by natural means, although with extraordinary skill and speed,[31] but are actually illusions. Scholastic thinkers too asserted

---

28. 'iubeoque … solum manesque exire sepulcris [I bid … the ghosts to come forth from their tombs]' (*Metamorphoses*, Book VII, 205–6).
29. See Clark, *Thinking with Demons*, pp. 161–78.
30. 'We must believe with absolute conviction that almighty God can do everything he wishes … but demons of course can't create things; if they do anything of this sort, in the area now under discussion, it's only in appearance they transform those things created by the true God, so that they seem to be what they are not [Firmissime tamen credendum est omnipotentem Deum posse omnia facere quae voluerit … Nec sane daemones naturas creant, si aliquid tale faciunt, de qualibus factis ista vertitur quaestio; sed specie tenus quae a vero Deo sunt creata commutant, ut videantur esse quod non sunt]'; Augustine, *De Civitate Dei*, Book XVIII, xviii; see also Augustine, *De Civitate Dei*, Book X, xii, and *De Divinatione daemonum*, iii.
31. The argument is an important one for Scot in *Discoverie*, who argues that the feats attributed to witches are miraculous, and that this cannot be, as only God can work miracles.

that the devil works by illusion.[32] These illusions were thought to be brought about by diabolic interference with the imagination, or deception of the sense of sight. In addition, early modern Protestants claimed that miracles, necessary in the days of Christ's ministry and the establishment of the early church, were now ceased. In a letter to the young Prince Henry, King James writes, 'Ye have ofte hearde me saye that most miracles nou a dayes proves but illusions.'[33] Shakespeare knows that miracles have ceased, as he says so twice, in *Henry V* (I, i, 68) and *All's Well* (II, iii, 1). For both demonological and Protestant reasons, miracles are likely to turn out to be false wonders.

This chapter turns finally to the curious ontological nature of some Shakespearean figures and situations which have appeared in it: a fictitious uncle who then appears in Arden, a non-existent statue and its 'real' author (Julio Romano died in 1546), imaginary devils on imaginary cliffs, and resurrections of the living. Similar situations, brought about by magic, are frequent in *The Tempest*: spirits pretending to classical goddesses, daughters who were not after all lost in storms, and a shipwreck caused by magic which never happened, although the audience and Miranda could have sworn that it did. The ship we heard and saw split in the play's first and most naturalistic scene, with that curiously convincing and specific stage direction '*Enter Mariners wet*' (SD I, i, 50), is reported by the Boatswain in V, i, as 'tight and yare and bravely rigged as when / We first put to sea (V, i, 224–5). Whether or not in the play's fiction the ship really sank, that representation on stage in I, i, would be exactly the same. The same is true of Hermione's statue and Dover cliff in *King Lear*: whether or not they exist, and in terms, as it were, of the reality of the fiction of both plays, these could only exist on the Globe or the Blackfriars stage in the way they did. A 'real' Dover cliff could only have been constituted in the theatre by a bare stage and Edgar's marvellous description (IV, v, 11–24), just as it is in Edgar's deception of his father about a Dover cliff which is not there. Similarly the process of Hermione's statue 'really' coming to life would be constituted by the boy actor who had played Hermione in the first half of the play now playing a statue becoming Hermione.

---

32. See, for example, Aquinas' frequent assertions that magic and demons work 'through some illusion [per quandam illusionem]', 'through some imaginary appearance rather than in reality [secundum phantasticam apparitionem magis quam secundum veritatem]' (*De malo*), 'through illusion and not by a real effect [per illusionem et non per effectus veritatem]', and 'by some deceitful illusion [per aliquam praestigiosam illusionem]' (*De potentia Dei*).

33. BL MS Harley 6986, art. 40, quoted in Kittredge, *Witchcraft*, p. 319.

A major difference between magic in these two late plays is apparently that in the fictional world of *The Winter's Tale* the magic is not real and in *The Tempest* it is. However, we have seen in a number of places the difficulty of such a clear distinction in the case of supernatural or quasi-supernatural events. Prospero uses his 'real' magic to perpetrate a series of deceptions and produce apparitions not of a real sea-nymph, harpy or the goddess Ceres, but Ariel impersonating these figures. And what did happen to Hermione? The two images of Hermione we hear about in the play, the apparition to Antigonus and Julio Romano's statue, serve to confuse her history, and Hermione's account to Perdita is not exactly explicit:

> For thou shalt hear that I,
> Knowing by Paulina that the oracle
> Gave hope thou wast in being, have preserved
> Myself to see the issue. (V, iii, 125–8)

Hermione only promises Perdita and us an explanation which we never hear. Although we tend to assume she has been alive and in hiding for sixteen years, the wonderfully equivocal reflexive construction 'have preserved myself', suggesting both agency and being acted upon, is not giving much away.

In dramatic terms Shakespeare wanted magic for the effect of wonder, prepared for in Paulina's demand that the statue's audience awake its faith (V, iii, 94–5), both the prerequisite and consequence of working a miracle, and her implicit direction of our response in 'Strike all that look upon with marvel' (V, iii, 100). But *The Winter's Tale*, V, iii, arguably the most satisfying comedic ending in Shakespeare, is actually, like the end of *As You Like It*, an apparent miracle which is only a false wonder: a series of natural events, a trick, mystified by talk of magic. And do the characters on stage at the end of *The Winter's Tale*, apart from Hermione and Paulina, recognise that there has been no marvellous and magical event? And has there not been one?

Neither magic nor the devil can create. Shakespeare probably knew this technicality. When Antipholus of Syracuse asks Luciana: 'Are you a god? Would you create me new? / Transform me, then, and to your power I'll yield' (*The Comedy of Errors*, III, ii, 39–40), which seems informed by the idea that the creation, and hence real transformation of creatures, is only possible to the deity. The idea was originally Augustinian, but became a demonological commonplace. Shakespeare may well have read Reginald Scot's *Discoverie of Witchcraft* (1584) before writing *The Comedy of Errors*, and may have been influenced by Scot's discussion

of transformations in Book V, which has many examples of men transformed into asses, a recurrent fear of the Dromios.[34] Scot too argues that
to believe witches can transform men into beasts denies the unique
power of an omnipotent God, for that would be 'to attribute that to a
creature, which onelie belongeth to God the creator of all things'.[35] In
The Tempest Prospero's description of Alonso's sinister political scheming
may take up the same ideas, for Alonso 'new created / The creatures that
were mine, I say: or changed 'em, / Or else new formed 'em' (I, ii, 81–3).
As a result of this the devil was often described from Tertullian onwards
only as God's imitator, *diabolus simia Dei*. Devils, and magicians with
their aid, thus produce effects which seem real but are not. But the
means by which they work may still be thought wonderful. For example,
magic cannot change a man into a beast, but with the devil's aid can
make it seem that this has happened, by cleverly manipulating natural
forces. Similarly the operations of magic are deceptions. For instance,
words have no power in themselves, as Dr Faustus discovers: they are a
counterfeit means by which Satan deceives us. The power of magic to
work effects is an illusion: it can only operate through the power of the
devil, often by means of an arrangement, which is itself a trick. To the
orthodox, magic was itself a series of endlessly receding deceptions and
illusions. Magic in *The Winter's Tale* and *The Tempest* has this nature;
apparent wonders which actually always have another explanation; in
The Winter's Tale a benevolent deceit cloaked in magic; in *The Tempest* a
series of spectacular shows engineered by a magician and a spirit.

Some writers specifically use the comparison of the illusions of spirits
and of the theatre, even as Propsero does (V, i, 148–56). The following is
an example from an English translation of a French book of wonders,
Edward Fenton's *Certaine Secrete Wonders of Nature* (1569), which translates Pierre Boaistuau, *Histoires Prodigieuses* (1560):

> It is an easie thing (saith [Augustine]) for the wicked sprites with
> their bodies of ayre, to do many marvellous and fearfull things,
> which exceede the compasse of oure understanding, ... And if
> sometime (saith he) we be drawne into admiration with the viewe
> of straunge thinges presented upon theatres or stages, which also
> we woulde not believe thoughe they were tolde us by others
> bycause they are so farre withoute the compasse of our under-
> standing, why ought we to finde it straunge if Divels and their

---

34. See Roberts, 'The descendants of Circe', esp. pp. 192–9.
35. Scot, *Discoverie*, V, iii.

Aungels (with their bodyes of the Elemente) do abuse our fragilitie in shewing us visions, Idols, and figures).[36]

This idea of spirits operating through the medium of air is an important one (it provides the conceit for Donne's 'Air and Angels'), especially in the way that they deceive us with false wonders. It is also an idea informing one of the most famous parts of Prospero's admission of the illusions of his magical masque:

These our actors,
As I foretold you, were all spirits, and
Are melted into air, into thin air. (IV, i, 148–50)

This passage may have taken the idea immediately from King James's *Dæmonologie*,[37] where James too gives an explanation of spirits using the air to create illusions for magicians:

he will guard his schollers with fair armies of horsemen and footemen in appearance, castles and forts: Which all are but impressiones in the aire, easilie gathered by a spirite, drawing so neare to that substance himselfe: ... And yet are all these thinges but deluding of the senses, and no waies true in substance, as were the false miracles wrought by king *Pharaoes* magicians.[38]

In a famous passage in Sidney's *Apology* the poet grows another nature, imitating God's creation of Eden, and claims his operations surpass those of nature. Throughout the late plays magic operates as a metaphor for both the aspirations and limitations of the poet's powers. Like magic, early modern fiction and theatre produce curious effects simultaneously real and unreal, in which an audience experiences not miracles but only wonders.

---

36. Fenton, *Certaine Secrete Wonders*, fol. 90.
37. See Latham, '*The Tempest*'.
38. James VI and I, *Dæmonologie*, I, vi, p. 22.

PART III
HISTORY AND INTERPRETATION

8

POSTCOLONIAL SHAKESPEARE: BRITISH IDENTITY FORMATION AND *CYMBELINE*

Willy Maley

Recent work in Shakespeare studies has begun to address the complexity of the multi-national milieu in which Shakespeare wrote.[1] The chief aim of this chapter, in the light of this fresh scholarship on the multiple historical contexts of Shakespeare's texts, is to articulate two current critical paradigms – postcolonial theory, and the new British history of the seventeenth century that revolves around the question of the 'British Problem'.[2] Precisely because both approaches have their limitations – postcolonial theory tends to confuse England with Britain and to confine itself largely to the nineteenth and twentieth centuries, skipping the Renaissance, while historians of the British Problem concentrate almost exclusively on the decades of the middle part of the seventeenth century, skirting the sixteenth – they can be seen to impinge in important ways upon the late plays. I want to stake a claim for the space of 'Britain' in

---

1. For recent interventions addressing the multiple national contexts of Shakespeare's drama see Hawkes, 'Lear's maps'; Hamilton, '*The Winter's Tale* and the language'; Holderness, '"What ish my nation?"'; Kurland, '*Hamlet* and the Scottish succession?'; Norbrook, '*Macbeth* and the politics of historiography'; Wortham, 'Shakespeare, James I'.
2. On the British Problem see for example Russell, *The Fall of the British Monarchies*. For a compelling and profound literary perspective see Baker, *Between Nations*. Equally impressive is Highley's *Shakespeare, Spenser*. On postcolonialism see, for example, *Postcolonial Criticism*, eds Moore-Gilbert, Stanton and Maley.

the time of Shakespeare as an exemplary postcolonial site. Drawing on the new British history, I shall maintain that this revisionist scholarship on the 1640s can be instructively read back into the early part of the seventeenth century, a time when England was moving from postcolonial nation to empire state. Drawing on postcolonial theory, specifically the notion of 'mimicry', I shall argue that the process of national liberation in an early modern English context involves a repetition of the colonial project, a common feature of postcolonial discourse. This act of repetition – greatly feared and eagerly awaited in equal measure – is implicit in Shakespeare's Roman / British plays.

The formation of the British state, an experience characterised by successive crises of sovereignty, was both a prerequisite to empire *and* an act of empire in itself. The very legislation that freed England from Roman authority, the Act of Restraint of Appeals (1533), did so by declaring England to be an empire in its own right. The word 'empire' in this context 'designated a sovereign territorial state which was completely independent of the pope and all foreign princes'.[3] Claire McEachern has pointed up the irony of a 'nation' being founded as an 'empire', and noted the extent to which England was here defining itself in relation to Rome.[4] McEachern identifies the risk of repetition implicit in such a move: 'To call England an empire is to announce political sovereignty in the term by which it was known. Crucially, it is an announcement based as much in a competitive, mimetic resemblance to foreign authority as in a rejection of it' (p. 2). This 'competitive, mimetic resemblance' is at the heart of Shakespeare's late plays, especially those that deal directly with the formation of the British state. There is also a mimetic desire, a desire to emulate a Roman achievement about which there is deep ambivalence. A state forged in Wales and subsequently fitted with parts in Scotland before being exported to Ireland had an obvious blueprint. Britain was made in Rome. This was a problem for those English writers who feared that their country was in danger of being consumed by an enlarged state whose imperialist aspirations came to resemble all too closely those of its Roman counterpart, a rejuvenation rather than a rejection of Empire.

Concepts of anachronism and disjuncture are useful in thinking about Shakespeare's late plays, which resonate with belatedness and untimeliness.[5]

---

3. Levack, *Formation of the British State*, p. 2.
4. McEachern, *Poetics of English Nationhood*, p. 1.
5. See Parker, 'Preposterous estates' and 'Romance and empire'. If this chapter owes much to Parker's concept of 'preposterousness' then I am equally indebted to McEachern's notion of 'anachronism'.

Samuel Johnson castigated *Cymbeline* for its 'confusion of the names and manners of different times', but Shakespeare's justification of an innovative political union by representing it as a process of reunion demanded exactly such a level of con-fusion.[6] According to Richard Hosley, in the introduction to his edition of the play, 'Johnson's aversion to the violent yoking together of Roman Britain and Renaissance Rome reveals a characteristic blindness to the essence of romance.'[7] Conversely, one could argue that the romance of empire is complicated by the act of betrayal, of two-timing. An anti-imperialist, anti-Roman Englishness yields to an imperial Britishness that emulates, even as it opposes, its former tyrant. England, Rome and Britain constitute a love triangle that can only end in tears for at least one party. In the first chapter of her book on Shakespeare's last plays, Frances Yates writes of 'The Elizabethan revival in the Jacobean Age', and argues that 'there was built in to the basically Protestant position of the Queen as representative of a pure reformed Church which had cast off the impurities of Rome, this aura of chivalric Arthurian purity, of a British imperialism, using British in the mythic and romantic sense which it had for the Elizabethans'.[8] This 'mythic and romantic sense' has always been inseparable from the modern economic sense, and it proved to be ideologically, as it was etymologically, inseparable from its Roman model. Romance is Roman. For Jacobeans in particular, struggling to come to terms with a new-found British identity, Arthurian romance could not conceal the outlines of a Roman tragedy. Philippa Berry, in a compelling essay on *Macbeth*, has shown how deeply embedded in early modern culture were notions of historical repetition: 'We can identify the existence of what can be termed "double time" in several of Shakespeare's histories, tragedies and Roman plays ... whereby the particular historical time of the play is implicitly paralleled or repeated by recent or near-contemporary political moments.'[9] Berry argues that the British monarchy in the Scottish play 'is mysteriously dependent upon its opposite yet originating shadow: the tyrannical and bloody image of a Scottish or Celtic king' (p. 387). I shall make a related case for *Cymbeline*, but as a dramatic endorsement of the Roman roots of Britishness, rather than a repudiation of its Celtic fringe.

Berry points out that in debates on Anglo-Scottish union the two kingdoms were often depicted as brothers (p. 385). In *Cymbeline* three

6. *Johnson on Shakespeare, The Yale Edition of the Works of Samuel Johnson*, vol. VIII, p. 908.
7. *Cymbeline*, ed. Hosley, p. xxxv.
8. Yates, *Shakespeare's Last Plays*, p. 17.
9. Berry, 'Reversing history', p. 373.

versions of union coexist in the shape of a marriage threatened then resolved, long-lost brothers reunited with their natural father, and a *pax Britannica* that mirrors the *pax Romana* of pre-Reformation days. The play's complexity stems in part from its multilayered treatment of the problem of British origins and the troubled issues of union and empire. The emphasis is on continuity within change, so that Britishness is seen as the resumption of a historical process rather than an absolute break with the past. Roger Warren, in his edition of *Cymbeline*, speaks of 'the view of ancient Britain in the play – independent, yet related to the Roman empire' (p. 37). It is the fraught nature of the British post-colonial condition – 'independent, yet related' to its Roman counterpart – that Shakespeare is addressing with a subtlety suited to the subject. Always one to make a drama out of a crisis, Shakespeare takes the intractable historical material of union and state formation as his text. Giacomo is not the only Italian intriguer at large. The bard of Britain is himself performing sleights of hand, affirming a British monarchy that sees its reflection in Rome. What we are presented with in *Cymbeline* is a Union Jack in the box, a surprise package that delivers a sucker punch, a play that ostensibly celebrates the union of England and Scotland but which figures it, provocatively and controversially, cloudily enwrapped in a *rapprochement* between Britain and Rome. In a neat reversal, a newly expanded state is projected backward into Roman times, stealing James VI and I's thunder, and giving all tribute to the reign of Caesar. With a foot in both camps, Roman Britain and Reformation England, *Cymbeline* marks the accession of James not as the advent of the Other, succeeding through some bizarre dynastic accident, but as the eternal return of the Same, coming to fruition ripely and rightly through ancient lineage.

Cymbeline is a nativity play, but it deals not with the birth of Christ, but with the birth of Britain, a birth that is not virgin but Virgilian. The contention of Emrys Jones that *Cymbeline* has to be read in its Jacobean context in order for its meaning and significance fully to be grasped has met with resistance, as have all topical readings of Shakespeare's plays.[10] Roger Warren maintains that this, possibly Shakespeare's most complex drama, needs no interpretative key, 'since the play creates, arguably to a greater extent than many of Shakespeare's other plays, its own self-sufficient theatrical world, requiring no explanation beyond itself' (p. 63). This strikes me as a very British perspective, one that projects its own expansive insularity onto the text. Where Warren sees the location of the play within an immediate historical context as a mere embellish-

---

10. Jones, 'Stuart *Cymbeline*'.

ment on the part of the playwright, I would want to argue for a central and profound preoccupation with origin myths and ideas of union as structuring the action of the play.

In an essay entitled 'Shakespeare, James I and the Matter of Britain', Christopher Wortham took three early Stuart plays by Shakespeare – *King Lear*, *Macbeth* and *Antony and Cleopatra* – written roughly between 1604 and 1607, and argued strongly for their topicality.[11] One could make a case for seeing three later Stuart plays – *Cymbeline*, *The Tempest* and *Henry VIII*, written around 1609–13 – as meditations on the origins of Britishness, ancient and early modern, from Roman times to the Henrician Reformation and beyond to the Union of Crowns under James VI and I and the Anglo-Scottish colonisation of Ireland that union engendered. These plays are postcolonial in so far as Shakespeare is working through England's post-Reformation history, the history of a nation wrested from an empire that copied (in true deconstructive fashion) the thing to which it was ostensibly opposed, a history in which a new English nation grew into an empire virtually overnight, then sealed its fate through an act of union that resulted in a net loss of English sovereignty in favour of a British empire modelled on the Roman one that had only just been shaken off. At the end of *Cymbeline*, a play whose themes are reunion, reunification, repatriation and reconciliation, this is presented positively, but its covert reintroduction of Catholicism by the back door would be interpreted much less generously and optimistically by those whose insular idea of Englishness did not extend to Britain. Even the seventy years of apparently unadulterated Englishness between 1533 and 1603 were complicated by the fact that England had 'pales', 'marches' and 'borderlands' in its possession, territories that both supplemented and suppressed the development of Englishness.

The greatest ruse of anglocentrism is its eccentricity, its facility for displacing issues of identity onto England's neighbours and colonies, and thereby setting itself up as a standard or norm. Part of the Stuart Myth of course was to portray Britishness as a kind of homecoming. British identity is represented – like Protestantism, in fact – as a return to an original wholeness, to unity and integrity, to a pre-existent identity that was dormant during centuries of foreign tyranny, Roman and Norman (French). This Britishness is recycled, at the same time as it is collapsed into an Englishness that is literary and cultural, mythical and romantic. Modern critics tend to do what early modern writers specialised in –

11. Wortham, 'Shakespeare, James I'.

project into the past something that is new, strange and foreign and thus make it familiar, recognisable, in short, domesticated.

The history of late Shakespeare, of Jacobean or Stuart Shakespeare, is, like the history of England, nasty, British and short. Crucified between Rome and Britain, England was divested of its new-found sense of selfhood. *Cymbeline* seems obsessed with the very idea of Britain, its intangibility. Innogen, who 'chose an eagle' who is also a lion, asks:

> Hath Britain all the sun that shines? Day, night,
> Are they not but in Britain? I' th' world's volume
> Our Britain seems as of it but not in't,
> In a great pool a swan's nest. Prithee think
> There's livers out of Britain. (III, iv, 137–41)

The mere incantation of the name of Britain, the watery grave of the dying Swan of Albion, serves to give it a force in language that is otherwise lacking. The delivery or deliverance of Britain is bound up with fantasy. Britain seems of the world but not in it precisely because it is an invention, and one with which Shakespeare's culture is only just coming to terms.

In *Cymbeline*, it is a question of autonomy and independence from Rome, but at the same time the imperial design was patented by Rome, and thus Britain pays tribute by default. Tribute and attribution are crucial to the drama. The villains of the piece are those, like the Queen, who refuse to give credit where credit is due. For example, Cloten refuses to pay tribute to Rome, saying:

> Britain's a world
> By itself, and we will nothing pay
> For wearing our own noses. (III, i, 12–14)

Cloten is forswearing his own nose, or cutting it off to spite his face, because Britain may be a world by itself, but it is a world made in the graven image of the empire that conquered it of old, and from which it has freed itself only to be chained afresh. To deny this is to deny one's paternity and one's birthright. Paradoxically the real slaves are those who misread their own history. The solution to Britain's Roman legacy is not to shake it off, not to renounce Rome, but to succeed it, to step into its shoes, easier now that the imperial leather is on the other foot.

Cymbeline was written at a time when a new British imperial monarch with two sons, one the Duke of Albany, the other Prince of Wales, had effected a union between two warring kingdoms – Scotland and England – and made possible the conquest of a third, Ireland. Where

Lear had divided the ancient kingdom of Britain with disastrous consequences, Cymbeline preserves its integrity while keeping the peace with Rome. It is hard not to hear a contemporary resonance in the closing speeches of Shakespeare's king of Britain:

> Well,
> My peace we will begin; and Caius Lucius,
> Although the victor, we submit to Caesar
> And to the Roman empire, promising
> To pay our unwonted tribute, from the which
> We were dissuaded by our wicked queen.,
> Whom heavens justice both on her and hers,
> Have laid most heavy hand. (V, iv, 460–6)

The Soothsayer, Philharmonus, then hails a new Roman Britain, one that both pays tribute to Rome, and yet is paid tribute by Rome, as Rome's successor:

> The fingers of the powers above do tune
> The harmony of this peace. The vision,
> Which I made known to Lucius ere the stroke
> Of this yet scarce-cold battle, at this instant
> Is full accomplished. For the Roman eagle,
> From south to west on wing soaring aloft,
> Lessened herself, and in the beams o' th' sun
> So vanished; which foreshadowed our princely eagle,
> Th'imperial Caesar, should again unite
> His favour with the radiant Cymbeline,
> Which shines here in the west. (V, iv, 467–77)

When Cymbeline follows this with a declaration that 'A Roman and a British ensign wave / Friendly together' (V, iv, 480–1), he is ironically pointing up an imperial conjunction that would raise the troubled ghosts of religion and nationalism for years to come. A Brutus killed Caesar, only to become another Caesar.

In *Cymbeline*, the soothsayer foretells that when 'from a stately cedar shall be lopped branches, which, being dead many years, shall after revive, be jointed to the old stock, and freshly grow, then shall Posthumus end his miseries, Britain be fortunate and flourish in peace and plenty' (V, iv, 438–42). A 'stately cedar' might suggest a state that ceded, in the sense of ceding territory, in this case a state that ceded branches – limbs or members – that are now being grafted back onto the main body of the state. The Soothsayer elaborates:

> The lofty cedar, royal Cymbeline,
> Personates thee, and thy lopped branches point
> Thy two sons forth, who by Belarius stol'n,
> For many years thought dead, are now revived,
> To the majestic cedar joined, whose issue
> Promises Britain peace and plenty. (V, iv, 454–9)

Multiplicity and plurality are the key to understanding Britishness. At the close of *Henry VIII* Cranmer's prophecy tells of how James will 'make new nations' (V, iv, 52). This proliferation of polities is a recurrent theme of the late plays, with union and plantation supplanting succession as the touchstone of sovereignty. The ceding of authority implicit in the transition from Tudor to Stuart government, and from English to British identity, was represented as a reunification and reinforcement of identity. As England receded, Britain was heralded as an outgrowth of an originary Englishness, as though the non-English nations of the flowering British state were branches of an English family tree. The cedar is invoked once more at the end of *Henry VIII*, where Cranmer's prophecy foresees James VI and I branch out:

> He shall flourish,
> And like a mountain cedar reach his branches
> To all the plains about him. Our children's children
> Shall see this, and bless heaven. (V, iv, 52–5)

Union and empire inevitably invoked images of amplification and expansion, and metaphors of natural growth abound in the literature of the period. In *The Tempest* the Duke's followers say of his venture:

> SEBASTIAN   I think he will carry this island home in his pocket, and give it to his son for an apple.
> ANTONIO   And sowing the kernels of it in the sea, bring forth more islands.
>
> (II, i, 95–8)

You reap what you sow. Linkage can entail shrinkage as well as growth. Colonies are both a necessary supplement – they shore up a deficiency in identity, or displace differences (for example, class) – and also dangerous supplements, as they can become sites of resistance to an imagined and imposed unity. A loss of sovereignty can follow when the latter end of a commonwealth forgets its beginning. *Cymbeline* offers an avenue out of English insularity and isolation, but all roads lead to Rome.

I want to conclude by looking very briefly at some prophetic writings of the seventeenth century that can be read in relation to Shakespearean prophecy in the late plays, specifically *Cymbeline* but also *Henry VIII*.[12] We can learn from the future, as well as the past, and by focusing on the drama of British sovereignty as it unfolded in the turbulent years following Shakespeare's death we can see more clearly how difficult his task was, and how heretical his approach. As the jailer says in *Cymbeline*, 'what's past is, and to come the discharge' (V, iii, 262). Prophecy, like theatre, is a kind of heresy, a form that allowed many women writers access to the male domain of history, and facilitated political interventions that might otherwise have been denied. Prophecy is a form in which the nation is figured, contested and invented. It points to the future but is anchored in the past. What is past is prophecy. In the middle of the seventeenth century England found itself on the horns of a dilemma, torn between insularity and expansion, and haunted by empire and union. The constitutional crisis of the 1640s galvanised many writers, and it was a crisis that was often expressed in the form of allegory and prophecy:

> So againe looking backe to *Daniel* touching the *little Horne* declaring or sounding the brevitye of great *Brittaines* Monarchie, (*Whose looke more stoute then his fellows*) more over thus I considered the *Hornes, and there came up another little Horne, before whom three of the first Hornes were pluckt up by the rootes*, the truth of it as much to say, *That he the first Heire of the red rose and the white*. Whose ISUE three of them Crown'd Princes childlesse, *deceasing without Heires of their body*, the Crown of *England* fell to *Scotland*, and great *Brittaine so stiled*, then wherefore blazoned by those great *Beasts foure being from the name of Bruite derived*, whose *Unicorns* Horne become as short as his fellowes.[13]

This prophecy was made in 1644 by Lady Eleanor Davies (1590–1652), addressing – in fact, blessing – her daughter, Lucy, Countess of Huntingdon. Stitching together the story of Jacob and his sons (Genesis 29–45) and the beasts of Daniel's vision (Daniel 7), Davies offers a radical English Protestant critique of a Britishness that threatens to repeat the worst excesses of the Roman Empire. For English Catholics, those whom the Reformation had effectively rendered strangers in their own country, a change of state and an outward expansion into empire, with its echoes

12. On prophecy as a vehicle for women writers in the Renaissance see Chedgzoy, 'Female prophecy'. See also Garber, '"What's past is prologue"'; Mack, 'Women as prophets'. In a postcolonial context prophecy is also a vital force for change, and plays a part in numerous national liberation struggles. See West, *Prophesy Deliverance!*.
13. Eleanor Davies, 'Her blessing' (1644), *Prophetic Writings*, p. 123.

of times past and opportunities for an intermingling of otherness, might have appeared inviting, suggesting an embracing of Europe after being disenfranchised. For Davies, the phrase 'Roman Britain' conjures up images of the present and a fateful future rather than the past. What is past is prologue. Endings are beginnings. These are old paradoxes.

In her defiance of Britishness and defence of Englishness Davies belongs to a tradition, one that would include Milton, of besieged English Protestantism convinced that the expansion of the Tudor state in the wake of the Reformation had actually stifled rather than stiffened the process of Reformation and that the advent of Stuart rule had smothered a new-born Englishness. In her blessing of her daughter, so different from Cranmer's blessing of Elizabeth in Shakespeare's *Henry VIII*, Davies reminds her readers that the offspring of the father of the Reformation have failed to reproduce, resulting in the adoption of a child of empire, a British infant that apes Rome, fostering dissent.

Whereas the prophecies of Cranmer at the close of *Henry VIII* and the Soothsayer at the close of *Cymbeline* hold out the promise of a fruitful future (both refer to a cedar that will have its branches restored), Davies sees something ceded, or surrendered, rather than seeded, or planted. When James accedes, England gives ground, or cedes. Davies, writing on the eve of what a modern anglocentric critical perspective calls the 'English Civil War' or the 'English Revolution' – she conversely alludes to 'Three devided kingdoms rent in peices' – discerns in the dynastic accident that brought James to the 'English' throne the seeds of destruction. As the former wife of Sir John Davies, Attorney-General of Ireland and author of a prominent treatise on that country's conquest under James VI and I, Lady Eleanor was in a strong position to judge the progress of the British project.[14]

Davies's prophecy is, like many prophecies – including those that bring the curtain down on *Henry VIII* and *Cymbeline* – written after the fact. That is, the prophecies are histories, or reflections on events that have come to pass; they are epilogues rather than prologues. As well as playing with several senses of horn, Davies harps on the mythical meanings of Britishness. In her account, Bruite – Brute or Brutus – legendary founder of Britain, is changed from a brute to a beast, and one that recalls in too many respects the Beast of Rome, lately slain by England, now risen again in the guise of Britain. The risk of conversion, of becoming Roman, pervades *Cymbeline*. Posthumous cites Belarius, who urges his fellow Britons to 'Stand, / Or we are Romans (V, iii, 25–6).

14. Sir John Davies, *A Discovery of the True Causes* (1612).

Davies's lament for a lost England that has made a shameful conquest of itself through buying into Britishness is in keeping with a certain tradition of national narrative which figures the origin of the nation as a battle for recognition. Homi Bhabha remarks:

> In each case what is being dramatized is a separation – *between* races, cultures, histories, *within* histories – a separation between *before* and *after* that repeats obsessively the mythical moment of disjunction ... Colonial fantasy is the continual dramatization of emergence – of difference, freedom – as the beginning of a history which is repetitively denied.[15]

The crisis of the mid-seventeenth century that Davies records, and which she imputes to what historians now call the 'British Problem', is not new. As she herself maintains, its seeds were planted with the origins of the British enterprise, a Trojan Horse that brought the beast of Rome back into England, the gift of empire that undermines the nation in the name of enhancing it.

The birth of Britain was an event that provoked Shakespeare to word play as devious as that later deployed by Davies. The soothsayer's prophecy in *Cymbeline* plays upon the proper name of Posthumus Leonatus:

> Thou, Leonatus, art the lion's whelp.
> The fit and apt construction of thy name,
> Being *leo-natus*, doth import so much. (V, iv, 444–6)

Britain is a posthumous brute, rumoured abroad, part lion and part eagle, a rough beast that lurches towards London. Born in the breach between England and Rome, it serves to fill that breach with the English dead, or with the death of Englishness, the Pyrrhic victory that *Cymbeline* anticipates, celebrates and commemorates. By figuring Britain as a second coming, an ancient kingdom restored to its former glory, Shakespeare was playing into the hands of the Roman precedent.

Multiple kingdoms call for multiple contexts. Even before James's accession English writers were working within a state that was not self-contained, a state that harboured more than one nation, which included Wales and Ireland. In *Henry VIII* Katherine alludes to her husband's 'dominions' (II, iv, 14), and while the king himself speaks of 'kingdom' in the singular (II, iv, 191), he refers to 'realms' in the plural (II, iv, 194). France figures here, Wales too perhaps, and also Ireland, a lordship of the English crown from the twelfth century and a kingdom from 1541,

---

15. Bhabha, 'The other question', p. 171.

when Henry declared himself to be monarch of that realm. This raises the question of the integrity of Englishness. When was England itself alone, and when exactly was Britain conjured into being? Davies's prophecies, penned at the chilling denouement of a particular phase of 'the British experiment' or the British Problem, ought to send us back to other crises of national identities, points of rupture and fragmentation, moments when the state is 'disjoint and out of frame'. One such time is, obviously, the early seventeenth century, when a newly united kingdom was coming to terms with a mixing of identities, with an openness to a previously threatening other, and with a multiplication of national contexts.

Like Yeats's 'Leda and the Swan', stratified allegory rather than straightforward history can best capture the postcolonial condition, and its legacy of violence. Mastered by the brute blood of Rome, did England put on its knowledge with its power? The poet, the prophet and the playwright can more eloquently express the complexities of nationalism and colonialism than either criticism or historiography. One could draw an analogy between Joyce's sense of Ireland struggling under a double yoke of British and Roman imperialism and Davies's perception of England suffering from an identical underlying complicity. Joyce wrote: 'I confess that I do not see what good it does to fulminate against the English tyranny while the Roman tyranny occupies the palace of the soul'.[16]

How, finally, can one reconcile the voices of Shakespeare's optimistic imperialists with the dissenting tradition exemplified by a prophet of doom such as Eleanor Davies? One way of thinking about the differing attitudes to Englishness and Britishness that these writers exemplify is to accept the fact that disenfranchised communities respond in different ways to political change. Both Shakespeare and Davies, in the face of exclusion, could be seen to be voicing dissent, one championing a residual Catholicism that regarded British imperial interests as an opportunity for a more inclusive, more multicultural, more pluralistic, more European, more worldly state, more tolerant of religious difference than

16. Watson remarks of these lines: 'In fact, Joyce is most vitriolic about the Church precisely at those moments where he senses its identity and common cause with that other imperial tyranny; behind much of the Parnellite anti-clericalism he inherited from his father can be glimpsed a sense of thwarted nationalism raging before an unshakeable combination of forces.' See Watson, *Irish Identity*, p. 155, quoting James Joyce, 'Ireland, island of sages and saints', *The Critical Writings of James Joyce*, eds Ellsworth Mason and Richard Ellmann (Faber and Faber, London, 1959), p. 173.

was Reformation England, and the other advocating a radical Protestantist counter-tradition that saw history repeating itself, in the shape of a Brute this time rather than a Beast. Linda Colley's monumental study of the formation of British identity presents a providential Protestant view. Murray Pittock has tried to counter this anglocentric Tudor mythology with a peripheral Stuart vision that is Catholic, Celtic and Gaelic.[17] The truth lies somewhere in between. There is more than one way to be British, more than one variety of Britishness, and more than one form of resistance. The constant vacillation between nation, state and empire is the stuff of drama, and is dealt with in telling ways by Shakespeare. The casual slippage between 'English' and 'British' in current critical discourse notwithstanding, the cultural cross-fertilisations and constitutional – and chronological – double crosses of the seventeenth century continue to resonate. The discharge of history is not transparent, but remains clotted and ambiguous. Its colour and constituency are better known to the dramatist than to the critic or historian.

17. Colley, *Britons*; Pittock, *Inventing and Resisting Britain*.

9

HISTORY AND JUDGEMENT IN
HENRY VIII

Thomas Healy

I

MOPSA   I love a ballad in print, alife, for then we are sure they are
    true.
AUTOLYCUS   Here's one to a very doleful tune, how a usurer's wife
    was brought to bed of twenty money-bags at a burden, and how
    she longed to eat adders' heads and toads carbonadoed.
MOPSA   Is it true, think you?
AUTOLYCUS   Very true.

> (*The Winter's Tale*, IV, iv, 251–6)

2ND GENTLEMAN   [D]id you not late days hear
    A buzzing of a separation
    Between the king and Katherine?
1ST GENTLEMAN   Yes, but it held not;
    For when the king once heard it, out of anger
    He sent command to the lord mayor straight
    To stop the rumour, and allay those tongues
    That durst disperse it.
2ND GENTLEMAN   But that slander, sir,
    Is found a truth now.

> (*Henry VIII*, II, i, 147–54)

The Famous History of the Life of King Henry the Eighth, as *Henry VIII* was titled in the First Folio, was known to its first audiences in 1613 as *All Is True*. Various modern critics have assumed that this original name argues the play's claims to historical exactness, particularly in contrast to the glaring inaccuracies of Samuel Rowley's *When You See Me, You Know Me or the Famous Chronicle History of King Henry the Eight* (1605 but reprinted in 1613).[1] As the passages above demonstrate, though, what is true is something drama of this period understands as problematic, linked to the question of what audiences can believe or be made to believe. This chapter will contend that Shakespeare's and Fletcher's play determinedly sets out to provoke its audience to interrogate what is seen and heard and will try to provide some indications of why this questioning process is important. In doing so, it will maintain that the play participates in a widely used Reformation debate about the uses of history.

My argument begins from the premise that the dramatists are acutely aware of the inherent contradictions in the assertion that 'all is true': that this can appear either as the avowal of a singular, unique interpretation which the play may be proposed as attesting, or that in various ways the variety of differing perspectives on the events enacted, additionally subject to the contingent circumstances of an audience's understanding of them, might *all* be true. In a genre which commonly draws attention to its witnesses' credulousness about its fabrications, *Henry VIII* joins with other historical plays of this period in claiming 'truth' with the expectation of viewers both believing and disbelieving:

> Such as give
> Their money out of hope they may believe,
> May here find truth too. Those that come to see
> Only a show or two, and so agree
> The play may pass, if they be still and willing,
> I'll undertake may see away their shilling.
> (Prologue, ll. 7–12)

The extracts opening this chapter appear to offer vastly differing senses of what is true: one humorously emerging from the world of the naive simpleton, the other from a more sinister world of *realpolitik*. Yet *Henry VIII* challenges ready separations between a gullible faith in the fabulous among simple folk and more urbane attempts to manipulate public beliefs through political machination. In the play's opening scene,

---

1. See Foakes's introduction to *Henry VIII*, p. xxix; Gaspar, 'The Reformation plays', p. 207.

there is a crucial instance of this in the Duke of Norfolk's description of the meeting of the French and English kings at the Field of Cloth of Gold. Norfolk readily conjoins the exaggerated fabulousness of the pageantry with a cynical reflection on the political emptiness of this excessive display:

> To-day the French,
> All clinquant all in gold, like heathen gods
> Shone down the English; and to-morrow they
> Made Britain India ...
> The two kings
> Equal in lustre, were now best, now worst ...
> and being present both,
> 'Twas said they saw but one, and no discerner
> Durst wag his tongue in censure. When these suns
> (For so they phrase 'em) by their heralds challeng'd
> The noble spirits to arms, they did perform
> Beyond thought's compass, that former fabulous story
> Being now seen possible enough, got credit
> That Bevis was believ'd. (I, i, 18–38)

The chapbook world of popular romance represented by the exploits of Bevis of Hampton is aligned with the history of Henry VIII. But Norfolk's and his companions' celebratory tone rapidly transforms into one of hostility. The actuality of the displays at the Field of Cloth of Gold is that the nobility have financially impoverished themselves in a meaningless exercise, because the peace between France and England that it was supposed to represent was immediately abandoned. The whole event is concluded to belong to Cardinal Wolsey's vanity; rather than the stuff of romance it had 'poor issue' (I, i, 86). As we shall see, this scene is characteristic of a play which entices an audience to perceive events in a certain manner only to have their interpretation strained or contradicted. Attempts to unravel a consistent understanding of the events performed – a single narrative perspective on the meaning of this history – are futile. This is not to suggest the play as some postmodernist celebration of contingency. Rather, *Henry VIII* participates in patterns firmly established in contemporary historical drama and historiography, where recognising competing claims of historical truthfulness is seen as crucial in the developing of proper historical witness. Shakespeare and Fletcher are not claiming that there is no truth to be discovered; rather that it is a difficult but important pursuit, and one subject to revision within changing historical conditions.

II

A fear of secular and spiritual corruption arising from 'arbitrary government', that is despotic tyranny, is a central issue in *Henry VIII*. For the play, excess and tyrannical tendencies are pre-eminently associated with Cardinal Wolsey and the Roman Church's hierarchy. His ultimate rejection by Henry, along with Henry's support for Cranmer, might initially appear to celebrate the king as an instrument for furthering the course of true religion and liberty. But Henry's role in this play, and in other plays of this period dealing with his reign, is far from certain. Accepting that the nature of government and that of religion are closely intertwined, the king's actions do not inspire confidence in his position either as defender of English liberties or as defender of the faith. While it is clear the play is anti-Roman, its assurance about an English capacity for proper temporal or spiritual government is less apparent, and it is this arena that it is most challenging. Rejection of Rome does not imply certainty about events in England.

In staging these concerns, *Henry VIII* develops a number of issues which are familiarly echoed in a wide variety of texts from the mid-sixteenth century: a sense of 'true' Englishness based on an opposition to tyranny and Roman Catholicism; a belief that national integrity is threatened; the enticement of an audience to witness this by comprehending a particular projection of history. This is a pattern prominently established by John Foxe's influential *Acts and Monuments of these Latter and Perilous Dayes Touching Matters of the Church* (1st edition 1563). Foxe's *Acts and Monuments*, arguably the most significant and certainly the most widely dispersed historical account in early modern England, with seven editions by 1610, illustrates an important conjunction of facets common within such English writing of the sixteenth and seventeenth centuries: that in the minds of contemporaries secular issues of political theory and practice surrounding England's rejection of the Church of Rome were inseparable from supernatural questions associated with popery – in extreme cases the equation of it with the diabolical Antichrist.[2] Tyranny is not only an undesirable secular force but one filled with resonances of subjection to the diabolic. Allowing its presence in England will diminish political freedoms long struggled for; more sinisterly, such losses enable the forfeiture of religious reformation.

Although historians and literary critics have recognised that supernatural *historia* – or unfolding narrative – and secular history were

2. See Lake, 'Anti-popery'.

intertwined during the Renaissance, most have tended to witness this in terms of a lingering but evaporating legacy of *historia* being replaced by the emerging dominance of secular history, a process perceived as a sign of cultural development.[3] This is too crudely reductive a view and fails to reflect contemporaries' views. Foxe's *Acts and Monuments* is an illustration of how increasing attention to accurate assemblage of detailed evidence interacted with a theoretical perspective which witnessed history as an unfolding narrative whose 'meaning' was to be discerned in Scripture. Foxe's Protestant truths are corroborated not only in what his martyrs represented in their deaths – their participation in patterns to be discovered in the early church – but in the historiography itself, the methods Foxe consciously employs to record the evidence he collected about these occurrences. The meticulousness which Foxe sought (even to reporting opposing claims about what occurs) invites the reader to endorse a Protestant quest for accuracy in contrast to the fabulous claims made in Roman Catholic saints' legends.[4]

If, however, a grand historical pattern might be observed resulting from a conflict between spiritual forces of good and evil, this does not imply that Foxe or his contemporaries believed that determining the significance of different historical actions was straightforward. Through the three editions of *Acts and Monuments* he was personally responsible for (1563, 1570, 1583), Foxe continually reassesses the incidents he relates: a ready illustration of the ways contemporaries responded to an awareness that events were constantly open to reappraisal.[5] As Annabel Patterson has brilliantly demonstrated in *Reading Holinshed's Chronicles*, there was a deliberate attempt by the compilers of such chronicles – we can include the *Acts and Monuments* among these – to inculcate in the reader a recognition of the contingency of the significance of historical events.[6] Neither seeking to foster modern views of objective detachment, nor merely refusing to come to a decision about the meaning of an event, the chroniclers' endeavour was to promote the engaged reader, one actively weighing differing views. Motivated by an urgency to discern truths which ultimately had spiritual as well as secular implications, the chroniclers believed an individual's involvement in understanding

3. See Levy, *Tudor Historical Thought*; Burke, *The Renaissance Sense of the Past*. For a specifically Shakespearean orientation see Rackin, *Stages of History*, esp. pp. 1–85.
4. The best general introduction to Foxe is Wooden, *John Foxe*. See also Loades, *John Foxe*.
5. See Flech, 'Shaping the reader', and Betteridge, 'From prophetic to apocalyptic'.
6. Patterson, *Reading Holinshed's Chronicles*. For Foxe's similarities see Flech, 'Shaping the reader'.

history was crucial. Accepting a supernatural agency (both ungodly corruption and godly grace), the chroniclers imagined that knowing what secular events might signify had implications for readers well beyond those claimed by the modern historian. This imposed a duty on both historian and reader to negotiate history carefully. One particular factor prompting this conscientiousness was a perception that the diabolic used misrepresentation as a key element in its arsenal. Upon whose 'side' truth lay was a dilemma not to be swept away by overly selective or partisan accounts. Educating the reader to be able to grasp historical meaning, to negotiate contending representation with a careful weighing of alternatives, becomes one of the principal endeavours of contemporary English chroniclers.

If Annabel Patterson has argued this basis for historiography with Holinshed – one we can easily extend to include Foxe – it may also be readily observed with the contemporary history play. Thomas Dekker's *The Whore of Babylon* (*c*.1606) has some good illustrations of contemporary dramatists' alertness to England's opponents manipulating common materials to different ends, often deliberately adopting the same rhetoric and drawing on the same store of imagery.[7] Dekker succinctly demonstrates how Protestant England and the Roman Catholic Continent both employed the same claims against one another. At the play's start the Empress of Babylon claims of Elizabeth:

> That strumpet, that inchantresse (who, in robes
> White as is innocence, and with an eye
> Able to tempt stearne murther to her bed)
> Calls her selfe *Truth*, has stolne fair *Truths* attire,
> Her crowne, her sweet songs, counterfets her voyce,
> And by prestigious tricks in sorcerie
> Ha's raiz'd a base impostor like *Truths* father:
> This subtile Curtizan sets vp againe,
> Whom we but late banisht to liue in caues,
> In rockes and desart mountaines. (I, i, 56–65)

Dekker shows that it is the Empress of Babylon who is the 'subtle courtesan', but he draws attention to deception as one of the chief weapons in the wars of truth. Although in the *lectori* of his play, Dekker has absolved himself from his use of history in a cavalier fashion by proclaiming 'I write as a poet, not as a historian, ... these two do not live under one law', *The Whore of Babylon's* prologue indicates that Dekker is

7. All references are to Dekker, *The Whore of Babylon* in *The Dramatic Works of Thomas Dekker*, vol. II.

trying to educate the reader in a manner similar to that of the chroniclers:

> These Wonders sit and see, sending as guides
> Your Iudgement, not your passions: passion slides,
> When Iudgement goes vpright: for tho the Muse
> (That's thus inspir'de) a Nouel path does tread,
> Shee's free from foolish boldnes, or base dread.
> Loe, scorne she scornes and Enuies ranckling tooth,
> For this is all shee does, she wakens *Truth*. (ll. 20–6)

Encouraging judgement, and the difficulty in maintaining it in an environment subject to deception, is, indeed, a facet which marks out the English history plays of the late sixteenth and early seventeenth centuries and in which Shakespeare's fully participate. The only striking exception with *Henry VIII* among Shakespeare's other histories is in its dealing directly with events of Reformation history, and in its style more closely resembling that of other contemporary history plays, including *Sir Thomas More*, *The True Chronicle of … Thomas Lord Cromwell*, *If You Know Not Me You Know Nobody*, *When You See Me, You Know Me*, and *The Famous History of Sir Thomas Wyatt*. Many of these were multi-authored, most are difficult to date precisely and were frequently subject to later revision. However, they span approximately a twenty-year period from the mid-1590s (*Sir Thomas More*) to the mid-1610s (*Henry VIII*). Although they all share Protestant origins, and, as Julia Gaspar has demonstrated, a number appear to have been written in response to (or to take advantage of) events with strong Protestant connections such as the Essex rebellion or the Gunpowder plot, what is notable is how all of them do not reduce the history they perform to a narrow depiction of heroes and villains (Dekker's *Whore of Babylon* is, in fact, the most jingoistic among them) (pp. 190–216). All present puzzling scenes where an audience is posed with a series of problems in interpretation, both within the scene itself and in the scene's relation to others in the plays. All dramatise events or portray characters in manners that refuse narrow sectarian interpretations. Kathleen McLuskie's comment on *Sir Thomas Wyatt* can be said to refer to them all: 'this is a politics of negotiation among contradictory alternatives, aware of the realpolitik of competing hierarchies and establishment of legitimate authority'.[8]

It is worth considering a few examples from some of these plays as they help illustrate how *Henry VIII* participates in this drama. Comparisons

---

8. McLuskie, *Dekker and Heywood*, p. 40.

also help reveal the complexity of Protestant drama's historiography. One of the central concerns of Foxe's *Acts and Monuments* is to demonstrate true Catholic continuity in England against the false claims of the Roman Church. When practices could be argued as having been returned to purer, uncorrupted forms, the English Church generally promoted continuities, including ritualistic ones, with its past.[9] The vast majority of English people were used to the prescribed *Book of Common Prayer's* emphasis on this (for example, the creed's declaration 'I beleue one Catholike and Apostolike churche'). Further, Anglican opposition to the Roman Church did not automatically equate with wholesale xenophobia against those who continued to belong to it. The sympathetic presentation of the Spanish-born Queen Katherine in *Henry VIII*, for instance, finds ready parallels in these other history plays, emphasising the dramatists' refusal to collapse the implications of events into simple oppositions of the good versus the bad.

In Heywood's *If You Know Not Me You Know Nobody, part 1* (1605), for instance, there is a scene in which a Spaniard treacherously kills an Englishman: a dramatic instance apparently confirming xenophobic stereotypes. However, Philip of Spain (Mary Tudor's husband) immediately enters and, despite the pleas of Mary's English courtiers to pardon the Spanish villain, orders the murderer to be hanged. Throughout Heywood's play Philip works to try to reconcile Mary and the Princess Elizabeth against the machinations of Mary's English Roman Catholic faction, notably Stephen Gardiner. In Samuel Rowley's *When You See Me, You Know Me* (1605), while Wolsey is presented as uncompromisingly treacherous in his self-serving, Henry VIII is shown to be a figure wholly unable to control himself emotionally. The link between a failure of personal self-government with control of the realm is made explicit, drawing attention to Henry's inability to contain rebellion in Ireland. As Gordon McMullan's chapter in this collection demonstrates, Henry's lack of self-control is prominent, if more subtly so, in *Henry VIII*, and poses the same dilemma as Rowley's portrayal: is this a king unable to control his realm because of his inability to control himself? Is this a sound king who has been abused by false Roman Catholic clerical counsellors or one whose despotic tendencies allow popish corruption to flourish at his court?

Dekker's and Webster's *Sir Thomas Wyatt* (1607, reprinted 1612) is one

9. See Lake, *Anglicans and Puritans?*, and Tyacke, *Anti-Calvinists*, as examples of studies which have challenged the frequent critical assumption that the reformed English Church was essentially Calvinist in dispostion.

of the best examples of a play which develops around a shifting historical perspective, the succession of events performed complicating any
easy audience response. It opens with expressions of Wyatt's fierce loyalty
towards Mary Tudor's legitimacy. Having helped to confirm her claim to
the throne, Wyatt then turns to revolt against Mary because of his fears
over her Spanish marriage. His rebellion fails and though providing the
dramatists with an opportunity for some stirring nationalistic rhetoric, it
is not made explicit whether Wyatt's cause is justified. There is no doubt
that the play reveals the crowned Mary as increasingly disregarding her
obligations to tolerate her subjects' Protestantism. Nevertheless, the
dramatists are intent on preventing their characters from sliding into
reductive vehicles of Protestant saints versus Roman Catholic tormen-
tors. The dramatic effect of Mary's announcement of the restoration of
the monasteries, for example, is tempered by her insistence that she will
pay for these herself so as not to impoverish her subjects: hardly the
action of a unfeeling tyrant!

Centrally, though, Wyatt's defence of Mary's rights against Northum-
berland's and Suffolk's attempt to place Lady Jane Grey on the throne
early in the play has serious implications for his own rebellion's legitimacy. In one telling incident, Suffolk is betrayed by a servant he thought
he could trust. This elicits a denunciation of unreliable servants from
Suffolk, but more importantly it shows the servant despairing of his
deed and hanging himself. The parallels with Judas' betrayal of Christ are
glaring: yet Suffolk, too, has been a betrayer of Mary, motivated by the
prospect of familial advantage. Although presenting Wyatt's, Suffolk's,
Jane Grey's and her betrothed Guildford's deaths in manners clearly
derived from Foxe's accounts of Protestant saints in the *Acts and Monuments*, the play also promotes the centrality of loyalty, something all these
characters are to varying degrees culpable of breaking. Applauding the
maintenance of individual integrity – 'Ile dambe my soule for no man,
no for no man. / Who at doomes day must answere for my sinne?',
announces Wyatt early in the play – *Sir Thomas Wyatt* shows how acting
according to conscience's dictates is not a straightforward affair.[10] What is
genuine loyalty, what calculated action for political advantage, is not
easily distinguished.

To turn to *Henry VIII*, it is worth considering two scenes to demonstrate how the play may be seen to entice an audience to be ruled by
judgement rather than passion. Detailed consideration of these illustrates
how finely the dramatists have arranged their materials to resist simplistic

10. Dekker and Webster, *Sir Thomas Wyatt*, I, i, 34–5.

categorisation of the historical significance of what is performed. The first is the portrayal of the Duke of Buckingham's fall from favour and his execution for treachery (Acts I and II); the second Katherine's and Griffith's consideration of Wolsey after his death (IV, ii).

In the first case, the play initially appears to present Buckingham as the innocent victim of Wolsey's hatred. Norfolk counsels him that 'The state takes notice of the private difference / Betwixt you and the Cardinal. I advise you ... that you read / The Cardinal's malice and his potency / Together' (I, i, 101–6). Buckingham is shown to be unable to control his anger towards Wolsey, who arranges his arrest for treason. Despite acknowledging the duke's merits, Henry is persuaded of his guilt by Wolsey, who organises a succession of Buckingham's servants to testify against him.

Determined opponents though they are, it is interesting that the drama shows Buckingham and Wolsey closely paralleling one another. Both claim to be utterly loyal and accuse one another of treachery. Both are reported by various characters, including Henry, to be learned and eloquent. Both are quick to show excessive anger and yet, when their respective falls come, both demonstrate (or are reported as demonstrating) fortitude, forgiveness and the ability to meet their end with Christian resignation. The significant difference is that Buckingham dies protesting his innocence, Wolsey repenting his faults.

Superficially, therefore, it appears that Buckingham's truth is contrasted with Wolsey's duplicitiousness, the latter duping Henry through corrupting a succession of Buckingham's servants falsely to accuse the duke. Wolsey's contrivances have not convinced the people, though. The play employs a group of gentleman (who importantly meet again in IV, i, to opine on Anne's coronation) to comment on Buckingham's fall. They report the general attitude to Wolsey and the duke:

> All the commons
> Hate him perniciously, and o' my conscience
> Wish him ten faddom deep: this duke as much
> They love and dote on; call him bounteous Buckingham
> The mirror of all courtesy. (II, i, 49–53)

Crucially, while reporting this general opinion, they do not themselves pronounce unequivocally on Buckingham. The play refuses an unambiguous admission of Buckingham's innocence. The duke acknowledges he has been betrayed by his servants, but whether this is because they disclosed confidences or accused him falsely is unclear. Buckingham eloquently claims that he does not challenge the law because it has convicted him on evidence which appeared to be true but was in fact contrived. Should we accept, however, that his articulate speeches in II, i, are to be taken as an iteration of truth? The gentleman commentators give an audience reason to pause. The candour they manifest in their report of the progress of his trial reveals the dramatists' refusing to present this as a forthright instance of an English patriot destroyed by clerical treason. Although their report on the trial is lengthy, it is worth giving in full because it so aptly illustrates how judgement is called for in considering this scene. The first gentleman relates to the second how:

> The great duke
> Came to the bar; where to his accusations
> He pleaded still not guilty, and alleged
> Many sharp reasons to defeat the law.
> The king's attorney on the contrary
> Urg'd on the examinations, proofs, confessions
> Of divers witnesses, which the duke desir'd
> To have brought *viva voce* to his face;
> At which appeared against him his surveyor,
> Sir Gilbert Perk, his chancellor, and John Car,
> Confessor to him, with that devil monk,
> Hopkins, that made this mischief.
> 2ND GENTLEMAN   That was he
> That fed him with his prophecies.
> 1ST GENTLEMAN   The same;
> All these accus'd him strongly, which he fain
> Would have flung from him; but indeed he could not,
> And so his peers upon this evidence
> Have found him guilty of high treason. Much
> He spoke, and learnedly for life; but all
> Was either pitied in him or forgotten. (II, i, 11–29)

Buckingham's passionate defiance of his accusers may be a reflection of his truth, or it may be that rhetoric is his only weapon to fight a desperate defensive corner. The suggestion that Buckingham is trying to throw off his accusers but cannot may just as probably reflect that he did dabble in treachery. These gentlemen (their status is not wholly clear, but they do not seem to be courtiers) may be said to act as a fit audience to the drama of state which they witness and report on. Their discriminations may be seen as a guide for the larger audience of the play about the candour it should adopt.

The scene in *Henry VIII* which perhaps most vividly illustrates the dramatists' endeavours to develop considered judgement instead of an immediate emotional response to events is the discussion of Wolsey between Katherine and Griffith. After Wolsey's manipulation of her, Katherine's unsurprising response to news of his death is a catalogue of his faults. This focuses on Wolsey's skilful deceit, his two-facedness: something the audience has had ample opportunity to witness in the play. As a victim of Wolsey, and because of her presentation as an honest figure throughout the play, Katherine's summary of him might appear to articulate the play's general sentiment:

> His own opinion was his law: i'th presence
> He would say untruths, and be ever double
> Both in his words and meaning. He was never
> (But where he meant to ruin) pitiful:
> His promises were as he then was, mighty,
> But his own performance, as he is now, nothing.
> (IV, ii, 37–42)

In response Griffith, who is described as a gentleman-usher to Katherine, acknowledges Wolsey's faults, which revolved around his greed. But he balances this with Wolsey's virtues when it came to giving, highlighting his founding of colleges in Oxford and Ipswich, and his contrition at his end (IV, ii, 48–68). Katherine responds by hailing Griffith as an 'honest chronicler':

> After my death I wish no other herald,
> No other speaker of my living actions
> To keep mine honour from corruption,
> But such an honest chronicler as Griffith.
> Whom I most hated living, thou has made me,
> With thy religious truth and modesty,
> Now in his ashes honour. (IV, ii, 69–75)

Exploring this scene in relation to material in Holinshed's *Chronicles*, Annabel Patterson has noted how the play intelligently employs material from Hall and Campion which is separated in the Chronicles: 'someone highly intelligent and experienced in reading the Chronicles reversed their order, dramatised their disagreements, and rendered that disagreement, in terms of the philosophy of history, theoretical'.[11]

The scene continues, though, to develop our interest in how events may be characterised by its next presentation, which provides further

11. Patterson, "'All is true'", p. 153

credibility to Griffith as 'an honest chronicler' and which fulfils, in part, Katherine's desire to have Griffith as the 'speaker of my living actions'. Katherine falls asleep, we may even think for a few moments that she has died, and the audience is presented with a visionary dumb show which appears to reveal Katherine gaining a heavenly crown. Reporting the event, Katherine's own perspective on the spectacle provokes her to describe 'a blessed troup / Invit[ing] me to a banquet'; 'They promis'd me eternal happiness / And brought me garlands, Griffith, which I feel / I am not worthy yet to wear; I shall assuredly' (IV, ii, 87–92). Rather than acknowledging Katherine's apparent elevation to sainthood, though, Griffith offers another outlook on this event: 'I am most joyful, madam, such good dreams / Possess your fancy' (IV, ii, 93–94). Griffith's analysis of what has taken place unsettles the audience's own view of the dumb show: has this been a true vision or a staging of a fanciful dream? The former gives considerable support to a view of Katherine as a figure the play is celebrating for her religious life (and raising troublesome questions about Henry's divorce provoking religious alteration). If, on the other hand, what we have seen is a mere dream, Katherine might even appear guilty of a false humility, denying her worthiness while imagining herself attaining a heavenly crown. Actually, Griffith's response largely diffuses the vision's potential to either beatify or castigate Katherine. His pleasure at what he sees as good dreams possessing her fancy and offering solace to a character *in extremis* prompts considerable sympathy for her, while refusing to allow this scene to be claimed as her unequivocal apotheosis. If, as Katherine claims for Griffith, he speaks with 'religious truth and modesty', this truth is not inclined to hagiography. Even if we propose Griffith is not a true chronicler – misinterpreting both Wolsey and what has happened to Katherine – the play has once again skilfully refused to let an audience rest contented with any straightforward interpretation, even of the actions they themselves have just witnessed.

III

Exploring the large-scale use of prophecy in the writing of Reformation England, Patrick Collinson has noted that, despite an underlying sense of God's providence for England, this mode of writing is marked by being 'judgmental, inward-searching, and self-critical, not at all triumphalist'.[12] This distinction between a belief in the special position of England as a nation chosen by God and a refusal to bask in any

12. Collinson, 'Biblical rhetoric', p. 24.

assurance about this is an important modification to the concept of the elect nation frequently invoked in considering Protestant literature of this period.[13] If employing biblical prophecy to project England's future left contemporary commentators uneasy, this is true also of their readings of England's history. Foxe's *Acts and Monuments* is once again a key illustration of this, a work which embraces both history and prophecy.[14] While it is the case that Foxe celebrates England's opportunity to merge the invisible church of the godly – those who had maintained the true faith in times of persecution – with a newly cleansed visible church – the formal institutions of church and state – what is also readily apparent is the sense of uncertainty the *Acts and Monuments* conveys over whether this opportunity is being realised, an anxiety which displaces any jingoistic religio-national triumphalism. Notably in the 1570 and 1583 editions of his work, Foxe registers his concerns about a nation which, while enjoying God's special favour, does not seem to be living up to its responsibilities. Far from being overthrown, the Antichrist remains a powerful threat *in* the nation as well as across the Channel.

As we have seen, *Henry VIII* shares with other history plays of its period an interest in complex types, ones shifting in intricate historical circumstances. It attacks popery, but Wolsey is more than the figure of sedition from a Protestant morality tradition. A distinction is created between the promise of Wolsey's native gifts and his misuse of these in office, perhaps suggesting that in a state of proper religious and secular government a figure such as Wolsey would have been of value. His contrition at the end may even be taken to suggest that he has been the victim of popery's corrupting influence rather than its thorough representative. By following Wolsey's dismissal with his contrition to Cromwell and then the favourable report of his death by Griffith, the play presents his downfall as a personal tragedy. It makes it apparent that Henry's pursuit of private passion over Anne Boleyn may only accidentally, or – perhaps more exactly – providentially, result in England's good.

The misgivings that *Henry VIII* registers about how decisively Henry's court is intent on pursuing a reformation of religion is shared by other contemporary dramatists' – and historians' – presentation of his reign. Typically, these history plays celebrate the true advent of reformed

13. See particularly Haller, *Foxe's Book of Martyrs*. Haller's views have prominently influenced one of the few critical considerations of English Reformation history plays, Spikes, 'The Jacobean history play'.
14. See particularly Betteridge, 'From prophetic to apocalyptic'.

religion in England with either Edward VI under the tutelage of Cranmer (Rowley's *When You See Me, You Know Me*) or more commonly under Elizabeth (*If You Know Not Me You Know Nobody, Sir Thomas Wyatt, The Whore of Babylon*). Indeed, part of twentieth-century criticism's difficulties in attempting to locate an unambiguous Reformation dynamic in *Henry VIII* may result from the abiding Whiggish view of the Henrican Reformation, which has had notable currency since the 1950s but which does not appear to have been particularly shared among late sixteenth- and early seventeenth-century commentators.[15] Hindsight may enable some historians to declare an increasing Protestantisation in England from Henry's reign, but many contemporaries saw no such unstoppable direction: a source of anxiety or hope, depending on the individual's beliefs.

Henry VIII ends with a display of apparent Reformation prophecy, but one which reflects the self-critical fashion which Collinson sees as characteristic of the prophetic mode of this period. As with all the play's pageantry, the baptismal ritual, culminating in Cranmer's divination about the infant Elizabeth and England's future, is an uncertain spectacle. Once again, it poses challenging questions about what is true, notably highlighting the inseparability of secular questions of government and questions of supernatural conflict.

Cranmer's speech is rich in the resonance of supernatural prophecy ('Let me speak sir, / For heaven now bids me', V, iv, 14–15), and its promise describes a reign built round a political vision which emphasises the commonwealth ('In her days every man shall eat in safety / Under his own vine what he plants'; 'those about her / From her shall read the perfect ways of honour, / And by those claim their greatness, not by blood', V, iv, 33–8). Central to Cranmer's vision of the future Elizabeth and of her successor James is that the nation's welfare rests on resisting tyranny within its own government: 'She shall be lov'd and fear'd; her own shall bless her' (V, iv, 30).

If a case needs to made for *Henry VIII*'s Anglican Protestant vision of England, it rests in this final Act. Here the monarch recognises the fundamental virtue of the archbishop he has appointed to the governorship of the Church in England and protects him from the manoeuvring of evil counsellors. Henry and Cranmer display a model of loyalty and fidelity which reflects the reciprocal duties of their positions. Cranmer's

---

15. The most influential account of the increasing Protestantisation of the Reformation is Dickens, *The English Reformation*. This has been widely challenged: see Scarisbrick, *The Reformation*; Duffy, *The Stripping of the Altars*; and Haigh, *English Reformations*.

relies on interior spiritual qualities as an answer against his accusers; Henry points out that such a defence betrays little knowledge of the ways of the world and statecraft. It is these which the monarch offers his archbishop as protector: 'Thy truth and thy integrity is rooted / In us thy friend' (V, i, 114–15). In return, Cranmer plays the part of spiritual mentor, speaking for heaven in his projection of idealised monarchy under Elizabeth and James. In doing so, he apparently transforms Henry. As Gordon McMullan's chapter in this volume details, for most of the play Henry is shown not to possess the self-control which is the proper province of the masculine governor. At the conclusion, in response to Cranmer's predication he proclaims: 'O lord archbishop, / Thou has made me now a man; never before / This happy child did I get anything' (V, iv, 63–5). In exercising his authority in protecting Cranmer, confirming his governorship of the English church, Henry is rewarded by this church's blessing. Henry's concluding speech reinforces exactly this concept in declaring Elizabeth's baptism a holy/holi-day, employing language which demonstrates how the secular and spiritual state have apparently properly combined to promote a national sense of common accord, a general feast which renders concrete Cranmer's future prediction:

> This day, no man think
> 'Has business at his house; for all shall stay:
> This little one shall make it Holy-day. (V, iv, 74–6)

In the play Wolsey's and Gardiner's endeavours pursue the consolidation of their own and Rome's power through upsetting the proper function of monarchy, standing between king and the fit exercise of rule over his people (see esp. I, ii, 9–108). Cranmer's refusal to meddle in state politics, except as a prophet of the future, is in notable contrast and prompts the king to assume a more beneficent role as the state's temporal governor.

A contemporary audience witnessing this scene, though, would probably have raised some sceptical complications over this prophecy. Far from ushering in an era of peace and plenty, the Boleyn marriage was merely another chapter in the clashes among differing groups for power and control. Foxe's *Acts and Monuments* notably presents both Cranmer and Elizabeth as two of the most significant Protestant 'martyrs' of the Marian period (Heywood's *If You Know Not Me You Know Nobody, part 1* similarly portrays Elizabeth in this way). Cranmer's inspired projection of the future is refuted by historical experience, one which saw Cranmer's death at the stake. Henry's declaration of a holy/holi-day may be seen as drawing attention to this visual and rhetorical pageant as a show, an interlude in the reality of English history.

Henry VIII opens with Norfolk reporting events of the Field of Cloth of Gold, which event:

> Beyond thought's compass, that former fabulous story
> Being now seen possible enough, got credit
> That Bevis was believ'd. (I, i, 36–8)

The play concludes with a prediction that recreates the legend of the golden age, virtually the land of Cockaigne of the popular imagination. The events Norfolk reports in France are quickly deflated by the admission that the stuff of legend is subject to the laws of economics and politics: it has bankrupted the nobility and achieved nothing of substance. The Field of Cloth of Gold was only a show. The dramatists leave Cranmer's prediction of prosperity and political perfection unanswered except by the audience's own experience. The 'judgmental, inward-searching, and self-critical, not at all triumphalist' qualities which Patrick Collinson notes in this era's use of the prophetic mode prompt a response which would place current realities against what *should* have happened, emphasising that in failing to achieve the stability and plenty which *should* have arisen from Reformation, England's political and spiritual direction has yet to be fulfilled. To accept Cranmer's future vision of Elizabeth's and James's rule as a reflection of reality is to participate in the world of the credulous simpleton:

> Such as give
> Their money out of hope they may believe,
> May here find truth too. (Prologue, ll. 7–9)

First produced in 1613, *Henry VIII* appeared in a year in which London was filled with plays, pageants, masques and other spectacles to celebrate the marriage of the Elector Palatine to the Princess Elizabeth. Shakespeare's and Fletcher's use of extensive pageantry has helped prompt some critics to argue its appropriateness within these Stuart celebrations, ones which many contemporaries saw as strengthening Protestantism in Europe.[16] As Julia Gaspar has noted, though, a play centred on divorce would seem a poor choice for marriage celebrations (pp. 207–8). Even more so, the play's inquiry into, and scepticism about, the spectacles its drama encompasses renders it judgemental about attempts to present organised displays of royally sponsored 'truth'.

16. *Henry VIII*, ed. Foakes, pp. xxviii–xxxv.

Shakespeare's and Fletcher's clever deployment of commentators on events – Norfolk, Abergavenny and Buckingham on the Field of Cloth of Gold; the three gentleman who observe Buckingham's trial and Anne's coronation; Griffith's perspective on Wolsey and on Katherine's dream; Cromwell's counter to Gardiner's excessive condemnation of Cranmer – reflect the lack of any straightforward appraisal of what is displayed and, notably among the less exalted characters, demonstrate the importance of candour in the exercise of judgement.

Henry VIII and other contemporary history plays of this era confront attempts to reduce what is staged to narrow, jingoistic evocations of a Protestant celebration of England's divine destiny. Reflecting contemporary anxieties about whether England was acting out the *historia* which ideally belonged to the nation, these plays emphasise the need to be vigilant in interpreting history, acutely aware of both the secular and supernatural dangers in tyranny and popery. Despite Dekker's assertion that poets and historians do not live under the same law, these history plays share with chroniclers such as Foxe and Holinshed the desire to encourage a judgemental audience as witnesses to their work. *Henry VIII* is a further instance that the too readily accepted division between the didactic Protestant theatre of the early Reformation and the secular commercial theatre from the late 1580s continues to call out for whole-scale reassessment.[17]

17. Recent studies which have importantly begun this reassessment include White, *Theatre and Reformation*; McEachern, *The Poetics of English Nationhood*; and Diehl, *Staging Reform*.

10

'TO WRITE AND READ / BE HENCEFORTH TREACHEROUS': *CYMBELINE* AND THE PROBLEM OF INTERPRETATION

Alison Thorne

This play has many just sentiments, some natural dialogues and some pleasing scenes, but they are obtained at the expense of much incongruity. To remark the folly of the fiction, the absurdity of the conduct, the confusion of the names, and manners of different times, and the impossibility of the events in any system of life, were to waste criticism upon unresisting imbecility, upon faults too evident for detection, and too gross for aggravation.

Thus Dr Johnson on *Cymbeline* in 1756.[1] Reviewing the play's critical history since then, we might well conclude that in many ways it has not moved beyond the parameters established by Johnson's splendidly trenchant dismissal. Faced with its proliferating plots, its bewildering diversity of generic modes, unevenness of tone and blatant anachronisms, the play's critics have tended to fall back on one of two solutions: either they have conceded its radical decentredness and 'incongruity' along with Johnson, or they have abstracted one particular plot strand or set of generic conventions on the pretext that this embodies the play's essential interest – presenting it as primarily a fashionable experiment in pastoral tragicomedy, for example, or a historical play about emergent British

---

1. *Johnson on Shakespeare, The Yale Edition of the Works of Samuel Johnson*, vol. VIII, p. 908.

nationalism.[2] Alternatively, appeal has been made to some extra-dramatic fact unspecified in the text (such as Christ's birth during Cymbeline's reign, or James's self-styled role as the new peace-making Augustus Caesar), in a desperate attempt to impose cohesion on a work that, it is granted, might otherwise seem barely intelligible.[3] One aim of this chapter is to propose a fundamental reorientation of our approach to *Cymbeline*, away from this obsession with demonstrating the play's structural integrity or lack of it. This is not to say that our efforts to make coherent sense of the play are necessarily futile. Some of the most stimulating analysis of *Cymbeline* has sought to mediate between the psychoanalytic and historicist approaches that have dominated recent criticism, by expanding upon G. Wilson Knight's suggestive remarks regarding 'the close reference of the sexual to the national'.[4] Moreover, it could be said that such a holistic perspective is sanctioned by the play itself, given its many intimations of hidden links between the erotic, familial and political plots, as well as its preoccupation with the fragmentation of dismembered bodies, marriages, families and political alliances and their eventual reintegration. However, I do wish to argue that, instead of trying to solve the riddle of the play's 'meaning' by identifying the key to its multiplicity, we might more profitably attend to the ways in which this, the most elusive of Shakespeare's so-called 'romances', reflects ironically on the question of its own illegibility. Consideration should be given, in particular, to the play's staging of the problems and the pitfalls involved in interpretative practices, especially reading.

Leah Marcus's discussion of *Cymbeline* in her *Puzzling Shakespeare: Local Reading and its Discontents* provides a convenient starting point, inasmuch as it can be seen as illustrative of some typical failings in *Cymbeline* criticism, whilst also signalling a possible way beyond them. Marcus offers a detailed explication of the play as a transparent allegory

2. Among those critics who regard *Cymbeline* as predominantly a romance or pastoral tragicomedy are Nosworthy in his introduction to the Arden edition of the play, Harris, '"What's past is prologue"', and White, *'Let Wonder Seem Familiar'*, pp. 130–44; those who see it rather as a historical play concerned with British nationalism include Wilson Knight, *Crown of Life*, pp. 129–202, and Kahn, *Roman Shakespeare*, pp. 160–70. Seeking to reconcile these two models, Felperin argues that the play exploits the commonalities between biblical history, the Tudor myth of Britain's past, and romance narratives in order to produce what, paradoxically, 'is probably the most unified … romance that Shakespeare wrote' (*Shakespearean Romance*, p. 179).

3. See, e.g., Jones, 'Stuart *Cymbeline*', p. 89, and Goldberg, *James I*, p. 240.

4. *Crown of Life*, p. 149. Two outstanding examples of this productive synthesis of psychoanalytic and historicist approaches are Adelman, *Suffocating Mothers*, pp. 198–218, and Mikalachki, 'The masculine romance'.

of James VI and I's project for the Union of the Kingdoms, in which the
irate Jupiter descending with his thunderbolts is taken to represent James
and his vexed relationship with Parliament, while the conflicting political
and religious interests that stood in the way of the proposed unification
of England and Scotland are figured now by the beleaguered marriage
of Posthumus and Innogen,[5] now by the factionalism of Cymbeline's
Britain. At the same time, Marcus acknowledges that 'in some of its
episodes … the play stubbornly refuses to make sense at the level of
Stuart interpretation', locating this resistance to the 'authorised line' in a
number of riddling texts and symbolic visions that simultaneously cry
out for and frustrate interpretation.[6] Yet despite commenting percep-
tively on how such moments serve to foreground the problematic
nature of reading ('Reading in *Cymbeline* may be enticing, but it is also
directly and repeatedly thematized as fraught with dangers, almost inevitably "misreading"' (p. 140)), her argument, by subordinating such difficulties to its own drive to closure, suggests that they may ultimately be
overridden. If, however, we are to take the play's 'discomfort with the
interpretive process' seriously (p. 142), it must surely be admitted that
this constitutes more than a token or passing impediment to the kind of
reading Marcus performs on *Cymbeline*, a reading that seeks to resolve its
persistent absurdities and enigmas into a clear, univocal meaning. In this
chapter, I shall try to show how *Cymbeline* incorporates a reflexive, metacritical commentary on the hazards of interpretation through its reitera-
tive use of the interlocking tropes of reading, writing or narrating, and
seeing. By plotting the characters' individual histories in terms of their
encounters with a series of recalcitrant texts, I argue, the play dramatises
the risks posed by the sorts of reductive reading or overreading in which
not only the characters but the play's critics are prone to indulge.[7]

5. Following Warren's Oxford edition I have adopted 'Innogen' as the heroine's name, on
   the grounds that this spelling is historically apt, in recalling the legendary first queen of
   Britain, and that the Folio's 'Imogen' is probably an error. However, I have retained
   the original spelling of 'Iachimo', as against the 'Giacomo' of the Oxford editor.
6. Marcus, *Puzzling Shakespeare*, p. 110.
7. It is necessary to point out what is not included within the boundaries of this
   discussion: while I believe that *Cymbeline* offers ample warrant for my emphasis on
   reading and spectating as textually based activities, other important aspects of the
   play are sidelined here as a consequence, most obviously its theatrical self-consciousness and the whole question of staging. It is perhaps fair to say, though, that the
   critical attention devoted to these topics has tended in the past to occlude the play's
   rhetoricity, creating an imbalance which this chapter seeks in some measure to
   redress. One notable exception is Simon Palfrey's *Late Shakespeare*, which stresses the
   materiality, opacity and self-contradictoriness of the play's courtly language.

With the exception of Marcus's study, surprisingly little has been made of the conspicuous presence of letters in the play (which exceeds any requirements of the plot) and their association with other types of text that require decoding. In so far as it has been noticed at all, the phenomenon is regarded as one of the play's many unaccountable oddities, worthy only of passing mention. Yet this superfluous proliferation of letters, 'papers', books and tablets – at least nine of which are produced on stage, giving concrete form to the many additional references to the writing and reading of texts – would seem to point to the working out of some deeper preoccupation.[8] The opening scenes clarify the nature of that preoccupation; on several occasions textual objects and allusions are enlisted as a device for highlighting the degree to which identity, meaning and value are mediated by hermeneutic processes that prove to be highly suspect. From the first, Posthumus Leonatus is referred to as though he were a cryptic text, whose significance, not yet fully apparent, must be 'unfold[ed] ... duly' (I, i, 25–7). One gentleman confesses that he 'cannot delve him to the root' (I, i, 28), yet he and his fellow courtiers show few scruples about inferring Posthumus' worth from public 'report', from the 'catalogue of his endowments', wherein he may be 'peruse[d] by items' (I, iv, 5–6), and, most importantly, from Innogen's choice of him as a husband:

> To his mistress,
> For whom he now is banished, her own price
> Proclaims how she esteemed him; and his virtue
> By her election may be truly read,
> What kind of man he is. (I, i, 50–54)

Their often ambiguously phrased eulogies may make us somewhat uneasy, none the less. In particular, their emphasis on reading the outward graces of the still unknown, untested Posthumus in Platonic fashion as denoting inward virtue (I, i, 22–4; I, iv, 7–9) hints at the dangers lurking in this assumption of semiotic stability.[9] A similar disquiet is voiced by Iachimo in I, iv, when he exploits the fact that Posthumus' character is 'weighed rather by her [Innogen's] value than his own' in

8. In addition to the references given below, see I, i, 98–102, 172; I, iii, 2–4; I, vi, 10–11, 205–6; II, iv, 35, 184; III, i, 71–4; III, ii, 25; III, v, 2, 100–8; IV, ii, 385–7; V, iv, 279.

9. The assumption of a fixed correlation between the inner and outer person, which is central to the ideology of the late plays, is problematised throughout *Cymbeline*, most obviously when Innogen mistakes Cloten's headless body for that of Posthumus. Cf. III, iv, 46–9; V, i, 29–33; V, iii, 227–31; V, iv, 62–5.

order to contest this official reading, arguing that it 'words him ... a great deal from the matter' (ll. 13–15).

If Posthumus' worth is perceived, initially at least, as wholly determined by the 'estimation' that others, notably Innogen, choose to put on it, much the same may be said of Innogen herself. Although she, unlike Posthumus, imprints herself on our consciousness as an autonomous and highly individualised personality from the outset, her fate is chiefly dictated by the overblown praise of her admirers and, on the other side, by Iachimo's detractions (later echoed in a correspondingly extreme form by Posthumus), whereby competing versions of her feminine identity are circulated at large. (Her powerlessness to intervene in what is said of her in Rome, where her presence is registered only via others' reports or the letters she sends Posthumus, underscores this fact.) In a reworking of the male boasting contest which instigated the rape of Lucrece, one of Innogen's literary prototypes, in Shakespeare's poem of that name, Posthumus' rhetorical construction of his wife's identity puts her directly in jeopardy. His blazoning of Innogen's virtues in the wager scene emphasises the received correlation between praising and appraising in ways that objectify the beloved, converting her into a precious gem: 'I praised her as I rated her; so do I my stone' (I, iv, 73). The effect of this 'descent into shop talk', as Nancy Vickers remarks, is to position Innogen as a 'splendid jewel placed between buyer and seller', thereby awakening Iachimo's sexual cupidity.[10] It is not only the latter's desires that are disastrously aroused by Posthumus' epideictic rhetoric, however; his iconoclastic instincts too are provoked. As a dissenting reader, Iachimo again turns the discursively mediated and therefore contentious status of Innogen's qualities to his advantage, this time as a pretext for initiating the wager. Indeed, he is at pains to stress that it is not her chastity which is being put to the test, so much as Posthumus' overweening confidence, both in his exclusive right of possession and in his powers of judgement: 'I make my wager rather against your confidence than her reputation' (I, iv, 106). In these early scenes, our attention is repeatedly drawn to the judgements at stake in interpretative acts, suggesting that they will be an important factor in the characters' development and our assessment of it. Relative to Posthumus, who is completely taken in by Iachimo's 'false report' of his night in the royal bedchamber, Innogen proves a competent, even astute reader. She has little difficulty in seeing through Iachimo's parallel account of her husband's infidelity as a slanderous fabrication: 'Thou wrong'st a gentleman who is as far /

10. Vickers, '"The blazon"', p. 101.

From thy report as thou from honour' (I, vi, 145–6). Nevertheless, both Iachimo (I, iv, 17–21; I, vi, 171–6) and Cloten (III, v, 74–9) continue to cast aspersions on the quality of her judgement where Posthumus is concerned – and rightly so, as it turns out.

The prominence given to such forms of rhetorical mediation is most strikingly demonstrated in the bedroom scene, II, ii, where the act of rape is figuratively transposed onto the activities of writing and reading: writing, in that Iachimo's 'design' on entering Innogen's bedchamber is not sexual violation as such, but to 'write all down', making an 'inventory' of the 'contents o' th' story' (II, ii, 24–7) (a reference encompassing not only the contents of the room or the figured arras adorning it, but the 'story' fabricated from these details which will be recounted to Posthumus in II, iv); and reading, in the sense that Iachimo's intrusion is prefaced by Innogen's bedtime reading of Ovid's *Metamorphoses*, and itself takes the form of his perusal of Innogen's recumbent body, displayed to his voyeuristic gaze, and of the extraordinarily rich and equivocally suggestive narrative contexts which impinge on this.[11] The classical stories within which Iachimo's interpretative interaction with this corporeal text is inscribed articulate a range of masculine responses to the objectified, chaste female body.[12] Balanced against the outright violence of Tereus' rape of Philomel (the Ovidian account of which Innogen has just been reading) and Tarquin's assault on Lucrece (explicitly cited as a model by Iachimo) is the mode of aesthetic contemplation, compounded in equal measure of lubricity and awe, evoked by the various tales depicted in the tapestries and ornamental plasterwork of the bedchamber, images of 'chaste Dian, bathing' (as furtively gazed on by Actaeon perhaps) and of Cleopatra's encounter with 'her Roman'

---

11. An important precedent for embedding 'rape' within the context of reading and writing is provided by another Shakespearean text that alludes extensively to the stories of Philomel and Lucrece: *Titus Andronicus*. Not only is Lavinia's violated and horribly mutilated body mediated by Marcus's perverse *blazon* and by her other male kinsmen, who take it upon themselves to 'interpret all her martyred signs' (III, ii, 36), but she herself employs textual means to disclose her fate, guiding them to the relevant passage in a copy of the *Metamorphoses* and writing the names of her assailants in the sand. For an analysis of the role of literacy in this play and the humanist ideology of violence it sustains, see Eaton, 'A woman of letters'.

12. Traub argues that the 'metaphoric and dramatic transformation of women into jewels, statues and corpses' in Shakespeare's plays functions as a strategy for containing the 'erotic threat of the female body' (*Desire and Anxiety*, p. 26). Similar anxieties over the uncontrollable nature of female sexuality appear to motivate the reactions of Innogen's male suitors to her body (which is objectified in each of the ways specified by Traub) and their efforts to contain its meaning.

Antony at Cydnus. More than any other factor, it is this deflecting of direct action into narrative fantasy which gives the 'rape' scene its strangely oblique, dream-like quality. And it is perfectly in keeping with the textualised experiences enacted here that sexual desire should be gratified at the level of imaginative or narrative satiety, rather than through actual physical contact. Iachimo holds back even from kissing his victim.[13] Instead, he declares that he has 'enough' after having noted down sufficient details of Innogen's body and the furnishings of her chamber – those same descriptive details he will latter use to 'satisfy' Posthumus of his wife's infidelity (II, iv, 134). Moreover, this expression of satiated desire coincides, provocatively, with his discovery that the leaf of Innogen's copy of Ovid has been 'turned down / Where Philomel gave up' (II, ii, 45–6), at the place, that is, where she yields to Tereus' sexual advances.[14]

But what is it exactly that is being yielded here to Iachimo's inquiring gaze? Psychoanalytic critics have argued that the play operates according to the logic of displacement and condensation characteristic of dreams – a 'hermeneutic of dream analysis', as Ruth Nevo calls it – which allows Iachimo and Cloten to substitute for Posthumus, acting out his socially unacceptable desires by proxy.[15] This seems to me a useful way of accounting for the play's more baffling features, but one I would want to

13. The play's editors and critics sometimes assume otherwise (see, e.g., the Oxford edition, p. 130), but this seems to me contrary to the whole tenor of this scene, which eschews bodily contact for the mediated forms of Iachimo's fantasy, whilst also discounting the fact that his wish to touch is stated in the conditional (II, ii, 16).

14. By focusing on this moment in the story of Philomel (interestingly, omitted from Golding's translation), Iachimo's monologue obliquely raises the question of Innogen's guilt. That she may to some degree be complicit in the 'assault' is insinuated at various points in the text: e.g., it is hinted that she may be dreaming the incident (II, iii, 63), with the implication that it is her desires as much as Iachimo's / Posthumus' which are being enacted. However, Innogen indirectly rebuts this inference when justifying her blunt dismissal of another unwelcome suitor: 'But that you shall not say I yield being silent, / I would not speak' (II, iii, 92), she says to Cloten. Parallels may be noted here with *The Rape of Lucrece*, a text similarly preoccupied with the illegibility of corporeal (especially facial) signs that are supposed to be a reliable index of moral character. Conscious that her sad demeanour might be misconstrued as betokening her acquiescence in the rape (ll. 806–12, 1342–4), Lucrece intervenes before her suicide to set the record straight and dictate the exemplary meanings which should be read into her (dead) body.

15. Nevo, *Shakespeare's Other Language*, p. 66. Nevo is one of several critics who believe that the play's peculiarities only begin to make sense when looked at through the lens of (post-)Freudian dream analysis, including Schwartz, 'Between fantasy and imagination', Kirsch, *Shakespeare and the Experience of Love*, and Landry, 'Dreams as history'.

modify slightly. What links Innogen's three suitors or would-be assailants of her 'honour', I suggest, is their competitive vying for possession not so much of her 'dearest bodily part' as of its textual significance.[16] Hence Iachimo's jubilation on discovering those tell-tale 'corporal sign[s]' – the bracelet on Innogen's arm, and, more crucially, the mole secreted under her left breast – which promise to unlock her hidden meaning (II, iv, 119). Within the patriarchally inflected semiotic systems of the court, such signs are destined to be deciphered as synecdochic markers of her 'honour', of the chastity whose presence or absence is assumed to define female worth. His familiarity with this interpretative code assures Iachimo that the mere citation of these 'natural notes about her [Innogen's] body' (II, ii, 28), together with their attendant 'circumstances', will be sufficient to convince Posthumus that his wife has played the strumpet in his vacated bed (just as he will later be convinced of her death by the 'bloody sign' of the blood-stained cloth sent him by Pisanio). That Innogen's guilt or innocence will be decided by a process of rhetorical manipulation is repeatedly spelt out:

> POSTHUMUS   If you can *make't apparent*
> That you have tasted her in bed, my hand
> And ring is yours ...
> IACHIMO   Sir, my *circumstances*,
> Being so near the truth as I will make them,
> Must first *induce you to believe*; whose strength
> I will *confirm with oath*, which I doubt not
> You'll give me leave to spare when you shall find
> You need it not. (II, iv, 56–66; my italics)

True to prediction, Posthumus reads Innogen's 'incontinency' into the wealth of signifying 'particulars' supplied by Iachimo on his return to Rome, with an eagerness that supports Terry Eagleton's characterisation of sexual jealousy as a 'crisis of interpretation', more specifically, of 'over-reading'.[17] Posthumus' projection of his own anxieties into Iachimo's narrative may remind us of Othello, who was, of course, similarly inveigled into believing in his wife's adultery by Iago's crafty deployment of the strawberry-spotted handkerchief (also decodable as a symbol of female sexuality) and his heaping up of circumstantial evidence. In each case, seduction or rape has become a question of interpretative inference,

---

16. According to Schwartz, the question '[w]ho shall possess Innogen? To whom does she belong?' is a central issue of the play ('Between fantasy and imagination', p. 224)
17. Eagleton, *William Shakespeare*, p. 65.

sexual guilt a matter of rhetorical persuasion rather than direct proof.

Whatever their differences, Posthumus, Iachimo and Cloten are equally confident of knowing what that 'good sign', Innogen, means, even though their readings may shift over time. However, the 'knowledge' (epistemological as well as carnal) to which all three lay claim is called into question, both by our access to dramatic impressions of Innogen pointedly at variance with such readings and, more subtly, by the textual ambiguities with which her body becomes overlaid. These ambiguities can be seen, on one level, as symptomatic of an unresolved tension in the attitude of Innogen's male readers, whose fantasies regarding her oscillate between idealisation and degradation.[18] At one moment identified with the venality of 'Cytherea' (Venus), of Cleopatra and common 'tomboys' (whores), she is invested with the purer connotations of a 'heavenly angel' or 'goddess Diana' the next. In Iachimo's rapt vision, the 'mole cinque-spotted, like the crimson drops / I'th' bottom of a cowslip' (II, ii, 38–9) takes on eucharistic associations consistent with the web of religious allusion generated around her iconic form in the bedroom scene. Yet, in that his description of the mole also graphically evokes the female genitalia, it leaves room for Posthumus' reinterpretation of this bodily 'stain' as betokening a moral 'stain as big as hell can hold' (II, iv, 138–41). On another level, such verbal indeterminacy would appear to be a by-product of the laws of metonymic displacement governing the expression of these same masculine fantasies, or to put it rather differently, the play's dream logic. For, ironically, in revealing the pressure of unconscious desires, this process of displacement brings about a dispersal of meaning, a 'veering off of signification' that undoes any attempt to pin down Innogen's identity.[19] Thus, as I noted above, her 'honour' becomes linked with a succession of signifiers, attaching itself in turn to each of the 'moveables' within her chamber in addition to the mole and bracelet (that errant token whose loss makes Innogen fear lest it has 'gone to tell my lord / That I kiss aught but he' (II, iii, 144–5)), all

18. This conflicted perception of the heroine, and the ideology of sexual dualism it expresses, is of course nothing new in Shakespeare; parallels abound in, e.g., *Much Ado*, *Hamlet*, *Othello* and *The Winter's Tale*. Although Schwartz apportions the sublimation of sexuality to Iachimo and its defilement to Cloten, acting out different aspects of Posthumus' psyche ('Between fantasy and imagination', p. 231), in fact all three vacillate between these opposing impulses.

19. Lacan, 'The insistence of the letter', p. 92. I have found Lacan's linguistic reformulation of Freudian dream-analysis, according to which unconscious activity takes the form of a 'play of signification' organised by the figures of metaphor (condensation) and metonymy (displacement), especially helpful when trying to account for the diffused eroticism of II, ii, and II, iv.

of which serve, cumulatively, to incriminate her in Posthumus' eyes. In short, the slipperiness of this female text mocks the clumsy efforts of the male characters to master or appropriate it. And, in this respect, it seems calculated to reinforce our already awakened misgivings concerning the validity of reading as an exercise.

As is so often the case with Shakespeare, a change of topographical location brings a change of outlook. Innogen's journey from Lud's Town to Milford Haven, and Posthumus' return from Rome to Britain, in particular, prompt a rethinking of their former interpretation of events, but their new readings are no more securely grounded than their old. In her unfamiliar Welsh surroundings, Innogen is confronted by Pisanio with Posthumus' letter instructing her murder. Previously, she expressed a naive faith in her ability to decipher her husband's character from his 'characters' (III, ii, 27–9). But now the contents of his letter force a radical revision of that assumption, and lead her symbolically to discard her stash of letters from him – including presumably the bogus or 'feigned letter' that lured her to Milford Haven in the first place – as so much 'heresy':

> What is here?
> *She takes letters from her bosom.*
> The scriptures of the loyal Leonatus,
> All turned to heresy? Away, away,
> Corrupters of my faith, you shall no more
> Be stomachers to my heart. Thus may poor fools
> Believe false teachers. (III, iv, 80–5)

This discovery is not the prelude to some new enlightened state, however. For Innogen, by far the most clear-sighted character in the play, will soon be driven by the logic of Shakespeare's plot to commit the most embarrassing, the most humiliating of misreadings, when, in IV, ii, awakening from her drugged sleep beside the headless corpse of Cloten, she mistakes it for that of her husband and proceeds, on the basis of this fallacious inference, to accuse Pisanio wrongly of complicity in his death. Ironically, only her conclusion that 'To write and read / Be henceforth treacherous!' (IV, ii, 317–18) is sound. Given the duplicitous nature of all texts in the play, and the dangerous – indeed, potentially fatal – misconstructions they elicit, such scepticism would seem the only sensible position to adopt.

Posthumus similarly extricates himself from one misreading only to fall into others. Despite its new-found generosity of spirit, the moving outpouring of forgiveness towards Innogen which reintroduces him to us at the beginning of Act IV, after a long absence from the stage, is still based on the false premise of her guilt. Another interesting gloss on Innogen's predicament as a reader is supplied by Belarius and the princes. As a one-time favourite of Cymbeline, whose fair reputation or 'honour' (in the military sense) was impugned on the basis of a false report that he had treacherously consorted with the Romans, Belarius' case history closely parallels Innogen's. He tries to make the best of his exiled state by co-opting his uncouth surroundings for the homespun education he imposes on Guiderius and Arviragus. Thus he lectures his adopted sons on the importance of viewing things from the correct perspective so that their true value may be discerned, for 'To apprehend thus / Draws us a profit from all things we see' (III, iii, 10–21, 17–18). So too, he lets slip no opportunity to 'read' lessons out of the landscape, as well as out of his own 'corporal sign[s]', the scars imprinted on his body by Roman swords (III, iii, 55–64): traditional moral lessons regarding the corrupt ways of the court and the comparative wholesomeness of their rugged pastoral existence. Such expository dogmatism clearly provides Belarius with a necessary form of security, acts as a psychological refuge from an unpredictable world on a par with their mountain cave. But his sermonising does not go down at all well with the young princes. Having to depend on their tutor's (possibly biased) reporting for their whole understanding of life is, in their eyes, no substitute for direct experience, and they reject Belarius' suggestion that wisdom can be gleaned from this form of annotated or guided reading. On the contrary, they see themselves as locked in a 'cell of ignorance', which they can only break out of by exposing themselves to the vicissitudes of historical process – with all the epistemological hazards that involves. Again, we are more likely to find ourselves agreeing with the princes' pessimistic account of their state of knowledge than with Belarius' complacency regarding his competence as a reader, since the former, unlike the latter, is repeatedly borne out by events.[20] As the plot grows ever more tortuous and unexpected in its changes of direction, the characters are increasingly forced to confess their bewilderment. All are 'perplexed / Beyond self-explication' (III, iv, 7–8), or, like Innogen, trapped in a blinding fog they 'cannot look through' (III, ii, 78–80; cf. IV, iii, 36–46; V, iii, 239–44).

20. One need only consider the tissue of fallacies from which the princes' lives are constructed: they have no knowledge of their royal birth, of the true identity of Belarius or of the reasons for their being in Wales. In III, vii, they fail to recognise Innogen as a girl, let alone their sister, and will later wrongly assume her to be dead.

The 'extraordinary blindness' inflicted on every one of the characters without exception, and the growing sense of helplessness this breeds, raises important questions about what purpose, if any, interpretation serves in this play.[21] Why is the hermeneutic process foregrounded in this way when its outcome – in terms of moral profit or any other quantifiable benefit – is so disappointing compared to the amount of energy invested in it? In one sense, as we have seen, reading is figured as a powerfully instrumental activity with the capacity to remake or destroy whole lives. 'What shall I need to draw my sword? The paper / Hath cut her throat already' (III, iv, 32–3), asks Pisanio, observing the devastating effects of slander on Innogen. Yet, in other ways, reading conspicuously fails to conform here to any of the accepted criteria or ends associated with this activity in the period. It does not provide an effective vehicle for moral instruction or spiritual enlightenment, as the absurdity of Belarius' didactic ambitions illustrates. Nor does it result in any signifi-cant course of action, or (for that matter) produce a meaningful affective impact – strong emotions are aroused, but for the most part confused and misdirected.[22] The sole use which the characters' misconstructions appear to have is to interrogate their pretensions to human agency and knowledge.[23] In undermining their attempts to comprehend or exercise real influence over the direction of their lives, these misreadings raise the further issue of moral responsibility. When confronted, in V, iv, with evidence of the Queen's evil machinations against him and his family, Cymbeline reasons that he cannot be blamed for taking her at face value; it would, he says, have been 'vicious / To have mistrusted her' (IV, iv, 65–6), for 'Who i'st can read a woman?' (V, iv, 48). As self-exculpation goes, this may strike us as pretty feeble, but is it in the circumstances? Cymbeline has been regularly lambasted by critics for failing to learn anything much from his mistakes (in contrast to the other erring fathers of the last plays, notably Leontes and Prospero), yet the possibility of this generic outcome is invoked here, only to be dismissed. Victoria Kahn has argued that the primary purpose of reading, according to Renaissance theorists, was to educate the reader's practical judgement in

21. Frye, *A Natural Perspective*, p. 67.
22. On the various agendas associated with reading in the Renaissance period, see especially Grafton and Jardine, '"Studied for action"', and Jardine, 'Reading and the technology of textual affect'.
23. This can partly be explained as a convention of romance, which tends to downplay individual agency in favour of larger, supra-human forces, normally inaccessible to human consciousness. But in *Cymbeline* this motif is taken to almost parodic lengths.

ways that could be transferred productively to the sphere of political action.[24] But while the play's emphasis on individual judgement seems at first to confirm the relevance of this pedagogic model, implying that improved understanding, based in part on the acquisition of new reading skills, will offer some restitution for past wrongs and a bulwark against their recurrence, this possibility is largely negated by the collective failure of interpretation. In fact, the premature claims made – by Posthumus especially (I, iv, 44) – to 'mended judgement' are consistently ironised.

If the characters prove to be incapable of arriving at a valid interpretation of each other or events, perhaps Shakespeare's point is that this is not attainable by purely human means without the help of divine illumination. As has often been noted, it seems to be the play's policy to defer any real enlightenment until the complex denouement, when, following the spectacular descent of Jupiter, we (like the characters) finally get to see how the various plot strands fit together, outstanding errors and miscomprehensions are resolved, disguises shed and the true identity of individuals made known. As if to announce this new age of perspicacity, Guiderius is correctly identified by the 'sanguine star' (V, iv, 365) on his neck; the fantastic, ungovernable diffusion of meaning triggered by his sister's corresponding birthmark is replaced here by consensus. But while the fog lifts somewhat in the final scene, I would suggest that matters are clarified only at the most superficial level. For contrary to our generic expectations and to the assertions of many critics, the intervention of the deity and the series of 'recognitions' it precipitates do not lead to any transcendent insight or revelation – whether of the national destiny, the mystical essence of unity, or a new era of peace heralded by the imminent birth of Christ, to cite but a few of the anagogical readings critics have proposed. Or at least, they do not lead to any vision whose authority might be said to be beyond dispute. Given the play's interest in the problematics of reading, it is surely not fortuitous that the divine revelations bestowed on the characters in this scene are embodied in forms that expose them to the ambiguities of textual exegesis. Thus Jupiter's prophecy is transmitted in the shape of a riddlingly inscribed tablet laid on Posthumus' breast, creating yet another corporeal text whose 'senseless speaking' (V, iii, 241) both invites and defeats interpretation until the Roman soothsayer offers to explicate it. The soothsayer's own vision of the Roman eagle vanishing into the beams of the western sun is similarly opaque. It is initially glossed as an

24. Kahn, *Rhetoric, Prudence,* esp. Ch. 2.

omen of Roman victory (IV, ii, 347–53), but the soothsayer is forced to reconfigure it, in the light of subsequent events, as a sign that 'Th'imperial Caesar, should again unite / His favour with the radiant Cymbeline, / Which shines here in the west' (V, iv, 471–7). The teleological nature of this supposedly supernaturally inspired exposition puts us under strong pressure to accept its canonical status as the play's last will and testament. But, against this, it should be noted that prophecies are commonly represented as untrustworthy in the literature of the period, not so much vehicles of oracular truth as historical documents whose meaning can be infinitely wrested to suit the agenda of the moment.[25] In this context, the soothsayer's politically expedient decodings come across as no less flawed or provisional than the readings that precede them.

By way of conclusion, I wish to return briefly to the possible metacritical implications of the play's ongoing critique of interpretation outlined at the beginning of this chapter. One alternative line of approach open to us would be to argue that the security of comprehension denied to the characters is ultimately made available to the player's audience or readers: that it is *our* interpretative abilities that are being tested, *our* judgement that is being educated. But the play's dismantling of the reading process seems designed as much to challenge overconfidence in our own analytic powers as to undermine the smugness of its fictive readers. While it is unquestionably the case that we are put in possession of more knowledge than the latter, in many ways we are subjected to a similar ordeal: forced to engage with the play's ever-expanding frame of reference, its disconcerting shifts of location and time-frame, and its figurative iteration that appears to lead nowhere in particular – all of which disrupt our critical assumptions and resist our attempts to pattern them. As the critical history of *Cymbeline* demonstrates, there is a very strong temptation to escape this disorienting experience by attempting to nail down the text in the same logocentric fashion as a Posthumus or a Belarius, to rush to identify the key to its meaning in a way that forecloses on the laborious and always inconclusive process of interpretation. To do so, however, we must discount the play's many insoluble enigmas, the refusal of its embedded texts to submit to any univocal or definitive reading. But when due account is taken of these factors, we are still left with a question: is the play's ironic emphasis on its own unreadability anything more than a clever device to perplex and tease

25. See, e.g., Campbell, ed., *The Mirror for Magistrates*, pp. 127–8, 227–9, and Francis Bacon, 'Of prophecies' in *Essayes*.

us? If there is a larger purpose at work here, I suggest it is neither to obstruct nor to make fun of our compulsion to formulate readings, but rather to invite critical scrutiny of the motives which sustain them, while intimating that we overlook their provisionality and fallibility at our peril.[26]

26. It may be objected that since reading does not take place in a historical vacuum, it is never as open-ended as I imply, and that in practice such factors as the political context or the playing space in which the play was staged would have set certain limits to interpretation. But my aim has been to show not that the play's meaning is indeterminate, but that the play reflects on the conditions governing interpretative practice and its attendant risks. In so doing, it highlights the ways in which the production of meaning may be constrained by psychological or political imperatives, as well as the partiality and provisionality of the readings produced.

PART IV
ENDINGS AND BEGINNINGS

11

UNSEASONABLE LAUGHTER:
THE CONTEXT OF *CARDENIO*

Richard Wilson

Escorted by one hundred and forty 'poor men in gowns' who filed behind 'the chief mourner, Prince Charles', the coffin emerged from St James's Palace at ten in the morning to 'a fearful outcry among the people', and was wheeled to Westminster Abbey on a spectacular hearse flanked by six horses amidst an 'ocean of tears'. But though the cortège took four hours to assemble, and was a mile long, with two thousand mourners in black, what struck onlookers was the 'universal silence' that descended on the crowd, whose 'utter desolation' was 'as if they felt they own ruin in that loss'. 'I must confess never to have seen such a sight of mortification', recorded one official, 'nor never so just a sorrow so well expressed as in all the spectators whose streaming eyes made known how inwardly their hearts did bleed'. The funeral of James VI and I's eldest son, Henry, Prince of Wales, on 7 December 1612, was the occasion of an unprecedented display of grief on the streets of London, and was followed by a deluge of printed souvenirs perpetuating the misery of 'Great Britain's mourning garment'; 'Tears shed by his country for His Highness' dear loss'; 'England's sorrow for the death of this most virtuous and peerless Prince'; 'Great Britain all in Black for its incomparable loss'; 'The Muses Tears for the Loss of Hope ... Together with Time's Sobs'; and even 'His Three Sisters' Tears shed at the Funeral of Henry, Prince of Wales'. Campion, Chapman, Donne, Drummond, Heywood, Taylor, Tourneur, Webster and Wither all contributed to the myth that 'there were few', in the words of the funeral sermon, 'who mourned not bitterly and shed abundant tears'. But in fact one refusal to grieve in public provoked such resentment that 'the cry of "Poison!" was raised'. The king, who 'loathed the sight of mourning', remained at Kensington, where his chief concern was said to be that 'the wind blew through the walls' so much 'he could not lie warm in his bed.'[1]

While thousands queued at the Abbey to pay respects to a macabre waxwork of the prince, 'decked with robes, collar, crown and golden rod, as he went when he was alive', which was to lie in state inside the hearse until the end of year, courtiers who had expected a 'black Christmas' were caught by surprise. Though Queen Anne was said to have 'wept alone in her room', and publicists put it about that James repeatedly 'burst out crying, "Henry is dead"', the king's instant reaction was that his daughter Elizabeth's wedding to Prince Frederick of the Rhine must proceed as planned. Court mourning should have prevented the ceremony until June, but the date was confirmed as 14 February, St Valentine's Day; and in the meantime, John Chamberlain reported, 'they are very busy preparing plays and exercises', so that 'our Christmas can come to an end without the least show of any alteration in Court or town'. So, 'Christmas was kept as usual at Whitehall', and the climax of the forced festivities went ahead on 27 December, with a formal betrothal in the Banqueting House, '[i]n the presence of the King sitting in state'. There the dark side of this 'strangest winter that was ever seen' was symbolised by the groom's black velvet cloak, while 'to make an even mixture of joy and mourning', the bride trailed twenty yards of black satin behind a plume of white feathers. The couple had earlier prayed before the effigy of the dead prince, but now their tension found embarrassing release, when the Secretary of State read the service in such comic French that the two sixteen-year-olds collapsed into fits of 'unseasonable laughter', followed by many of the court. That night the king was also 'noticed to be extremely cheerful', as he enjoyed one of the 'fourteen several plays' performed at Whitehall by the King's Men in these weeks when Prince Henry's hearse stood beside his grave in the silence of the church.[2]

Throughout the Christmas celebrations of 1612 the catafalque of the Prince of Wales remained at Westminster alongside the sumptuous new

---

1. Isaac Wake to Lady Dudley Carleton, 19 December 1612, PRO, SP14/71, fol. 128; quoted in Strong, *Henry, Prince of Wales* , p. 7; Nichols, *The Progresses*, vol. II, pp. 502, 504–7.
2. Nichols, *The Progresses*, vol. II, pp. 503, 513–14; Strong, *Henry, Prince of Wales*, p. 220; Oman, *Elizabeth of Bohemia*, pp. 66–7.

tomb of his grandmother, Mary Queen of Scots, in which her body had been reinterred only a month before: '[t]he Tapers placed in the Cathedral smoking like an Offertory'. To David Bergeron, this mortuary chapel, where smoke formed 'a smouldering sacrifice for James's conscience', seems a perfect setting of a Shakespearean late play. For 'the royal family resembled a paradigm of tragicomedy' during this winter when '[t]wo great hopes were lost: one by death, the other by a marriage which separated parents from child'. Likewise, the motive for persisting with the entertainments, he infers, was 'the desire to transmute the tragedy of Henry's death into a romantic comedy, to create a fiction to displace difficult reality'. At this 'turning point for the Stuarts', when 'uncertainty clouded the kingdom', the tragicomic form answered the need expressed also in Donne's Epithalamium for Elizabeth, to heal the rift left by the disaster.[3] Alvin Kernan agrees with this analysis, and proposes *Much Ado About Nothing*, 'with its war between the sexes and multiple marriages', as 'the most obvious' choice of all the works staged between the funeral and the wedding.[4] No commentator has considered the topicality of the only play attributed to the leading playwrights, Shakespeare and Fletcher, specifically commissioned for the King's Men to present that fatal Christmas, and which might even have been a new variation of the old Elizabethan comedy to fit the tragic Jacobean circumstances. Yet from what we know about it, it was *Cardenio* which seems more than any other play listed in the season's repertoire to have straddled the mixed emotions of festivities concluded almost literally over a prince's dead body.

Though confidently dated to the second half of 1612, as the first of three known Shakespearean collaborations with Fletcher, no attempt has been made to contextualise *Cardenio* in relation to its sensational Jacobean occasion. The reason is that a historicist reading of this 'lost' tragicomedy has been obstructed by the debate over its text, which survives only in the transcription published by Lewis Theobald in 1728, as revised and adapted from a work 'Written originally by W. Shakespeare', under the perilous title of *Double Falshood: or, The Distrest Lovers*. The legend of how Theobald acquired no fewer than *three* manuscripts of the play, the best in the hand of a Restoration prompter, John Downes; who inherited it from the actor Thomas Betterton; who received it from an illegitimate daughter of Shakespeare; and of how this

---

3. Bergeron, *Shakespeare's Romances*, p. 160; Bergeron, *Royal Family, Royal Lovers*, pp. 74, 114–16.
4. Kernan, *Shakespeare, the King's Playwright*, p. 156.

copy was 'treasured up' in the library of the Covent Garden Theatre that burned down in 1808, has always seemed fanciful; but recent criticism has swung decisively towards Stephen Kukowski's verdict that 'the evidence makes it clear that the play cannot be a forgery'; that '[i]f not a forgery, then the case for it being a relic of *Cardenio* is very strong', and that 'from the various stages of revision ... Theobald did manage to salvage a few scraps of a Shakespearean original'. As Jonathan Bate likewise affirms, in *Double Falshood* 'one hears a faint cry of a play by Shakespeare and Fletcher trapped below layers of rewriting'. That stifled cry suggests the presence of at least the story-line of the 'lost' late play; but whatever value is attached to its language and style, it is ironically because so much of it sounds like Fletcher that readers are now increasingly convinced that some of the surviving text can be attributed to Shakespeare:

> It has verbal similarities to a number of Shakespearean plays ... which were frequently staged in Theobald's time. This suggests that it could be a good imitation. But then most of acts four and five are in a style highly reminiscent of the tragicomic romances pioneered by Fletcher ... If Theobald was fabricating a Shakespeare play, why on earth did he write the second half in the style of Fletcher?[5]

Double Falshood is full of Shakespearean and Fletcherian echoes that have led critics, Clifford Leech states, to near-unanimity that 'Theobald made use of a Jacobean original' which 'owed something to *All's Well That Ends Well*, *The Winter's Tale* and *Cymbeline*'. But the real justification for the leap of faith in Theobald's text is that this has slowly come to appear more plausible than even he could have hoped in the light of facts of which he was oblivious. Crucially, his firm denial of Fletcher's involvement was made at a time when '*nobody knew Shakespeare collaborated*', for, as Bate points out, had he been aware of joint-authorship of *Henry VIII* and *The Two Noble Kinsmen*, 'he would have been able to argue that marks of Fletcher's hand are proof of authenticity'.[6] Nor did he know that in 1653 the Stationers' Register had entered '*a history of Cardenio* by Mr Fletcher and Mr Shakespeare'; and that in 1613 the King's Men had been paid for twice performing their *Cardenna* or

---

5. Kukowski, 'The hand of John Fletcher', pp. 81–9, esp. 89; Bate, *The Genius of Shakespeare*, pp. 78–8 1. See also Metz, *Sources of Four Plays*, pp. 259–83; Muir, *Shakespeare as Collaborator*, pp. 148–60; Proudfoot, '*Henry VIII*', p. 293; Freehafer, '*Cardenio*', pp. 501–13.

6. Leech, *The John Fletcher Plays*, pp. 150–3; Bate, *The Genius of Shakespeare*, p. 79.

Cardenio, a drama presumably based on the tale of Cardenio in *Don Quixote*. Moreover, Theobald made nothing of this source, which he correctly connected with Thomas Shelton's 1612 version, the first English translation of Cervantes. Yet, as John Freehafer has noted, some of the Shakespearean echoes in the published work are, in fact, so closely related to Shelton, and 'so out of place in *Double Falshood*, that they can scarcely be anything but relics of a Jacobean play'.[7] The sheer accumulation of evidence is such, then, that Bate summarises a current consensus when he recommends the existing text for qualified admission to the canon:

> The probability of Theobald having fabricated a Shakespeare play, unintentionally written half of it in the style of Fletcher, and used for its source the very book which Shakespeare and Fletcher used for a play of whose existence he was ignorant, is infinitesimal. The inference has to be that Theobald's play is indeed a version of *Cardenio*, which Shakespeare and Fletcher must have written while Thomas Shelton's translation was new and popular.[8]

Like *Much Ado*, which was also twice acted at Christmas in 1612, the story of Cardenio is a variant of the 'broken nuptial' genre described by Carol Neely as designed to incite both male fantasy and female sympathy, by first giving women 'power to resist or alter courtship', and then taking it away when they resume the dance into marriage.[9] Such a plot might have seemed apt for a betrothal that resulted from the rejection of a parade of rival suitors, and that placed the Princess Royal in the liminality of one who walked ahead of all these men, but only until she married. As David Lindley says, '[i]t is unimaginable that Elizabeth would have rejected Frederick';[10] yet what is extraordinary about *Cardenio* as a wedding entertainment is that its happy ending depends not on the heroine's submission to filial duty, but on her unswerving resistance to an arranged alliance. In this play the action turns on Leonora's resolve to 'disappoint these nuptials', and 'fall a bleeding sacrifice' by stabbing herself at the altar, rather than acquiescing in the match with Prince Henriquez into which she is coerced by her father. This is also the point of the most important divergence from *Don Quixote*, where, just when she is expected to 'take out the poniard to stab herself', the bride answers the priest 'with a dismayed and languishing

7. Freehafer, 'Cardenio', p. 507.
8. Bate, *The Genius of Shakespeare*, p. 80.
9. Neely, *Broken Nuptials*, p. 53.
10. Lindley, *The Trials of Frances Howard*, p. 39.

voice, "I will'". For in the tragicomedy Leonora not only arms herself, but arranges for her lover, Julio, to hide behind the arras from which he leaps between bride and groom before they exchange vows. Just how exceptional this violent interruption is in Shakespeare Anne Jennalie Cook shows, by reminding us that though the plays 'provide few women whose marriages do not require the approval of some masculine figure', only Juliet and Capulet fail to reach the 'multilateral consent' that was the social norm.[11] And as Leonora protests to her father, his own marriage provides the model of such a conventional romantic solution:

> I conjure you,
> By all the tender Interests of Nature,
> By the chaste Love 'twixt you and my dear Mother,
> (O holy Heav'n, that she were living now!)
> Forgive and pity me. – Oh, Sir, remember,
> I've heard my Mother say a thousand Times,
> Her Father would have forced her Virgin Choice;
> But when the Conflict was 'twixt Love and Duty,
> Which should be first obey'd, my Mother quickly
> Paid up her Vows to Love, and married You.
> You thought this well, and she was praised for This;
> For this her Name was honour'd, Disobedience
> Was ne'er imputed to her, her firm Love
> Conquer'd whate'er oppos'd it, and she prosper'd
> Long Time your Wife. My Case is now the same;
> You are the Father which You then condemn'd;
> I, what my Mother was; but not so happy. (II, iii; p. 19)

Don Bernard's reply, that 'You have old Stories enough to undo you … Go, go your ways, and … get ready within these Two days to be married to a Husband you don't deserve … or, by my dead Father's Soul, you are no Acquaintance of mine' (II, iii; p. 20) affiliates him with Capulet as the most mercenary of Shakespearean fathers. And his aside that 'The Girl says right; her Mother … chose me purely to spight that surly Old Blockhead my Father-in-Law' (II, iii; p. 21) reveals why he thinks his daughter needs no 'Precedent' (II, iii; p. 20) in Elizabethan stories. For, as Leonora complains, in her mother's day 'the Choice were not so hard' (II, iii; p. 20) but the marriage market has since drastically curtailed the freedom of daughters: 'Int'rest, that rules the World, has

---

11. Cook, *Making a Match*, pp. 89–9 1. See also Ingram, *Church Courts, Sex and Marriage*, p. 136.

made at last / A Merchandize of Hearts: and Virgins now / Chuse as they're bid, and wed without Esteem' (II, iii; p. 20). This is an exchange, then, which confirms Lindley's claim that if the arranged match is a problem for modern audiences, '[i]t was problematic also in the seventeenth century', and that situates the play within the 'deeply embedded contradictions' of a moment when '[e]ven the King "fell to inveighing against the marriage of young couples before they became acquainted"'. By caricaturing patriarchy, *Cardenio* seems, in fact, to be aligned with George Wilkins' 1607 play *The Miseries of Enforced Marriage*, which, as Lindley points out, is an otherwise extreme exposé of 'the rights of parents to overrule children's affections'.[12] But in that play, as in *All's Well*, the victim of the arranged match is a bridegroom, and the question posed by *Cardenio* is how this drama of a reluctant bride could have been thought appropriate to the wedding of a Stuart princess. The answer may lie in the sponsorship of its sources, which Shelton dedicated to Theophilus, Lord Howard de Walden, the son of Thomas Howard, Earl of Suffolk and Lord Chamberlain.

In the spring of 1612, when Shelton's publisher, Edward Blount, presented a copy of the translation to their 'very good lord, the Lord of Walden', in the hope that he would 'lend it a favourable countenance, to animate the parent thereof to produce some worthier subject',[13] the Howard family was on the eve of its zenith. The Lord Treasurer, Lord Salisbury, died on 24 May, and until his own death in 1614, the serpentine Henry Howard, Earl of Northampton, would dominate the Privy Council. An English version of *Don Quixote*, published by a stationer who specialised in Continental best-sellers and himself translated works of Spanish *realpolitik*, slotted neatly into the pro-Spanish and crypto-Catholic culture of the Howard faction. Both Northampton, code-named El Cid, and his nephew Suffolk received yearly pensions from Madrid, and, as Linda Levy Peck details, patronised counter-Reformation art as well as Catholic charities.[14] The Castilian aesthetic of these grandees may thus explain why the new work performed for their first Christmas in power was the sole Shakespearean drama set in Spain, and one of the few Jacobean plays with sympathetic Spanish characters. So might the support they earlier gave for a match between Elizabeth and King Philip. But if the Howards did read *Don Quixote*, it was more probably their own domestic concerns that led to the earmarking of the

12. Lindley, *The Trials of Frances Howard*, p. 41.
13. Cervantes, *The History of Don Quixote*, pp. 3–4.
14. Peck, 'The mentality of a Jacobean grandee', pp. 148–68; Peck, *Northampton*, pp. 70–2.

story of the unwilling bride and her secret lover, and that ensured that in the staged adaptation the marriage vows were never spoken. For it would have been impossible for the Whitehall audience of *Cardenio* not to recognise in this torrid melodrama the case of Frances Howard, sister of Theophilus, whose arranged marriage to the Earl of Essex and intrigue with the royal favourite, Robert Carr, Viscount Rochester, were about to feature in the most lurid of all Jacobean scandals. Indeed, Frances's lawyers were already drafting grounds for annulment when the court heard Leonora rehearse her plea for the priority of lovers' oaths over legal enforcement:

> How may I be obedient, and wise too?
> Of my Obedience, Sir, I cannot strip me;
> Nor can I then be wise: Grace against Grace!
> Ungracious, if I not obey a Father;
> Most perj'ur'd, if I do. – Yet, Lord, consider,
> Or e'er too late, or e'er that Knot be ty'd,
> Which may with Violence damnable be broken,
> No other way dissever'd: Yet consider,
> You wed my Body, not my Heart, my Lord;
> No Part of my Affection. Sounds it well,
> That *Julio's* Love is Lord *Henriquez'* Wife;
> Have you an Ear for this harsh sound? (III, ii; p. 30)

'This comes of forcing Women where they hate' (III, iii; p. 35) Don Bernard admits, when the wedding he has engineered explodes; 'It was my own Sin; and I am rewarded' (III, iii; p.35). If Frances Howard's father did sponsor *Cardenio*, then this change of heart would seem to reflect what Lindley sees as 'signs of guilt among those who surrounded her for having married her off so young', and the volte-face her father and great-uncle managed during these months when the deaths of Salisbury and Henry, and her liaison with Carr, offered such a 'tremendous opportunity' to her clan. The play thus tends to confirm Lindley's thesis, in *The Trials of Frances Howard*, that, contrary to rumour, the affair took the Howards by surprise, and that divorce proceedings opened while they still despised the upstart Carr. Certainly, Leonora's courage reinforces Lindley's image of Frances as 'braver and more heroic' than her critics allowed,[15] while her characterisation as without 'Fervour … / Which Youth and Love kindle' seems designed to protect the real lovers from

---

15. Lindley, *The Trials of Frances Howard*, p. 85. Lindley supersedes Beatrice White, *Cast of Ravens*.

slander. In this romance the heroine is one whose 'Affection / Is such ... as will break untouch'd; / Dye frosty, e'er it can be thaw'd' (I, ii; p. 5), and her suitor an innocent bemused to be the centre of attention. In fact, it is with Julio's vacuousness that the text nods most towards the gossips. For when his father demands to know 'How comes the Duke to take such Notice of my Son?' (I, ii; p. 3) the youth answers that it is through being 'commended for my Seat, or mock'd' (I, ii; p. 4): a risqué joke about an episode when Carr first attracted James by falling off his horse. So, like Carr, the Cardenio-character here must solve a problem unmentioned in Cervantes, though crucial at the Stuart court: 'Which is better, to serve a Mistress, or a Duke?' (I, ii; p. 4). One function of this play is clearly to reconcile the choice:

> Duke, I obey thy summons, be its Tenour
> Whate'er it will: If War, I come thy Souldier:
> Or if to waste my silken Hours at Court,
> The Slave of Fashion, I with willing Soul
> Embrace the lazy Banishment for Life ...
> Tomorrow, Love; so runs the Duke's command;
> Stinting our Farewell-kisses, cutting off
> The Forms of Parting, and the Interchange
> Of thousand precious Vows, with Haste too rude.
>
> (I, ii; pp. 6–7)

In *Shakespeare's Romances and the Royal Family*, Bergeron has argued that 'events in the life of the Stuarts helped to shape the action of these plays' by prompting radical revision of sources.[16] If so, it is significant that while in *Don Quixote* Henriquez ensures his plan to marry Leonora remains 'unknown to his father' by keeping Cardenio 'out of his presence',[17] the first change made in the play is to put Julio in the pay of Duke Angelo as 'An honest spy' on the Prince (I, i; p. 3). The effect is not only to place the lovers under an omniscient benefactor, but to establish the monarch in opposition to his son. Critics have questioned the relevance of this familiar Shakespearean situation, which, as Freehafer observes, is '[i]ntroduced with evident loss of context and is scarcely referred to again';[18] yet nothing ties *Cardenio* more to its historical moment than the suspicion with which the Duke views Henriquez' activities, beginning with his scheme to take youths such as Julio 'riding

16. Bergeron, *Shakespeare's Romances*, p. 160.
17. Metz, *Sources of Four Plays*, p. 314.
18. Freehafer, 'Cardenio', p. 505.

in *France'* (I, ii; p. 3). For since Julio, like Carr, 'can no more but gallop a Hackney' (I, ii; p. 3) before crossing the Channel, this French interlude, which has no parallel in Cervantes, seems a transparent satire on the chivalric pretensions of the actual heir. As Roy Strong relates, Henry's ambitions were focused on a monumental riding school, built at St James's in 1609 to 'train youths of the Prince's circle in the new art' of dressage. Its master, St Antoine, had been trainer to Henry IV; and sure enough, *Cardenio* opens with Henriquez in Paris, 'buying coursers' and raising cavalry with the Duke's gold. It was 'because they did not desire to exalt him too high', the Venetian envoy relayed, that Henry was forbidden to ride in state;[19] but Theobald can hardly have been aware of this contentiousness when he published a text that begins with a prince pursuing the same mania, and his father voicing identical fears to a favourite son about his secret agenda:

> worthy the Man,
> Who, with my Dukedoms, heirs my better Glories …
> Like a fair Glass of Retrospection, Thou
> Reflect'st the Virtues of my early Youth;
> Making my old Blood mend its Pace with Transport:
> While fond *Henriquez*, thy irregular Brother,
> Sets the large Credit of his Name at Stake,
> A Truant to my Wishes, and his Birth.
> His Taints of Wildness hurt our nicer Honour,
> And call for swift Reclaim …
> But I, by Fears weighing his unweigh'd Course,
> Interpret for the Future from the Past,
> And strange Misgivings, why he hath of late;
> By Importunity, and strain'd Petition,
> Wrested our Leave of Absence from the Court,
> Awake Suspicion. (I, i; pp. 1–2)

It is the French locale of Henriquez' Hal-like truancy that cements this play into a Jacobean context. For according to biographers, it was Henry's hero-worship of his French namesake, who cultivated him and his circle, which most infuriated his father. And if *Cardenio* did open with a ruler spying on his son, to discover whether he 'Will, by the Vantage of his cooler Wisdom, / E'er-while redeem the hot Escapes of Youth' (I, i; p. 2), its scenario could hardly come closer to English politics in 1612, when the Prince was 'cut off from communication with the

---

19. Strong, *Henry, Prince of Wales*, pp. 63–5.

King; St James's Palace became an "opposition" to Whitehall; and Henry found himself in total isolation from the government'. In particular, Angelo's favouritism towards his preferred son, Roderick, echoes reports that James was not 'pleased to see the Prince so beloved of the people', and was 'growing Jealous' enough to warn that 'if he did not attend more earnestly' to orders, 'the crown would be left to his brother'. So, the 'unwonted strain' (I, i; p. 1) in this court parallels what Strong calls 'the cold war atmosphere' of a London where factions polarised around hopes pinned by the pro-French on Henry as Protestant champion, and by the pro-Spanish on Carr as a Catholic sympathiser. And it is the antagonism between these camps which seems to fuel the emnity between Julio and the Henriquez. So violent was Henry's loathing of his father's favourite that when one of his guards 'offered to kill him, the Prince [said], if there were cause, he would do it'; adding that 'if ever he were King, he would not leave one of that family [the Howards] to piss against the wall'. No wonder, then, that in this Spanish comedy a Francophile prince is so demonised, for by late-1612 the real Henry was lined up not only with his old playmate, the jilted Essex, but with Carr's own ex-boyfriend, Sir Thomas Overbury, in a 'deadly quarrel' with the lovers.[20] And it was, perhaps, this final personal betrayal that inflamed the grievance of the 'inj'ur'd Julio' (II, iii; p. 17):

> Is there a Treachery, like This in Baseness,
> Recorded any where? It is the deepest:
> None but Itself can be its Parallel:
> And from a Friend, profess'd! – Friendship? Why, 'tis
> A Word for ever maim'd; in human Nature
> It was a Thing the noblest; and 'mong Beasts,
> It stood not in mean Place: Things of fierce Nature
> Hold Amity and Concordance. – Such a Villany
> A Writer could not put down in his Scene,
> Without Taxation of his Auditory
> For Fiction most enormous. (III, i; pp. 25–6)

'No killing, *Julio*' (III, ii; p.28): Leonora's reversal of Hero's command to 'Kill Claudio' (*Much Ado*, IV, i, 288) reveals the collective anxiety about the murderous vortex which swirled around Frances Howard in these days when her family prepared to duel with the husband they reviled as 'My Lord the gelding'. 'If my Lord would draw sword in

20. Strong, *Henry, Prince of Wales*, pp. 14–15, 56–7; Lindley, *The Trials of Frances Howard*, p. 119.

defence of a good prick it were worth his pains ... but never such a poor pudding', Northampton taunted; and the gibe would seem to support those who see the homophobic violence of the case as a displacement of that 'fiction most enormous' which '[a] writer could not put down in his scene' without taxing his audience, but which *Cardenio* insinuates: namely, the homosexual relations of all the men, from Carr, Overbury and Northampton to Essex, Henry and, of course, the king.[21] It may be no coincidence, therefore, that the heroine of this play says she must think love 'a cordial' even 'When I see poison in't' (IV, i; p. 52), because within a year of its performance Overbury was to die of suspected poisoning by his former friend, and even the death of the prince was to be attributed to Carr. The king blocked the duel with Essex by imprisoning Frances' brother for 'daring to speak of drawing swords, especially at court, in favour of these foul things';[22] but the love that dared not speak in court all but does so in *Cardenio*, when the villain who seems a composite of Carr's accusers is accused of sodomy himself, on evidence of a love-letter to 'A young He-bawd' (V, ii; p. 60) he has 'bobb'd' (V, ii; p. 59). This 'minion' is, in reality, Henriquez' disguised mistress, Violante; but an astonishing scene that has no source (and cannot, surely, be by Theobald) comes close to flaunting what Carr must have preserved as his ultimate deterrent: the 'letter in his casket' compromising the King (V, ii; pp. 59–62).[23] At his trial, it was alleged that the fallen favourite had plotted to destroy the entire Stuart dynasty, and something of the danger he posed to his interrogators may indeed therefore be threatened when Julio bursts like some 'boisterous sworder' into the royal wedding:

> Ungen'rous Lord! The Circumstance of Things
> Should stop the Tongue of Question. – You have wrong'd me;
> Wrong'd me so basely, in so dear a Point,
> As stains the Cheek of Honour with a Blush;
> Cancells the Bonds of Service, bids Allegiance
> Throw to the Wind all high Respects of Birth,
> Title, and Eminence; and in their Stead,

---

21. Lindley, *The Trials of Frances Howard*, p. 125; McClung and Simard, 'Donne's Somerset Epithalamium', p. 95.
22. Somerset, *Unnatural Murder*, pp. 162–3, 354.
23. Somerset, *Unnatural Murder*, p. 61. The 'letter in Somerset's casket found by my Lord Coke' was never produced in court, 'but Sir Simonds d'Ewes maintained that James never forgave Coke for having uncovered such sensitive material, and that this was the reason for Coke's subsequent disgrace'.

Fills up the panting Heart with just Defiance.
If you have Sense of Shame, or Justice, Lord,
Forego this bad Intent; or with your Sword
Answer me like a Man, and I shall thank you. (III, ii; p. 31)

It is the incipient menace of *Cardenio*, with the hindsight of the Overbury affair, which suggests that the prime movers of the 1612 celebrations were those with least cause to mourn the prince: the Lord Chamberlain and the Howards. Some time in late summer, we might therefore speculate, the first three acts of this tragicomedy were sent from Shakespeare to be completed by Fletcher, for their urgency is signalled with a drumming providentialism typical of the late plays. Leonora has fainted at the altar; Julio has fled the city 'raging mad' (III, iii; p. 35); Violante, discarded by Henriquez, has walked into the wilderness; and the fathers are left to 'bid the Bell knoll' for death: 'Now I am like an aged Oak, alone, / Left all for Tempests' (III, iii; p. 35). But in returning to the theme of 'maimed rites' the author of *Much Ado* has this time been certain to preserve the lovers' faith, and what may be his last lines are ringing cues for the revelations of Fletcherian romance: 'You've equal Losses; urge no farther Anger. / Heav'n, pleas'd now at your Love, may bring again, / And, no Doubt, will, your Children to your Comforts' (III, iii; p. 36). If *The Tempest* can be keyed to James's project, in the autumn of 1611, to orchestrate a religious peace by tying his son to a 'strange bedfellow' from Italy,[24] then the play that followed remains as hopeful of detente. Its Catholic Car/denio may 'sollicit ev'ry Saint in Heav'n / To lend me Vengeance' on Henri/quez (IV, i; p. 42), but Shakespeare's fathers shake hands and agree to let 'Quest for our lost Friends' make 'Brothers of Us, whom our cross Fates / Could never join. What I have been, forget; / What I intend to be, believe and nourish; ... Time may beget a Wonder' (III, iii; pp. 36–7). A final Shakespearean couplet strews advice on the future king and queen of Bohemia which seems, by implication, more appropriate to the future Lord and Lady Rochester:

> This is only Counsel: ...
> ... Let not Rewards, nor Hopes,
> Be cast into the Scale to turn thy Faith
> Be honest but for Virtue's sake, that's all;
> He, that has such a Treasure, cannot fall.
> (III, iii; p. 38)

24. See Wilson, 'Voyage to Tunis'.

Shakespeare's Spanish offering for a German wedding appears to set the scene not only for a policy of religious toleration, but also for a dissolution of the marriage that was the greatest obstacle to the ascendancy of his patrons. Pursuing their factional priorities, Nottingham and Suffolk had succeeded with this play, it seems, in diverting the nuptials of 'the *Phœnix* of the Earth, / The Bird of Paradise' (IV, i; p. 40), into something like a technical deposition for their own impending divorce case. Richard Dutton has documented their vigilance in censoring hostile dramatisations of both their family's sexual and religious practices;[25] and *Cardenio* suggests that they were as active in the commission of favourable propaganda. For by disrupting Henriquez' marriage plans, rather than holding his peace, the English Cardenio defends his lover from any possible taint of adultery. Frances Howard's annulment would hinge on her claims of just such a non-consummation; but in the theatre the heroine's virginity can be preserved only at the cost of depriving the hero of provocation for his defining madness. The absence of this indispensable motive is never filled, as Fletcher takes the story up once again where Cervantes started, with lovelorn lads and cross-dressed lasses surprising the shepherds in Arcadia. Now the collaborator's signature salacity is all that is needed to strip them of their rustic garb and restore them to their reunited parents. But Echo has barely sounded in the baroque mountain scenes when these pastorals are truly broken. Suddenly, the text confides, 'a vacant Herse pass'd by / From Rites but new perform'd' (IV, i; p. 46). Just as finishing touches were being put to the wedding programme by the officers of the Lord Chamberlain, the Prince of Wales had died.

Commentators on *Cardenio* are baffled by the incongruity of the funeral hearse which is announced in Act IV and carried on stage for the denouement. In Cervantes the villain had 'entered the Abbey' where the bride hid after 'he found the gates open', and abducted her by force;[26] but in the Jacobean version Henriquez and his brother hire the 'opportune' hearse and pretend to 'transport a Body / As 'twere to's Funeral: and coming late by, / Crave a Night's Leave to rest the Herse i'th'Convent' (IV, i; p. 46). The episode takes place offstage, but when Leonora appears she has been 'snatch'd … from that Seat of Contemplation,' (V, i; p. 51) and is told that for love Henriquez has steeled himself 'To feign a corpse' and sleep in the 'Herse one night within your hallow'd Walls' (V, i; p. 51). This mysterious catafalque has indeed brought

25. Dutton, *Mastering the Revels*, pp. 198–201.
26. Metz, *Sources for Four Plays*, p. 360.

a 'black Christmas' to the bride, who is now 'veil'd' and escorted by 'Attendants as mourners' (V, i; p. 51); but a night in the Abbey has also transformed the Prince, who is ready to beg for pardon. 'Do you bring Joy or Grief my lord?' (V, ii; p. 55), asks old Camillo, when Roderick leads on the wanderers, presumed dead, in a cortège that 'Follows a Herse with all due Rites of Mourning' (V, ii; p. 55). The question is soon answered, when they unveil themselves to their parents, but the 'even mixture of joy and mourning' persists, emphasised by the 'vacant hearse' that stands throughout the reconciliation. Critics have scoured Cervantes in vain for the origin of this tableau. To Kenneth Muir, its symbolism is not properly developed, and there seems little point in reintroducing the hearse for the finale, and Harold Metz conjectures that 'the hearse was an invention of one of the writers ... or perhaps a bit of folklore folded' into the action.[27] In fact, there is no feature of *Cardenio* that links the play more concretely to its occasion, for at Whitehall in 1612 the empty bier could only have reminded the audience of the opportunities that attended that other cenotaph in the Abbey:

> A great stately hearse, built quandrangle-wise with six pillars, showing three to the view on each side four square, canopy-like, rising small on the top, trimmed and set thick within with diverse scutcheons, small flags and pennants of His Highness' and several arms of the Union chained... with his motto, Fax *mentis honestae Gloria*, and that of the funeral hearse, *Jurat ire per altum*.[28]

'His glory... fitted him for heaven': if Theobald's text is faithful to *Cardenio*, then its emotions do seem to register the ambivalence of those who organised the funeral towards this 'flower of his country and admiration of the world'. In Strong's opinion, 'To the King, terrible as it may seem, the death of the Prince was to come as a relief',[29] and the tragicomedy catches this callousness in its last scenes, which, having first consigned Henriquez to a coffin, and then resurrected him to accusations that he has 'abused Men, Women, and Children' (V, ii; p. 60), crown his rivals with the Duke's approval: 'E'en as you are, we'll join your Hands together. / A Providence above our Pow'r rules all' (V, ii; p. 63). Critics liken this scapegoating to the disgrace of Bertram, but the cruelty is closer to the triumphalism with which, after Henry's death, Carr and his in-laws manoeuvred for Overbury's removal: first to Russia,

27. Metz, *Sources for Four Plays*, p. 2.
28. Nichols, *The Progresses*, vol. II, p. 501.
29. Strong, *Henry, Prince of Wales*, pp. 15, 225.

and when he evaded that posting, to the Tower. Sir Thomas had been confident that, knowing what he did, Carr 'would not dare to leave him' for 'that base woman'; but the disappearance of the prince left him isolated, and by June 1613 the Howards could relax that '[n]ot a man enquires after him, nor doth the Lord Carr miss him'. The prisoner could utter all the 'undecent and unmannerly speeches' he liked about his prosecutors, but they would not save him.[30] Likewise, in the play, the eclipse of Henriquez and his faction is hailed as a judicial *fait accompli*: 'When Lovers swear true Faith, the list'ning Angels / Stand on the golden Battlements of Heav'n / And waft their Vows to the Eternal Throne' (V, ii; p. 63). Thus, the panel of elders assembled in *Cardenio* anticipates the 1613 nullity commission, in ruling that 'Lovers have Things of Moment ... More than a Prince, or dreaming Statesman know: / Such Ceremonies wait on *Cupid*'s throne' (I, ii; p. 7). It was the triumph of this tragicomedy, it must have seemed, to raise loves like Carr's above the laws of 'a Prince, or dreaming Statesman'.

'Make thy fair Appeal / To the good Duke', *Cardenio* assures the court, 'and doubt not but thy tears / Shall be repaid with Interest from his Justice' (V, i; p. 54). If this play was a fanfare for Carr's alliance with the Howards, then that may explain its instant suppression, for this is a text that knows how much such 'gawdy Days' (III, ii; p. 27) depend upon the goodwill of an Angelo. It was one of the paradoxes of James's infatuations, however, that he was 'free from jealousy when his favourites acquired wives',[31] and Fletcher and Shakespeare optimistically reproduce this quirk with the Duke's generosity to Julio. Parents, he orates, are 'Heav'n's Lieutenants: / Made Fathers ... but to steer / The wanton Freight of Youth thro' Storms and Dangers' (V, ii; pp. 56–7); so at the close he speeds the divorcés on their travels, hoping the 'griev'd Lovers' in the audience, 'that your Story read, / Wish, true Love's Wand'rings may like yours succeed' (V, ii; p. 64). It is to be presumed that two, at least, of those 'griev'd lovers' took heart from this annulment. The late plays insistently remind us that 'A man may weep upon his wedding day' (*Henry VIII*, prologue, l. 32); and if Hermione's statue was added to *The Winter's Tale* in 1613, as Bergeron has argued, to signify a welcome end to the court's winter of mourning,[32] then it may be no surprise that in *Cardenio* an 'opportune' hearse was the centre of such 'unseasonable laughter'. Yet for all the dancing on the graves of their enemies, the

30. Somerset, *Unnatural Murder*, pp. 125–6, 130, 132.
31. Somerset, *Unnatural Murder*, p. 123.
32. Bergeron, *Shakespeare's Romances*, p. 160.

sponsors of 'This Bus'ness so discordant' (III, ii; p. 28) should also have been warned of their own nemesis. The premonition comes when the Duke first sets eyes on the page 'bobb'd' by Henriquez, and enthuses, 'What's thy Name Boy? ... A pretty Child. / Where wast thou born? ... What are thy Friends? / ... How camest thou hither? how, to leave thy Father?'. In the play, this Florio, born 'On t'other Side the Mountains', is a girl (V, ii; p. 59); but his living counterpart had no such disadvantage. Even as Carr enjoyed the fiction, the real Florio was being groomed for his appearance. He came from Leicestershire, his friends were Prince Henry's mourners, his family had been paid to dress him for the court, and his name was George Villiers.

12

TEARS AT THE WEDDING:
SHAKESPEARE'S LAST PHASE

Julia Briggs

Although the romances – *Pericles, Cymbeline, The Winter's Tale, The Tempest* – are commonly thought of as his last works, Shakespeare wrote or contributed to three further plays, performed, in all likelihood, during the winter of 1612/13 and the following summer, and it is these – the lost play of *Cardenio, Henry VIII* and *The Two Noble Kinsmen* – that actually constitute the final phase of the canon. If we make an imaginary reconstruction of *Cardenio*, drawing upon its origin in Shelton's translation of *Don Quixote* (1612) and Theobald's 1728 reworking of the play as *Double Falshood: or, The Distrest Lovers*,[1] these plays focus upon common themes of conflict and rivalry between friends, the blindness of love, betrayal, social division and tearful weddings (*Henry VIII* and *The Two Noble Kinsmen* both allude to weddings in their prologues), while their actions are played out in a bleak and confusing universe in evident contrast with those of the romances that precede them, actions governed by Prospero posing as Destiny, or by the pagan gods, Diana, Jupiter and Apollo, who perform the role of benevolent providence within them. By contrast, the 'last' late plays form a distinctive group that questions

---

1. Richard Wilson's chapter in this volume sets out the arguments for Theobald's play *Double Falshood* being derived from a lost original by Fletcher and Shakespeare, the plot of which was taken from the tale of Cardenio in the recently translated first part of Cervantes' *Don Quixote*.

and even mocks the optimistic assumptions of their predecessors, their words like those of Mercury, 'harsh after the songs of Apollo'. The comprehensive generosity of the romances culminating in 'Pardon's the word for all' or 'You precious winners all' gives place to a logic of exclusion, in which Anne Bullen can only triumph at Katherine's expense, Ferdinando at Cardenio's, Palamon at Arcite's; a world in which to win involves a kind of loss: 'For what we lack / We laugh, for what we have are sorry' (*The Two Noble Kinsmen* V, iv, 132–3).

In this distinctive development, the plenitude of alternatives, available in earlier Shakespearean comedy and the consciously artificial optimism of the romances, is finally withdrawn. The rival forms of Christianity established by the Reformation, the rival lovers of whom only one can be chosen in marriage, pose stark alternatives, but this time, there is no 'having your cake and eating it', such as the comedies had afforded, no happy endings in which lovers and friends are reconciled, or loved boys painlessly transformed into marriageable women. The exclusiveness of marriage now parallels that of religion: although more than one faith – or more than one lover – may be dreamed of and pursued, such alternatives cannot be easily reconciled or enjoyed. Typically, Shakespearean comedy recognised and celebrated the multiple aspirations of the imagination: incompatible desires were united in a single love object, or were magically metamorphosed, or both; the wronged or the dead were restored beyond all hope. The world of the final plays is altogether more stark: a single choice precludes alternatives and the mere act of choosing may itself become a torment. Emilia, defeated by her efforts to decide between the two kinsmen, painfully acknowledges the impossibility of choice:

> 'Alas, I know not!' ...
> What a mere child is Fancy,
> That, having two fair gauds of equal sweetness,
> Cannot distinguish, but must cry for both!
> (*The Two Noble Kinsmen*, IV, ii, 51–4)

The harshness and arbitrariness of choice is most vividly dramatised in *The Two Noble Kinsmen*, where it was picked up and mocked by Ben Jonson in his comedy *Bartholomew Fair*, first performed on 31 October 1614. Here the desirable heiress, Grace Wellborn, agrees to choose between her rival suitors, Quarlous and Winwife, but since she can see no very evident points of difference between them, she suggests that each writes a name on a set of tables, and 'the next person that comes this way' shall be asked to choose between them. One of the names chosen refers explicitly to Shakespeare's play:

QUARLOUS   Well, my word is out of the *Arcadia*, then: 'Argalus'.
WINWIFE   And mine out of the play, 'Palemon'.[2]

The absence of compromise or of redemptive forces in the final plays has contributed to a critical reluctance to concede them standing or significance within the canon, let alone the status of a distinctive new development within it.[3] They are now generally accepted as collaborations with John Fletcher,[4] and this has made it easier to ignore, marginalise or discount them. Yet the qualities of moral realism and metaphysical emptiness that characterise them are not obviously explicable in terms of Fletcher's contribution, or especially evident in his work elsewhere.[5] There are grounds for regarding these qualities as distinctively Shakespearean, their affinities lying with the ironised failures of providence in *Lear*, the perfunctory marriages at the end of *All's Well* or *Measure for Measure*, or the inescapable 'history' of *Troilus and Cressida*. Although a number of their scenes have been persuasively attributed to Fletcher, this chapter examines these final plays in terms of their Shakespearean workmanship.

It does not seem possible to establish for certain the chronological order in which these three plays were composed, though all three were written and performed between the winter of 1612/13 and October 1614, when *Bartholomew Fair* was staged. *Cardenio* (or *Cardenno* or *Cardenna*) may well have been the first written, followed by *Henry VIII* or *All Is True*, and finally, *The Two Noble Kinsmen* (see Introduction, p. 2 n. 3). *Cardenio* is examined in detail by Richard Wilson elsewhere in this volume; though I shall consider particular features that it shares with *Henry VIII* and *The Two Noble Kinsmen*, my focus is primarily on them, and to a lesser extent on some of the interpretations they have

---

2. Jonson, *Bartholomew Fair*, IV, iii, 67–9.
3. This suggestion has occasionally been made with reference to *The Two Noble Kinsmen*, though not to the group as a whole. See, for example, N. W. Bawcutt in the introduction to his edition of the play: 'It is tempting to speculate whether Shakespeare was moving off in a new direction', p. 46.
4. On Fletcher's hand in *Henry VIII*, see Hoy, 'The shares of Fletcher and his collaborators'; Masten, 'Beaumont and/or Fletcher'; Hope, *The Authorship of Shakespeare's Plays*; McMullan, '"Our whole life is like a play"'. On Fletcher's hand in *The Two Noble Kinsmen*, see Hoy and Hope, and also Potter's helpful summary in her edition (pp. 16–34). (Fletcher's joint authorship was announced on the title page of the 1634 Quarto text.) In relation to *Cardenio*, see Kukowski, 'The hand of John Fletcher'.
5. McMullan in *The Politics of Unease* is exceptional in emphasising Fletcher's ability to 'create a distinct unease in audience and critic alike' (p. x); he sees *The Two Noble Kinsmen* as sufficiently typical to end his account by citing Palamon's disillusion at V, iv, 110–12 (p. 261).

occasioned. At present neither play has achieved full canonicity, though they have been marginalised on somewhat different grounds.

Henry VIII has always had the securer position as a result of its inclusion in the First Folio, the earliest and most powerful guarantor of authenticity. Until the mid-nineteenth century, its canonical status remained unquestioned,[6] and was reinforced by the wonderful acting roles it affords. Hugh Richmond[7] has recently described its stage history; it became popular at the end of the nineteenth century and during the first half of the twentieth; Henry Irving and Forbes Robertson played Wolsey and Buckingham in 1892; Beerbohm Tree played Wolsey in 1910 and Sybil Thorndike played Katherine in 1925. Tyrone Guthrie produced the play three times, on one occasion with Charles Laughton as Henry VIII; more recent productions include that of Trevor Nunn in 1969, with Donald Sinden and Peggy Ashcroft, and Royal Shakespeare Company productions by Howard Davis in 1983 and Greg Doran in 1996.

G. Wilson Knight, the critic who may be said to have isolated and characterised the mode of the romances, particularly revered *Henry VIII*, reading it as a celebration of kingship and national values. For him, it represented the summit of Shakespeare's art, combining the transcendent themes of the romances that preceded it with the patriotism of the histories. In it, Shakespeare's 'bark has come to harbour. He returns to a national theme ... and deeply loads it with orthodox Christian feeling. Here the extravagances and profundities of the great sequence come, at the last, to rest.'[8] '*Henry VIII* is no mere historical pageant: it is far nearer a prophetic document, possessing a similarly culminating importance' (pp. 76–7). For Wilson Knight, Cranmer's prophecy of peace (V, iv, 17–55) assumed a general and contemporary application, rather than making particular reference to a revival of interest in Elizabeth, or to James's carefully balanced foreign policy. Its force seemed to him only enhanced by the coming of war in 1939, mystically representing the underlying aims of British foreign and colonial policy. In the dark days of July 1941, Wilson Knight staged a programme of readings at the Westminster Theatre entitled *This Sceptered Isle*.[9] A third of it was dedicated to 'The Royal Phoenix' and consisted of Buckingham's farewell (II, i) and Cranmer's

6. Serious doubts began with J. Spedding, 'Who wrote Shakespeare's *Henry VIII?*', pp. 115–24, 381–2.
7. Richmond, *Henry VIII*. See also Odell, *Shakespeare from Betterton to Irving*; Sprague, *Shakespeare's Histories*.
8. Wilson Knight, *The Olive and the Sword*, p. 68.
9. See Wilson Knight, *Principles of Shakespearean Production*.

prophecy (V, iv), followed by Queen Elizabeth's prayer before the Armada.

Wilson Knight firmly dismissed all claims that Henry VIII was the product of collaboration with Fletcher: it was 'Shakespeare's crowning achievement, though the understanding of it has been hampered by an utterly unfounded rumour that some scenes are un-Shakespearean'.[10] He showed no such confidence in *The Two Noble Kinsmen*, however, despite the presence within it of that sea imagery that he considered such a constitutive element of Shakespearean drama. Unlike *Henry VIII*, *The Two Noble Kinsmen* was not included in the First Folio, although it has as strong a claim to be considered as Shakespearean as *Pericles*, which Wilson Knight regarded as canonical.[11] *The Two Noble Kinsmen* was first published in quarto in 1634, and is described on its title page as 'Presented at the Blackfriers by the Kings Majesties servants, with great applause: Written by ... Mr John Fletcher, and Mr William Shakspeare'. Serious consideration of it as a Shakespearean play begins with William Spalding's *Letter on Shakespeare's Authorship of 'The Two Noble Kinsmen'* (1833).[12] The fullest account of the problems it poses is provided by Paul Bertram in *Shakespeare and 'The Two Noble Kinsmen'*,[13] though Bertram argues strenuously for Shakespeare's sole authorship. Wilson Knight's response to Bertram's account was to praise his lucid deployment of the evidence for Shakespeare as the author of *Henry VIII*.[14]

Wilson Knight's reluctance to engage with *The Two Noble Kinsmen* was not ultimately due to its exclusion from the First Folio or to its collaborative nature (since similar objections could be made to *Pericles*), but was more probably due to its failure to yield that sense of an ultimately benevolent order so strongly evident in the preceding romances, and which he also identified in Cranmer's prophecy at the end of *Henry VIII*, although the play as a whole arguably shares something of the dark and troubled vision that made him reject *The Two Noble Kinsmen*, conscious that it lacked the sense of spiritual or even of explicitly Christian values that he and his disciples had defined as

10. Wilson Knight, *The Olive and the Sword*, p. 76.
11. For example in Wilson Knight, *The Crown of Life*.
12. Spalding, *A Letter on Shakespeare's Authorship*.
13. Bertram, *Shakespeare and 'The Two Noble Kinsmen'*.
14. Wilson Knight, *Shakespeare and Religion*. The selectivity of Wilson Knight's response to Bertram may be judged from the single reference to *The Two Noble Kinsmen* to appear in this book: it is listed in the index under the name of John Fletcher. While he welcomed Bertram's arguments on behalf of *Henry VIII*, it was too late for him to reconsider Shakespeare's authorship of *The Two Noble Kinsmen*.

characteristic of Shakespeare's late plays. There was a strong critical investment in rounding off Shakespeare's career on an upbeat note, whether one of ultimate optimism (with tragicomedy figured as its characteristic generic expression) or of mystic faith associated with the presence of a benign world order, and of the 'clearest gods'. *The Two Noble Kinsmen* and *Henry VIII* were often thought to lack 'unity of conception and design'[15] (a criticism then also levelled against the problem comedies). Their evident bleakness and moral confusion became less threatening if they could be consigned to the margins, as only doubtfully Shakespearean, rather than as sources for the playwright's definitive and final statement on life. In their turn, new historicist, postmodern and deconstructive approaches registered unease with such appeals to the transcendent, and thus contributed to the comparative neglect of the romances in the final quarter of the century, a neglect addressed by the present collection of essays.

Conventionally *The Tempest*, with its epilogue of farewell and departure, had been regarded as Shakespeare's last play, but for Wilson Knight, that position was held by *Henry VIII* on the somewhat narrow basis of Cranmer's prophecy, which he read as a celebration of the sanctity of the monarchy and its commitment to defend justice and democracy. His views were influenced by the propagandists of Elizabeth I, writing at a comparable moment of national crisis in the late 1580s, when despite Spanish threats, the English were 'neither to be molested with broils in their own bosoms, nor threatened with blasts of other borderers; but always, though not laughing, yet looking as through an emerald at others' jars' (in the words of John Lyly).[16] In the later years of the twentieth century, a reaction against imperial pride has set in, accompanied by a distrust of nationalism and a cynicism about the royal family; *Henry VIII* has lost popularity, joining *The Two Noble Kinsmen* as a play of interest primarily to specialists, though Wilson Knight was to restate his sense of its prophetic significance during the Falklands campaign of 1982. By this time it looked eccentric enough for Terence Hawkes to include it in an account of the political and cultural (mis)appropriations of Shakespeare.[17]

Wilson Knight's several accounts of *Henry VIII* celebrate the centrality of monarchy, while side-stepping the more difficult question of how the play represents the events it records, and in particular how far Henry

15. Made of *Henry VIII* by Frank Kermode, 'What is Shakespeare's *Henry VIII* about?', p. 48 (cited by Bertram, *Shakespeare*, p. 151).
16. Lyly, *Euphues and his England*, vol. II, p. 210.
17. Hawkes, 'Swisser-Swatter', p. 43.

can be exonerated from responsibility for the deaths of Buckingham, Katherine and Wolsey (and, by extension, those of Anne Bullen, Cromwell and the Earl of Surrey yet to come). Since the play was written for performance by the King's Men, it could scarcely avoid celebrating the monarchy, but in view of Cranmer's prophetic encomia of Elizabeth and James, it is legitimate to enquire 'Whose monarchy?'.[18] The play sets an orthodox acceptance of Henry's achievement as the initiator of the English Reformation in conflict with spiritual values that pull in an altogether different direction, casting doubt on Henry's personal integrity and incidentally displaying strong Catholic sympathies.

In all three plays, the painful exclusiveness of choice remains a central issue: Grace's choice between Quarlous and Winwife in *Bartholomew Fair* deliberately vulgarises the moment in *The Two Noble Kinsmen* when Emilia is forced to choose between Palamon and Arcite. In Cervantes' tale of *Cardenio*, and in *Double Falshood*, Don Ferdinando (Henriquez, in Theobald's version) is torn between Dorotea (Theobald's Violante), whom he has seduced, and the reluctant Luscinda (Leonora), herself in love with Cardenio (Julio);[19] in *Henry VIII*, the King must choose between his faithful old Queen, Katherine, and the beautiful, young Lady Anne, between spring and autumn, and, even more crucially, between the old Catholic Church and the rising Protestant faith. His choices are further complicated by his responsibility to maintain national security by providing his kingdom with a male heir, so that the transference of desire from the ageing wife of his youth to a younger woman who will renew his sexual energies is not merely biologically understandable, it also promises the renewal and revitalisation of the kingdom in the process.

The contrast between Lady Anne and Queen Katherine inevitably invites comparison with Perdita and Hermione in *The Winter's Tale*, and there are particularly close parallels in the way that the wronged queens Katherine and Hermione conduct themselves at their respective trials, displaying a moving combination of dignity and devotion. But whereas in *The Winter's Tale* the queens of spring and autumn are both restored to

18. Henry VIII figured in the preface to Sir Walter Ralegh's *History of the World* as a stereotypical tyrant: 'if all the pictures and Patternes of a mercilesse Prince were lost in the World, they might all again be painted to the life, out of the story of this King' (p. 56). Robert Cecil referred in Parliament to Henry VIII as 'a child of lust and man of iniquity' (Cecil, *Proceedings in Parliament*: I am grateful to James Knowles for this reference).

19. In citing names used in *Don Quixote*, I have adopted the spellings given in Thomas Shelton's 1612 translation.

Leontes, Paulina and the waiting court, in *Henry VIII* they are fatal
alternatives to one another, locked in a competition that neither will
ultimately survive. Queen Katherine's resignation and ultimate acceptance of her fate leaves her as the play's moral victor, a secular saint
triumphing in the midst of adversity and treachery, which she recognises, and ultimately even forgives (IV, ii, 75). Katherine is endowed with
a moving eloquence, a language that, like Hermione's, conveys a blend
of self-control and passion in its measured rhythms. By contrast, her
maid of honour, Anne Bullen, is laconic, speaking only when required
to. In the scene where she first meets the King (I, iv), she speaks no more
than sixteen words, and none of them in his presence. The brevity of her
part gives her a mysterious, even an enigmatic air: in production, she
may appear unusually modest and shy, or else her silence may speak an
eloquent language of the body, a sly flirtatiousness.

In II, iii, the only scene where Anne speaks at any length, she plays
Desdemona to the Old Lady's Emilia in a conversation that recalls the
Willow scene of *Othello* (IV, iii), a dialogue between innocence and
experience in which coming events cast their shadows before:

> ANNE　　　By my troth and maidenhead,
> 　　I would not be a queen.
> OLD LADY　　　　　　　Beshrew me, I would,
> 　　And venture maidenhead for't, and so would you.
>
> 　　　　　　　　　　(II, iii, 23–5)

The intimacy of two women chatting is vividly evoked, and Emilia's
colloquial 'Come, come, you talk' (IV, iii, 25) is echoed by Anne's 'How
you do talk!' (II, iii, 44). Yet there are significant differences, too. Where
Emilia wonders at Desdemona's innocence, the Old Lady refuses to
believe in Anne's, and her speech continues, 'so would you / For all this
spice of your hypocrisy' (II, iii, 25–6). Hypocrisy was a favourite accusation made against the exponents of the Protestant faith, and while 'spice'
can be defined as 'a touch or trace', it also includes a suggestion of
excitement or arousal, then as now.[20] Othello accuses Emilia of being
the traditional bawd that she in fact is not, but the Old Lady, with her
heavy innuendo, her punning on 'queen' and 'quean',[21] is altogether
more knowing: her dismissal of Anne's disclaimers works to undermine
them, as do Anne's three protesting oaths, 'I swear again, I would not be
a queen / For all the world' – oaths that we know she is soon to break.

20. See OED, sense 5, 1.b.
21. See footnote to II, iii, 36–7, in Foakes's edition.

The Old Lady glosses Anne's words as less than the full truth, suggesting that she is as sexually responsive ('saving your mincing', II, iii, 31) and ambitious as the next court lady, while Anne's flat denials lack the shocked surprise that characterises Desdemona's responses to Emilia. The scene opens with Anne expressing her sympathy for the Queen's plight, and closes with her acceptance of the title of Marchioness of Pembroke, and perhaps the suggestion, by way of a quibble on 'the fair conceit / The king hath of you' (II, iii, 74–5), that she is already pregnant. The Old Lady's innuendo and venality (at V, i, 171–6, she expresses her disappointment with the hundred marks she is given for bringing news of the birth of Henry's daughter) indirectly suggest the presence of those qualities in Anne, since in drama, servants often shadow or figure aspects of their employers. There is a marked contrast between the Old Lady and the servants who wait upon Katherine, notably the good Griffith, who responds to Katherine's criticisms of Wolsey with an apology on his behalf (IV, ii, 48–68). Patience, who has few lines to speak, is as significantly named as Macbeth's officer Seyton or Antony's servant Eros, both of whom appear for the first time late in their respective plays and have little more to do than prepare their masters for their deaths.

Anne's association with the transient glories of this world, and Katherine's with the 'eternal happiness' of the next, are further polarised by the juxtaposition of Anne's temporal coronation at Westminster (IV, i) with Katherine's visionary coronation by 'a blessed troop' of spirits in the following scene (IV, ii, 87). The elaborate stage directions provided for both these sequences reflect the primacy of spectacle and pageant within the play, whether reported, as is the Field of Cloth of Gold (I, i), or enacted, as are the masque at the Cardinal's (I, iv), the ceremony of Katherine's trial at Blackfriars (II, iv) or the contrasting coronations of Anne and Katherine (IV, i and ii).

The dialogue preceding Anne's coronation (IV, i, 1–36) reflects the way in which the play's most spectacular moments constantly question and even undermine themselves, acting as a reminder that this happy event was only made possible by Henry's divorce from Katherine. The concept of divorce is first introduced by Buckingham, in a farewell speech that registers Henry's severity, if not his abuse of authority. Buckingham compares his fate with that of his father at the hands of Richard III: 'I had my trial . . . which makes me / A little happier than my wretched father' (II, i, 118–20). 'The long divorce of steel' (II, i, 76), the phrase that he uses of his execution, anticipates the literal divorce of Katherine, the metaphorical divorce of Wolsey, and the great divorce of the old church from the new, Catholic from Protestant, Gardiner from Cranmer.[22] The prologue has already warned the audience not to expect laughter; rather, they would see:

> How soon this mightiness meets misery:
> And if you can be merry then, I'll say
> A man may weep upon his wedding day.
> (Prologue, 30–2)

The Gentlemen who witness Anne's coronation acknowledge Katherine's sufferings while simultaneously praising Anne's virtues, though here as earlier (for example at II, iii, 76–9, and III, ii, 50–2), their praise is coloured by the expectation that her physical attractions betoken fruitfulness. The Second Gentleman further undermines his praise with a cynical reference to the conscience of the King:

> Sir, as I have a soul, she is an angel;
> Our King has all the Indies in his arms,
> And more, and richer, when he strains that lady;
> I cannot blame his conscience. (IV, i, 44–7)

The suggestion that Henry has made a convenience of his conscience[23] is present from his first account of its awakening (II, iv, 168) when, far from resisting the imputation of his daughter Mary's illegitimacy, his conscience became the instrument that would ensure her disinheritance. Its convenience to him is pointed up not only by the Second Gentleman's words, quoted above, but also in Suffolk's rephrasing of the Lord Chamberlain's observation:

> It seems the marriage with his brother's wife
> Has crept too near his conscience.
> SUFFOLK (*Aside*)   No, his conscience
> Has crept too near another lady. (II, ii, 16–18)

---

22. On the significance of divorce in the play as a whole, see Anderson, *Biographical Truth*, Ch. 8, pp. 126–7.
23. On the play's play on conscience see Anderson, *Biographical Truth*, pp. 128–30. McMullan has also analysed the meaning of conscience, showing how it is 'detached from its ostensibly higher meaning and degraded to the level of the material', in his article '"Swimming on bladders"', p. 219. He argues convincingly that Anne and Henry's desire for her are represented in terms of earthly and bodily analogies. But he also observes that 'Rather than differentiating between them, the play seems perversely and deliberately to blur the differences between Katherine and Anne' (p. 222). My own account considers these differences to be fundamental and structural.

The usefulness of conscience as a cover for the workings of desire becomes a repeated theme, suggested by Henry's description of it as 'a tender place' (II, ii, 143), and in the very next scene it is implicit in the Old Lady's warning to Anne that she will accept the king's gifts:

> OLD LADY   the capacity
> Of your soft cheveril conscience would receive,
> If you might please to stretch it.
> ANNE   Nay, good troth.
> OLD LADY   Yes troth and troth; you would not be a queen?
> (II, iii, 31–3)

The nature of Henry's desire for Anne is further emphasised at the Cardinal's masked ball, where disguise diminishes individual responsibility, and allows greater freedom to libidinal energies. Yet although Katherine's virtues are underwritten by the spiritual order, they do not have the last word in the play. With her death, a new figure of integrity emerges, a second, and this time a Protestant martyr, Thomas Cranmer, who endorses the birth of the Princess Elizabeth with a biblical promise of peace to come, when:

> every man shall eat in safety
> Under his own vine what he plants, and sing
> The merry songs of peace to all his neighbours.
> (V, iv, 33–5)

Cranmer's prophecy, drawing upon a range of Old Testament imagery, validates an alternative and Protestant reading of the play, recasting the birth of Elizabeth as a sign of the intervention of a merciful God who is not blind to the sins of Henry and Anne but makes fortunate their fall, so that it bears fruit for the Protestant faith (and so further illuminating the several links made between Anne's beauty and her fertility). Katherine's mystic vision of her own apotheosis gives place to a promise of a Protestant future, and the two faiths are left competing for the play's meaning, thus justifying its alternative title, 'All Is True'.[24] The opposed and irreconcilable versions of the truth that arose from Henry's Reformation are played out in terms of the practical dilemma created by Henry's desire for Anne, with its accompanying and necessary divorce – for Western marriage is as exclusive an institution as religion. Henry is

---

24. Anderson notes that the contradictory truths of the play render this title 'not false, but ironic', *Biographical Truth*, p. 126. See also Woodhuysen, '*King Henry VIII* and *All Is True*', pp. 217–18.

divided between two women, who represent two opposing faiths. The play's action takes place within the uncompromising order of history, and its unresolvable questions are disguised or distanced through the use of spectacle or vision. The representation of marriage as a painful dilemma, an occasion for tears as much as for joy, associated with conflicts of value and an uncertain spiritual order, is also characteristic of *The Two Noble Kinsmen* (although within the mode of romance it is worked out rather differently), as well as in what can be reconstructed of *Cardenio*.

There are evident difficulties in any such a reconstruction, since *Cardenio's* sources, Cervantes' complexly interwoven narrative of *Don Quixote* and Theobald's play *Double Falshood*, differ from one another in a number of respects, from details of plot development to the characters' names: in Theobald, Cardenio has been renamed Julio, and presumably all the other name changes (such as that of the villain, Don Ferdinand, to Henriquez) were made at the same time. Theobald's play has lost the irony at the expense of romance that characterises Cervantes' inset narrative, and his text is disappointingly lacking in wit, vigour or bite; it is hard to hear Jacobean energies beneath the often predictable rhythms. Yet even in its mangled state, it shares a striking number of themes with *The Two Noble Kinsmen*, including male rivalry and betrayal, imposed marriage, madness and the effect of class difference upon marriage. The last is also an issue in *Henry VIII*, where Wolsey's fall comes about through the failure of his marriage plans for Henry, whom he had intended to remarry to 'the Duchess of Alençon, / The French King's sister' (III, ii, 85–6; compare II, iii, 39–41), instead of a mere lady in waiting, 'A creature of the queen's, Lady Anne Bullen' (III, ii, 36). He expostulates against her:

> The late queen's gentlewoman? a knight's daughter
> To be her mistress' mistress? the queen's queen?
>
> > (III, ii, 94–5)

Further parallels link Theobald's Duke Angelo (Don Riccardo in Cervantes) and the Theseus of *The Two Noble Kinsmen*, while both Violante/Dorotea and the Jailer's Daughter suffer the same stigma, 'Th' Obscureness of her Birth' (*Double Falshood*, I, iii; p. 10). The Jailer's Daughter, like Julio/Cardenio, goes mad among the woods and wild places, and her strange talk of horses (*The Two Noble Kinsmen*, V, ii, 45, 55, 61–7) distantly echoes his wild talk of horsemanship in the mountains (*Double Falshood*, IV, i; p. 40). The introduction into the tale of Palemon and Arcite of a sub-plot concerning the Jailer's Daughter, rejected because of her low birth (like Violante/Dorotea), and going mad in the wilderness (like Julio/Cardenio), suggests that *The Two Noble Kinsmen* was written after *Cardenio* and drew upon some of its effects.

In his account of *Cardenio*, Richard Wilson points out one very curious addition to Cervantes' narrative that appears in *Double Falshood*: Henriquez, with his brother Lord Roderick, abducts Leonora from the convent where she has taken refuge, appropriating a hearse as a way of entering its hallowed walls: 'And, opportune, a vacant Herse pass'd by / From rites but new perform'd' (IV, i; p. 46). Their stratagem works, and the hearse accompanies Lord Roderick into the final recognition scene, where we learn that he is 'attended well: and in his Train / Follows a Herse with all due Rites of Mourning' (V, ii; p. 55), while later in the same scene Leonora insists upon a period of mourning for 'my murther'd *Julio*, – / … For such sad Rites must be perform'd, my Lord, / E'er I can love again' (V, ii; p. 57). A comparable insistence upon the necessity of performing mourning rites is carried over into the opening scene of *The Two Noble Kinsmen*, where Theseus' wedding procession is interrupted by three mourning queens who plead with him to delay his marriage and help them to confer proper burial upon the bodies of their husbands, left exposed upon the field of battle. Theseus accedes to their prayers and in the resulting battle, the two kinsmen are themselves left for dead and placed upon hearses (I, iv), to be followed in the next scene by the 'Queens with the hearses of their knights, in a funeral solemnity' (I, v, 0.1–2). The incongruous combination of hearses, mourning rites and weddings that haunts these plays links them with that strange period of 'funerals and hornpipes' that followed the sudden death of Prince Henry in November 1612, when the king and court were divided between mourning his loss and the need to press on with the politically controversial marriage of Princess Elizabeth to Frederick, Elector Palatine, eventually celebrated on 14 February 1613.[25] Allusions to Princess Elizabeth in Cranmer's prophecy, as well as to the self-renewing bird, the phoenix, evidently include topical references as well.

The wedding procession of Theseus and Hippolyta in the opening scene of *The Two Noble Kinsmen* is further darkened by Theseus' recollection of meeting one of the unburied kings, Capaneus. He tells the widowed queen, 'The day / That he should marry you, at such a season / As now it is with me, I met your groom' (I, i, 59–61), denouncing the effects of Time's ravages upon her. *The Winter's Tale* had presented Time

---

25. Links between *The Two Noble Kinsmen*, Prince Henry's funeral and Princess Elizabeth's wedding are examined by Bradbrook, *The Living Monument*, p. 236, and Wickham, 'The Two Noble Kinsmen', pp. 167–96.

very differently: emblematically speaking, Truth was the daughter of Time, the revelation that Time begot or brought forth. The sub-title of Greene's *Pandosto*, Shakespeare's source for *The Winter's Tale*, was 'The Triumphs of Time', and Time appears as Chorus to the play, healing old wounds and restoring lost happiness. In *The Two Noble Kinsmen* it has become the destroyer ('tempus edax rerum'), as Theseus exclaims: 'Oh, grief and time, / Fearful consumers, you will all devour!' (I, i, 69–70). Such a view is closer to that of the sonnets or *Troilus and Cressida* than of the romances.[26]

The interrupted and darkened marriage celebrations in *The Two Noble Kinsmen* are prolonged into the play's central scenes, where the School-master puts on an entertainment for the gentry in the form of the May Game. Here the unaccountable absence of Cecily allows the Jailer's Daughter to become the centre of the dance, a figure of chaos at the heart of order. Dances of madmen to celebrate marriage in Renaissance drama occur elsewhere, but they tend to be ominous, significant subversions of the social order that is figured in the marriage ceremony, as in Middleton and Rowley's *The Changeling*, where 'the madmen's morris' (IV, iii, 65) had been planned for the ill-fated marriage of Beatrice to Alsemero. The Jailer's Daughter's, like Cardenio – or Ophelia or poor Barbary in Desdemona's song – has run mad for love, conceiving an unrequited passion for Palamon while he was her father's prisoner. He exploits her affection to gain his freedom, but then takes no further interest in her. Even before she helps him to escape, she recognises the social distance between them, and the effect it is bound to have on their relationship:

> 'Tis odds
> He never will affect me: I am base,
> My father the mean keeper of his prison,
> And he a prince. To marry him is hopeless;
> To be his whore is witless. Out upon't.
>
> (II, iv, 1–5)

Desire does not only break up friendships, it also cuts across the social order. In more optimistic scenarios, it merely threatens to do so, as does Perdita's love for Florizel; lack of social status may be compensated for by moral worth, as in the case of Posthumus Leonatus, the gentleman

26. Edwards has written of *The Two Noble Kinsmen* that it 'seems to me to give the most cynical assessment of the progress of life since the writing of *Troilus and Cressida*', in 'On the design of *The Two Noble Kinsmen*', p. 105.

loved by the King's daughter Innogen, in *Cymbeline*. But there are no mitigating circumstances in *The Two Noble Kinsmen*, and the love of the Jailer's Daughter for Palamon is never requited (in this respect differing sharply from that of Violante/Dorotea). According to the Doctor, she must be deceived into accepting her rustic Wooer as Palamon, if she is to recover. The audience cannot tell how far or how long she remains deceived.

Like Helena in *All's Well*, the Jailer's Daughter challenges both class rules and traditional notions of gender behaviour, but to no end since she cannot attract Palamon's love – indeed she scarcely attracts his attention, except in so far as her plight resembles his own: 'her kind of ill / Gave me some sorrow' (V, iv, 26–7). She hardly exists for him, just as he hardly exists for Emilia, though both are vividly present to the audience. Love is thus represented as a potentially tragic fantasy built around an unknowing and undesiring object, even a form of solipsism, figured in the play's two pointed references to Narcissus (at II, ii, 119–20, and IV, ii, 32). Palamon and the other courtiers give their purses to the Jailer for his Daughter's dowry at V, iv, 31–3 (overlooking the fact that at IV, i, 21–4, Palamon, 'Not to be held ungrateful to her goodness, / Ha[d] given a sum of money to her marriage'). The Doctor recommends defloration as the traditional cure for this severe case of green sickness. While Emilia must be married, whether she will or no, the Jailer's Daughter is hurried off to anticipate her marriage with her Wooer, a surprising development, in view of the concern with continence before marriage shown in the preceding romances. Further tears are threatened as the Jailer's Daughter, after inviting her Wooer to sleep with her, touchingly warns him 'But you shall not hurt me . . . If you do, love, I'll cry' (V, ii, 111–12).

Both the Jailer's Daughter and Emilia criticise the values of chivalry and the social order that prevail within the play, the one perhaps unwittingly, the other from knowledge. Not only does Emilia not wish to marry at all (as in the play's source), but she cannot bear to watch the tournament set up to enable one of the knights to win her hand in marriage. She denounces its outcome, implicating the gods in permitting such cruelty:[27]

Is this winning?
Oh, all you heavenly powers, where is your mercy?

---

27. Elsewhere in the play, the gods appear as men's herdsmen (I, iv, 4–6) and even as their hunters (V, i, 131–2). See Bawcutt's introduction to his edition, pp. 26, 38.

But that your wills have said it must be so, . . .
I should and would die too. (V, iii, 138–40, 144)

Emilia's reluctance to marry is established in the first act, where she describes her relationship with the dead Flavina as an irreplaceable friendship, one that may be compared with that of Theseus and Pirithous (I, iii, 55–82):

> HIPPOLYTA   ... this high–speeded pace is but to say
>   That you shall never, like the maid Flavina,
>   Love any that's called man.
> EMILIA   I am sure I shall not. (I, iii, 83–5)

As in *The Winter's Tale* (I, ii, 67–75), there is a suggestion that true and perfect friendships belong to a world of lost, homosocial innocence, perhaps recalled at III, iv, where the kinsmen get drunk together and are briefly reunited in 'laddish' reminiscences until Palamon reverts to Emilia, the object of their rivalry (III, iv, 45, etc.).[28] Emilia's contentment with her own single state gives place to a sense of alarm at having to choose between the two kinsmen. As in the play's source, Chaucer's *Knight's Tale*, the gods cannot satisfy the irreconcilable prayers of all three protagonists, but the aftermath of the tournament is harsher in the play, since, in a notable departure from Chaucer, Theseus has condemned the loser to instant death: V, iv, begins with the entry of 'Palamon and his Knights, pinioned; Jailer, Executioner, Guard', bringing the axe and the block.

The world of *The Two Noble Kinsmen* is a bleak one – much bleaker than that of Chaucer's *Knight's Tale*, which at least affords the Boethean consolation that worldly desires are not to be enjoyed; by contrast with spiritual desires, they cannot be satisfied by their very nature, yet while earthly love can only lead to regret, for Chaucer there is a world without change or loss elsewhere. The ending of *The Two Noble Kinsmen* is one of the harshest in the canon, directly comparable to that of *Troilus and Cressida* (Shakespeare's other adaptation from Chaucer) or *Timon of Athens*. The play's most recent editor, Lois Potter, admits to finding the ending 'deliberately abrupt and frustrating' (in a footnote to V, iv, 137), and it is very far removed in tone from the sequence of recognitions that close *Cymbeline*, Caliban's resolve to 'seek for grace', or the reunions that crown *The Winter's Tale*.

As an end to Shakespeare's career and an appropriate farewell to the stage, *The Two Noble Kinsmen* looks a strong candidate in terms of its

28. See Abrams, 'Gender confusion and sexual politics in *The Two Noble Kinsmen*', pp. 69–77.

evident continuities with the rest of the canon: its gathers up many earlier themes and motifs, reworking them in distinctly sombre colours. Far more than does *The Tempest*, *The Two Noble Kinsmen* enacts a purposive rewriting of the devices of rhetoric and order imposed through ceremonial and ritual that had characterised the romances.[29] This act of rewriting/unwriting extends further back into Shakespearean drama, so that the play's opening sequence looks back to the masque of Hymen with which *As You Like It* had ended, and perhaps also the wedding masque of Ceres that Prospero mounted to entertain Ferdinand and Miranda. The play as a whole is closely linked with *A Midsummer Night's Dream*, which also opens with preparations for the wedding of Theseus and Hippolyta, and includes rival lovers fighting in a wood, and rustic entertainments to divert the ducal couple. Like *Love's Labours Lost* it focuses on male friendship, including a Schoolmaster as master of the revels; as well as the similar title, it shares a number of plot features with *Two Gentlemen of Verona*, including friends turned rivals in love, and an escape to the woods (in both, associated with the indulgence of atavistic and anti-social impulses). There are further affinities with *The Winter's Tale* where the male bonding of Leontes and Polixenes is interrupted by the fall into heterosexual desire, with disastrous consequences in both.

At the heart of both *Henry VIII* and *The Two Noble Kinsmen* lies a profound perception of human division and separation, a sense of the limitations set upon happiness when nothing can be gained without a corresponding loss. This insight is painfully voiced by Arcite at the very moment of his triumph in the lists:

> Emilia,
> To buy you, I have lost what's dearest to me,
> Save what is bought. (V, iii, 111–13)

And it is restated by Palamon, as he mourns his dying friend:

> Oh, cousin!
> That we should things desire, which do cost us
> The loss of our desire! That nought could buy
> Dear love, but loss of dear love.[30] (V, iv, 109–12)

---

29. See Wickham, '*The Two Noble Kinsmen*', esp. pp. 179–81; Bawcutt in his edition, p. 17.
30. Note the play in both quotations on 'dear' meaning both 'loved' and 'expensive', made explicit through the verb 'buy'. Arcite's opening words in the play are 'Dear Palamon, dearer in love than blood / And our prime cousin.' (I, ii, 1–2).

In George Eliot's *Daniel Deronda*, the hero explains to Gwendolen (whom he has first seen at the gambling tables in the opening chapter) exactly why he dislikes gambling so much: 'There are enough inevitable turns of fortune which force us to see that our gain is another's loss: – that is one of the ugly aspects of life.'[31] Although there is no presiding deity in Eliot's fictional world, Deronda's words strike a note of dignity and compassion that contrast markedly with the helpless and uncomprehending submission voiced in Theseus' closing speech:

> Oh, you heavenly charmers,
> What things you make of us! For what we lack
> We laugh, for what we have are sorry, still
> Are children in some kind. Let us be thankful
> For that which is, and with you leave dispute
> That are above our question. (V, iv, 131–6)

No one in the seventeenth century could have imagined a world without God, as George Eliot did, a world where meaning is what we must construct for ourselves rather than what has been constructed for us, but *The Two Noble Kinsmen* comes as close as its moment allowed to questioning the existence of a benevolent providence, and in the process generated for itself a dramatic structure that enacts and even reinforces that doubt. In this respect, it anticipates, albeit at an enormous distance, the dramatic structures of Samuel Beckett, as it registers the brave new direction taken in this, the last of the late plays.

31. Eliot, *Daniel Deronda*, Book IV, Ch. 29, p. 337.

BIBLIOGRAPHY

PRIMARY

Alciato, Andrea, *Emblemata* (Leyden, 1608)

Alexandria, Clement of, *The Instructor*, in *The Writings of Clement of Alexandria*, trans. William Wilson, 2 vols (Edinburgh: T. & T. Clark, 1867), vol. I

Anon., *The Seed*, trans. I. M. Lonie, in G. E. R. Lloyd (ed.), *Hippocratic Writings*, trans. J. Chadwick, W. N. Mann, I. M. Lonie and E. T. Withington (Harmondsworth: Penguin, 1978)

Anon., *The Quenes Maiesties Passage through the Citie of London to Westminster the Day before her Coronacion* (1559), facsimile, ed. James M. Osborn, intro. Sir John Neale (New Haven: Yale University Press for the Elizabethan Club, 1960)

Anon., *The Description of a Monstrous Pig* (London, 1562) [Huth 50/39]

Anon., *The True Reporte of the Forme and Shape of a Monstrous Childe, Borne at Muche Horkesleye* (London, 1562) [Huth 50/36]

Anon., *The Forme and Shape of a Monstrous Child Borne at Maydstone in Kent* (London, 1568) [Huth 50/38]

Anon., *The Ancient, Famous, and Honourable History of Amadis of Gaule*, Books I–IV (London, 1619)

B., H., *The True Discription of a Childe with Ruffes Born in the Parish of Micheham in the County of Surrey* (London, 1566) [Huth 50/34]

Bacon, Francis, *The Essayes or Councels, Civill and Morall*, ed. M. Kiernan (Oxford: Oxford University Press, 1985)

Bale, John, *The First Partes of the Actes or Unchast Examples of the English Votaries* (London, 1548)

Bale, John, *The Pageant of Popes, Contayninge the Lyves of All the Bishopes of Rome* (London, 1574)

Beaumont, Francis, *The Masque of the Inner Temple and Gray's Inn*, ed. Philip Edwards, in *A Book of Masques*, eds Stanley Wells and T. J. B. Spencer (Cambridge: Cambridge University Press, 1967), pp. 131–42

Beaumont, Francis, and John Fletcher, *Select Plays*, ed. M. C. Bradbrook (London and New York: Dent, 1962, repr. 1970)

Bullough, Geoffrey, ed. *Narrative and Dramatic Sources of Shakespeare*, 8 vols (London and Henley: Routledge and Kegan Paul, 1957–75)

Campbell, Lily B., ed. *The Mirror for Magistrates* (Cambridge: Cambridge University Press, 1938)

Campion, Thomas, *The Lord Hay's Masque* (1607), in David Lindley (ed.), *Court Masques* (Oxford: Oxford University Press, 1995)

Campion, Thomas, *Lord's Masque* (1613), in *The Works of Thomas Campion*, ed. W. R. Davies (London: Faber, 1969)

Castiglione, Baldassare, *The Book of the Courtier*, trans. Thomas Hoby, ed. Virginia Cox (London and Vermont: Dent, 1994)

Cecil, Robert, Speech to House of Lords, 3 May 1610, in *Proceedings in Parliament 1610*, ed. Elizabeth Read Foster, 2 vols (New Haven: Yale University Press, 1966), vol. I, pp. 231–2

Cervantes, Miguel de, *The History of Don Quixote of the Mancha Translated from the Spanish of Miguel de Cervantes*, trans. Thomas Shelton, ed. James Fitzmaurice-Kelly, 2 vols (London: David Nutt, 1896)

Chapman, George, *The Widow's Tears*, ed. A. Yamada (London: Methuen, 1975)

Chaucer, Geoffrey, *The Riverside Chaucer*, ed. F. N. Robinson, gen.ed. Larry D. Benson (Oxford: Oxford University Press, 1987, 3rd edn)

Cicero, *Tusculan Disputations*, trans. J. E. King (London: William Heinemann; New York: G. P. Putnam's Sons, 1927)

Cicero, *De Re Publica, De Legibus*, trans. Clinton Walker Keyes (London: William Heinemann; New York: G. P. Putnam and Sons, 1928)

Cicero, *Brutus, Orator*, trans. H. M. Hubell (Cambridge, Mass., and London: Harvard University Press, 1939)

Cleland, James, *The Institution of a Young Noble Man* (Oxford, 1607)

Clifford, Lady Anne, *The Diaries of Lady Anne Clifford*, ed. D. J. H. Clifford (Stroud: Alan Sutton, 1990)

Coleridge, Samuel Taylor, *Shakesperean Criticism*, 2 vols, ed. Thomas Middleton Raysor (London: Everyman Library; New York: Dutton, 1960, repr. 1967)

Cope, Antony, *The Historie of Two the Most Noble Capitaines in the World* (London, 1544)

D., John, *A Description of a Monstrous Chylde, Borne at Chychester in Sussex* (London, 1562) [Huth 50/33]

Daniel, Samuel, *The Vision of the Twelve Goddesses*, ed. J. Rees, in *A Book of Masques*, eds S. Wells and T. J. Spencer (Cambridge: Cambridge University Press, 1967), pp. 17–42

Daniel, Samuel, *Tethys' Festival*, in *Court Masques*, ed. D. Lindley (Oxford: Oxford University Press, 1995), pp. 54–65

Davies, Lady Eleanor, *Prophetic Writings of Eleanor Davies*, ed. Esther S. Cope (New York and Oxford: Oxford University Press, 1995)

Davies, Sir John, *A Discovery of the True Causes Why Ireland was Never Entirely Subdued, nor Brought Under Obedience of the Crowne of England, untill the Beginning of his Majesties Happie Raigne* (London, 1612)

Dekker, Thomas, *The Whore of Babylon*, in *The Dramatic Works of Thomas Dekker*, ed. F.

Bowers (Cambridge: Cambridge University Press, 1953–61), vol. II (1955)

Dekker, Thomas, and John Webster, *Sir Thomas Wyatt*, in *The Dramatic Works of Thomas Dekker*, ed. F. Bowers (Cambridge: Cambridge University Press, 1953–61), vol. I (1953)

Dryden, John, 'Defence of the Epilogue on the Second Part of the Conquest of Granada' (1672), in *Essays of John Dryden*, ed. W. P. Ker (Oxford: Clarendon Press, 1900)

Eliot, George, *Daniel Deronda*, ed. Terence Cave (Harmondsworth: Penguin, 1995)

Elyot, Thomas, *Boke Named the Gouernour* (London, 1531)

Erasmus, Desiderius, *The Colloquies of Erasmus*, ed. and trans. Craig R. Thompson (Chicago and London: University of Chicago Press, 1965)

Erasmus, Desiderius, *Collected Writings of Erasmus: Adages, II.vii.1 to III.iii.100*, trans. M. M. Phillips (Buffalo and London: University of Toronto Press, 1982)

Fenton, Edward, *Certaine Secrete Wonders of Nature, Containning a Description of Sundry Strange Things* (London, 1569)

Fletcher, John, *The Woman's Prize*, ed. George B. Ferguson (The Hague: Mouton, 1966)

Fletcher, John, *The Maid's Tragedy*, in *Dramatic Works in the Beaumont and Fletcher Canon*, gen. ed. Fredson Bowers, vol. II (Cambridge: Cambridge University Press, 1970)

F[ullwood], W[illiam], *The Shape of Two Monsters* (London, 1562) [Huth 50/37]

Golding, Arthur, trans. *The XV Bookes of P. Ouidius Naso, Entituled Metamorphosis* (London, 1603)

Greene, Robert, *Penelope's Web*, in *The Life and Complete Works in Prose and Verse of Robert Greene*, ed. Alexander B. Grosart, 12 vols (London and Aylesbury: Huth Library/ Hazell, Watson and Viney, 1881–3), vol. V

Greene, Robert, *Pandosto. The Triumph of Time*, in *An Anthology of Elizabethan Prose Fiction*, ed. Paul Salzman (Oxford: Oxford University Press, 1987)

Guarini, Giambattista, *The Compendium of Tragicomic Poetry* (1599), in *Literary Criticism from Plato to Dryden*, ed. and trans. Allan H. Gilbert (New York: American Book Co., 1940)

Guazzo, Stefano, *The Civile Conversation of M. Steeven Guazzo*, trans. George Pettie (London, 1581)

Harsnet, Samuel, *A Declaration of Egregious Popish Impostures* (London, 1603)

Heywood, Thomas, *The Golden Age*, in *The Dramatic Works of Thomas Heywood*, ed. R. H. Shepherd, 6 vols (London: J. Pearson, 1874), vol. III

Heywood, Thomas, *The wise-woman of Hogsdon*, in *Thomas Heywood: Three Marriage Plays*, ed. Paul Merchant (Manchester: Manchester University Press, 1996)

Hoby, Lady Margaret, *Diary of Lady Margaret Hoby 1599–1605*, ed. Dorothy M. Meads (London: Routledge, 1930)

Holland, Henry, *A Treatise against Witchcraft* (Cambridge, 1590)

James VI and I, *Dæmonologie*, ed. G. B. Harrison (London: Bodley Head, 1929)

James VI and I, *Basilikon Doron*, in *Political Works of James I*, ed. Charles Howard McIlwain (Cambridge, Mass.: Harvard University Press, 1918; repr. New York: Russell and Russell, 1965)

Johnson, Samuel, *Johnson on Shakespeare*, ed. A. Sherbo, intro. Bertrand H. Bronson, 2 vols (New Haven: Yale University Press, 1968), vols VII and VIII of *The Yale Edition of the Works of Samuel Johnson*

Jonson, Ben, *Ben Jonson*, eds C. H. Herford and P. Simpson, 11 vols (Oxford: Clarendon Press, 1925–52)

Jonson, Ben, *Bartholomew Fair*, ed. E. A. Horsman (London: Methuen, 1960; repr. Manchester: Manchester University Press, 1979)

Jonson, Ben, *The New Inn*, ed. M. Hattaway (Manchester: Manchester University Press, 1984)

Jonson, Ben, and others, *The Masque of Oberon*, ed. P. Holman, in *The Masqve of Oberon*, Musicians of the Globe, cond. Prickett (Phillips CD 446217–2, 1997)

Lavater, Ludwig, *Of Ghostes and Spirits Walkyng by Nyght*, eds J. Dover Wilson and May Yardley (Oxford: Shakespeare Association, 1929)

Lyly, John, *Euphues and his England*, in *The Complete Works of John Lyly*, ed. R. Warwick Bond, 3 vols (Oxford: Clarendon Press, 1902)

Lyly, John, *Euphues: The Anatomy of Wit. Euphues and his England*, eds M. W. Croll and H. Clemons (London: Routledge, 1916)

Marlowe, Christopher, *Doctor Faustus, A- and B-texts (1604, 1616)*, eds David Bevington and Eric Rasmussen (Manchester and New York: Manchester University Press, 1993)

Marshall, William, *Goodly Prymer in Englyshe* (London, 1535)

Marston, John, *Histriomastix*, in *The Plays of John Marston*, ed. H. Harvey Wood, 3 vols (Edinburgh: Oliver and Boyd, 1930)

Marston, John, *The Entertainment at Ashby*, in *The Poems of John Marston*, ed. A. Davenport (Liverpool: Liverpool University Press, 1961)

Mellys, John, *The True Description of Two Monstrous Children* (London, 1566) [Huth 50/35]

Middleton, Thomas, and William Rowley, *The Changeling*, ed. N. W. Bawcutt (Manchester: Manchester University Press, 1958, repr. 1979)

Nichols, John, *The Progresses, Processions, and Magnificent Festivities of King James the First, &c.*, 4 vols (London: Society of Antiquaries, 1828)

Nims, John F., ed. *Ovid's 'Metamorphoses': The Arthur Golding Translation, 1567* (Macmillan: London and New York, 1965)

Ovid, *Metamorphoses*, Books I–VIII, trans. Frank Justus Miller (Cambridge, Mass.: Harvard University Press, 1951)

P., I., *A Meruaylous Straunge Deformd Swyne* (London, n.d.) [Huth 50/42]

Peele, George, *The Old Wives Tale*, ed. Patricia Binnie (Manchester: Manchester University Press, 1980)

Perkins, William, *A Discourse of the Damned Art of Witchcraft* (Cambridge, 1608)

Puttenham, George, *The Arte of English Poesie*, eds Gladys Doidge Willcock and Alice Walker (Cambridge: Cambridge University Press, 1936)

R., C., *The True Description of this Marueilous Straunge Fishe* (London, 1569) [Huth 50/41]

Ralegh, Sir Walter, *The History of the World*, ed. C. A. Patrides (London: Macmillan, 1971)

Rich, Barnaby, *Rich's Farewell to Military Profession*, ed. Thomas Mabry Cranfill (Austin: University of Texas Press, 1959)

Scot, Reginald, *Discoverie of Witchcraft* (London, 1584)

Shakespeare, William, *The Works of Shakespear*, ed. Sir Thomas Hanmer, 6 vols (Oxford, 1743–4)

Shakespeare, William, *The Works of Shakespeare*, ed. F. W. Moorman (London: Methuen, 1912)

Shakespeare, William, *William Shakespeare: The Complete Works*, eds Stanley Wells and Gary Taylor (Oxford: Clarendon Press, 1988)

Shakespeare, William, *The Norton Shakespeare*, gen. ed. Stephen Greenblatt (New York and London: W. W. Norton, 1997)

Shakespeare, William, *The Comedy of Errors*, ed. R. A. Foakes (London and New York: Methuen, 1962)

Shakespeare, William, *Cymbeline*, ed. J. M. Nosworthy (London and New York: Routledge, 1955, repr. 1989)

Shakespeare, William, *Cymbeline*, ed. Richard Hosley (New York: New English Library, 1968)

Shakespeare, William, *Cymbeline*, ed. Roger Warren (Oxford: Clarendon Press, 1998)

Shakespeare, William, *Henry VIII* (or *All is True*), ed. R. A. Foakes (London: Methuen, 1957)

Shakespeare, William, *Macbeth*, ed. N. Brooke (Oxford: Clarendon Press, 1990)

Shakespeare, William, *Pericles*, ed. F. D. Hoeniger (Methuen: London, 1963)

Shakespeare, William, *The Tempest*, ed. F. Kermode (London and New York: Methuen, 1954, rev. 1958)

Shakespeare, William, *The Tempest*, ed. Stephen Orgel (Oxford: Clarendon Press, 1987)

Shakespeare, William, *The Winter's Tale*, ed. J. H. P. Pafford (London and New York: Methuen, 1963)

Shakespeare, William, *The Winter's Tale*, ed. Stephen Orgel (Oxford: Clarendon Press, 1996)

Shakespeare, William, and John Fletcher, *The Two Noble Kinsmen*, ed. Richard Proudfoot (London: Edward Arnold, 1970)

Shakespeare, William, and John Fletcher, *The Two Noble Kinsmen*, ed. N. W. Bawcutt (Harmondsworth: Penguin, 1977)

Shakespeare, William, and John Fletcher, *The Two Noble Kinsmen*, ed. L. D. Potter (London: Routledge, 1997)

Sidney, Sir Philip, *An Apology for Poetry*, ed. Geoffrey Shepherd (Manchester: Manchester University Press, 1973)

Sidney, Sir Philip, *The Countess of Pembroke's Arcadia*, ed. Maurice Evans (Harmondsworth: Penguin, 1977, repr. 1987)

Spenser, Edmund, *The Faerie Queene*, ed. A. C. Hamilton (London and New York: Longman, 1977)

State Papers, *Calendar of State Papers: Venetian, Vol. X: 1603–1607*, and *Vol. XI: 1607–10*, ed. H. Brown (London: HMSO, 1900 and 1904)

Strachey, Lytton, *Literary Essays* (London: Chatto and Windus, 1961)

Theobald, Lewis, *Double Falshood; or, The Distrest Lovers ... Written Originally by W. Shakespeare; and now Revised and Adapted to the Stage by Mr. Theobald*, facsimile ed. K. Muir (London: Cornmarket Press, 1970)

Traheron, Bartholomew, *A Warning to England to Repente, and to Turne to God from Idolatrie and Poperie* (Wesel, 1558)

Trismegistus, Hermes, *Hermetica: the Greek Corpus Hermetica and the Latin Ascelpius in a New English Translation, with Notes and Introduction*, ed. Brian P. Copenhaver (Cambridge: Cambridge University Press, 1992)

Turner, William, *A New Booke of Spirituall Physik for Dyverse Diseases of the Nobilitie and Gentlemen of Englande* (n.p., 1555)

Virgil, *Eclogues, Georgics, Aeneid I–VI*, trans. H. R. Fairclough (Cambridge, Mass.: Harvard University Press; London: William Heinemann, 1960)

Weigall, Rachel, 'An Elizabethan gentlewoman: the journal of Lady Mildmay, circa 1570–1617 (unpublished)', *Quarterly Review*, 428 (1911), 119–38

Whittinton, Robert, *The Thre Bookes of Tullyes Offyces Both in Latyne Tonge and in Englysshe* (London, 1534)

SECONDARY

Abrams, Richard, 'Gender confusion and sexual politics in *The Two Noble Kinsmen*', in *Drama, Sex and Politics, Themes in Drama* 7, ed. James Redmond (Cambridge: Cambridge University Press, 1985), pp. 69–76

Adelman Janet, *Suffocating Mothers: Fantasies of Maternal Origin in Shakespeare's Plays, 'Hamlet' to 'The Tempest'* (London and New York: Routledge, 1992)

Anderson, Judith, *Biographical Truth: The Representation of Historical Persons in Tudor–Stuart Writing* (New Haven: Yale University Press, 1984)

Attridge, Derek, 'Puttenham's perplexity: nature, art, and the supplement in Renaissance poetic theory', in *Literary Theory/Renaissance Texts*, eds Patricia Parker and David Quint (Baltimore: Johns Hopkins University Press, 1986), pp. 257–79

Auerbach, Erich, *Mimesis: The Representation of Reality in Western Literarture*, trans. Willard R. Trask (Princeton, N.J.: Princeton University Press, 1968)

Baker, David J., *Between Nations: Shakespeare, Spenser, Marvell, and the Question of Britain* (Stanford, Calif.: Stanford University Press, 1997)

Barkan, Leonard, '"Living sculptures": Ovid, Michelangelo and *The Winter's Tale*', *English Literary History*, 48 (1971), 639–67

Barkan, Leonard, *Transuming Passions: Ganymede and the Erotics of Humanism* (Stanford, Calif.: Stanford University Press, 1991)

Baroja, Julio Caro, *The World of the Witches*, trans. O. N. V. Glendinning (Chicago: University of Chicago Press, 1964)

Barroll, Leeds, *Politics, Plague, and Shakespeare's Theater: The Stuart Years* (Ithaca, N.Y., and London: Cornell University Press, 1991)

Barton, Anne, 'Leontes and the spider: language and speaker in Shakespeare's last plays', in *Shakespeare's Styles: Essays in Honour of Kenneth Muir*, eds Philip Edwards, Inga-Stina Ewbank and G. K. Hunter (Cambridge: Cambridge University Press, 1980), pp. 131–50

Bate, Jonathan, *Shakespeare and Ovid* (Oxford: Clarendon Press, 1993)

Bate, Jonathan, *The Genius of Shakespeare* (London: Picador, 1997)

Battenhouse, Roy, '*Measure for Measure* and King James', *Clio*, 7 (1978), 193–215

Baughan, Denver Ewing, 'Shakespeare's confusion of the two Romanos', *Journal of English and Germanic Philology*, 36 (1937), 35–9

Baum, Pauli Franklin, 'The young man betrothed to a statue', *Papers of the Modern Language Association*, 34 (1919), 523–79

Bentley, Gerald Eades, 'Shakespeare and the Blackfriars Theatre', *Shakespeare Survey*, 1 (1948), 38–50

Bentley, Gerald Eades, *The Jacobean and Caroline Stage*, 7 vols (Oxford: Clarendon Press, 1941–68), vol. VI, *Theatres* (1968)

Bergeron, David M., *Shakespeare's Romances and the Royal Family* (Lawrence, Kans.: University of Kansas Press, 1985)

Bergeron, David M., *Royal Family, Royal Lovers: King James of England and Scotland* (Columbia: University of Missouri Press, 1991)

Berry, Philippa, 'Reversing history: time, fortune and the doubling of sovereignty in *Macbeth*', *European Journal of English Studies*, 1 (1997), 367–87

Bertram, Paul, *Shakespeare and 'The Two Noble Kinsmen'* (New Brunswick, N.J.: Rutgers University Press, 1965)

Bethell, S. L., *'The Winter's Tale': A Study* (London, New York and Toronto: Staples Press, 1947)

Betteridge, Tom, 'From prophetic to apocalyptic: John Foxe and the writing of history', in *John Foxe and the English Reformation*, ed. David Loades (Aldershot: Scolar Press, 1997), pp. 210–32

Bhabha, Homi K., 'The other question: difference, discrimination and the discourse of colonialism', in *Literature, Politics and Theory: Papers from the Essex Conference, 1976–84*, eds Francis Barker, Peter Hulme, Margaret Iversen and Diana Loxley (London: Methuen, 1986), pp. 148–72

Billington, Sandra, *Mock Kings in Medieval and Renaissance Drama* (Oxford: Clarendon Press, 1991)

Bradbrook, M. C., *The Living Monument: Shakespeare and the Theatre of his Time* (Cambridge: Cambridge University Press, 1976)

Brown, Cedric, 'Milton's *Arcades*: context, form and function', *Renaissance Drama*, new series, 8 (1977), 245–74

Burke, Peter, *The Renaissance Sense of the Past* (London: Edward Arnold, 1969)

Butler, Martin, *Theatre and Crisis, 1632–1642* (Cambridge: Cambridge University Press, 1984)

Chambers, E. K., *The Elizabethan Stage*, 4 vols (Oxford: Clarendon Press, 1923)

Chambers, E. K., *William Shakespeare: A Study of Facts and Problems*, 2 vols (Oxford: Clarendon Press, 1930)

Chedgzoy, Kate, 'Female prophecy in the seventeenth century: the instance of Anna Trapnel', in *Writing and the English Renaissance*, eds William Zunder and Suzanne Trill (London and New York: Longman, 1996), pp. 238–54

Chew, Samuel C., *The Virtues Reconciled: An Iconographic Study* (Toronto: University of Toronto Press, 1947)

Clark, Stuart, *Thinking with Demons: The Idea of Witchcraft in Early Modern Europe* (Oxford: Clarendon Press, 1997)

Clarke, Kate, 'The Russell women as literary patrons, 1570–1620: a reconsideration of the role of gender in the kinds of dedicated works', paper given at the Women, Text and History seminar, Merton College, Oxford University, 17 October 1989

Clarke, M. L., *Classical Education in Britain, 1500–1900* (Cambridge: Cambridge University Press, 1959)

Colie, Rosalie L., *The Resources of Kind: Genre-Theory in the Renaissance*, ed. Barbara K. Lewalski (Berkeley, Calif., Los Angeles and London: University of California Press, 1973)

Colie, Rosalie, *Shakespeare's Living Art* (Princeton, N.J.: Princeton University Press, 1974)

Colley, Linda, *Britons: Forging the Nation, 1707–1837* (New Haven and London: Yale University Press, 1992)

Collinson, Patrick, 'Biblical rhetoric: the English nation and national sentiment in the prophetic mode', in *Religion and Culture in Renaissance England*, eds Claire McEachern and Debora Shuger (Cambridge: Cambridge University Press, 1997), pp. 15–45

Colvin, Howard M., D. R. Ransome and J. Summerson, eds, *The History of the King's Works, Volume III: 1485–1660, Part 1* (London: HMSO, 1975)

Cook, Ann Jennalie, *Making a Match: Courtship in Shakespeare and his Society* (Princeton, N.J.: Princeton University Press, 1991)

Cox, John D., *Shakespeare and the Dramaturgy of Power* (Princeton, N.J.: Princeton University Press, 1989)

Crane, Mary Thomas, 'Linguistic change, theatrical practice, and the ideologies of status in *As You Like It*', *English Literary Renaissance*, 27 (1997), 361–92

Cressy, David, 'Purification, thanksgiving and the churching of women in post-Reformation England', *Past and Present*, 141 (1993), 106–46

Davenport-Hines, Richard, *Sex, Death and Punishment* (London: Collins, 1990)

Davies, Neville H., 'Jacobean *Antony and Cleopatra*', *Shakespeare Studies*, 17 (1985), 123–58

Dickens, A. G., *The English Reformation* (London: Fontana, 1964; 2nd edition, 1989)

Dickey, Stephen, 'Language and role in *Pericles*', *English Literary Renaissance*, 16 (1986), 550–66

Diehl, Hutson, *Staging Reform, Reforming the Stage: Protestantism and Popular Theatre in Early Modern England* (Ithaca, N.Y., and London: Cornell University Press, 1997)

Dollimore, Jonathan, *Radical Tragedy: Religion, Ideology and Power in the Drama of Shakespeare and his Contemporaries* (New York, London, Toronto, Sydney and Tokyo: Harvester Wheatsheaf, 1984, repr. 1989)

Donaldson, E. Talbot, *The Swan at the Well: Shakespeare Reading Chaucer* (New Haven: Yale University Press, 1985)

Duffy, Eamon, *The Stripping of the Altars: Traditional Religion in England, 1400–1580* (New Haven and London: Yale University Press, 1992)

Dutton, Richard, *Mastering the Revels: The Regulation and Censorship of English Renaissance Drama* (Basingstoke and London: Macmillan, 1991)

Eagleton, Terry, *William Shakespeare* (Oxford: Blackwell, 1986)

Eaton, Sara, 'A woman of letters: Lavinia in *Titus Andronicus*', in *Shakespearean Tragedy and Gender*, eds Shirley Nelson Garner and Madelon Sprengnether (Bloomington and Indianapolis: Indiana University Press, 1996), pp. 54–74

Edwards, Philip, 'On the design of *The Two Noble Kinsmen*', *Review of English Literature*, 5 (1964), 89–105

Edwards, Philip, *Shakespeare: A Writer's Progress* (Oxford and New York: Oxford University Press, 1986)

Elton, G. R., 'Tudor government: the points of contact III. The court', *Transactions of the Royal Historical Society*, 26 (1976), 211–28

Evans, Maurice, 'Elizabethan spoken English', *Cambridge Journal*, 4 (1950–1), 401–14

Ewen, C. L'Estrange, *Witchcraft and Demonianism* (London: Heath Cranton, 1933)

Felperin, Howard, *Shakespearean Romance* (Princeton, N.J.: Princeton University Press, 1972)

Felperin, Howard, '"Tongue-tied our queen?" The deconstuction of presence in *The Winter's Tale*', in *Shakespeare and the Question of Theory*, eds Patricia Parker and Geoffrey Hartman (New York and London: Methuen, 1985), pp. 3–18

Finkelpearl, Philip J., '"The comedians' liberty": censorship of the Jacobean stage reconsidered', *English Literary Renaissance*, 16 (1986), 123–38

Finkelpearl, Philip J., 'Two distincts, division none: Shakespeare and Fletcher's *The Two Noble Kinsmen* of 1613', in *Elizabethan Theater: Essays in Honor of S. Schoenbaum*, eds R. B. Parker and S. P. Zitner (Newark: University of Delaware Press, 1996), pp. 184–99

Flech, Susan, 'Shaping the reader in the *Acts and Monuments*', in *John Foxe and the English Reformation*, ed. David Loades (Aldershot: Scolar Press, 1997), pp. 52–65

Fleming, Juliet, 'The ladies' man and the age of Elizabeth', in *Sexuality and Gender in Early Modern Europe: Institutions, Texts, Images*, ed. James G. Turner (Cambridge: Cambridge University Press, 1993), pp.158–81

Fletcher, Anthony, *A County Community in Peace and War: Sussex 1600–1660* (London: Longman, 1975)

Foucault, Michel, *The Use of Pleasure* (*The History of Sexuality*, vol. 2), trans. Robert Hurley (Harmondsworth: Penguin, 1992)

Fowler, Alaistair, *Kinds of Literature: An Introduction to the Theory of Genres and Modes* (Oxford: Clarendon Press, 1982)

Freedman, Barbara , 'Shakespearean chronology, ideological complicity, and floating texts: something is rotten in Windsor', *Shakespeare Quarterly*, 45 (1994), 190–210

Freehafer, John, '*Cardenio*, by Shakespeare and Fletcher', *Proceedings of the Modern Language Association*, 84 (1969), 501–13

French, Peter, *John Dee: The World of an Elizabethan Magus* (London, Boston, Melbourne and Henley: Routledge and Kegan Paul, 1972)

Frey, Charles H., '"O sacred, shadowy, cold and constant queen": Shakespeare's imperiled and chastening daughters of romance', in *The Woman's Part: Feminist Criticism of Shakespeare* (Urbana, Ill.: University of Illinois Press, 1980), pp. 295–313

Frey, Charles H., ed. *Shakespeare, Fletcher and 'The Two Noble Kinsmen'* (Columbia: University of Missouri Press, 1989)

Frye, Northrop, *A Natural Perspective: The Development of Shakespearean Comedy and Romance* (New York: Columbia University Press, 1965)

Frye, Northrop, *The Anatomy of Criticism: Four Essays* (Harmondsworth: Penguin, 1957, repr. 1990)

Garber, Marjorie, '"What's past is prologue": temporality and prophecy in Shakespeare's history plays', in *Renaissance Genres: Essays on Theory, History, and Interpretation*, ed. Barbara Kiefer Lewalski (Cambridge, Mass.: Harvard University Press, 1986), pp. 301–31

Gardiner, Samuel R., *History of England from the Accession of James I to the Outbreak of Civil War, 1603–42*, 10 vols (London: Longman, 1905)

Gaspar, Julia, 'The Reformation plays on the public stage', in *Theatre and Government Under the Early Stuarts*, eds J. R. Mulryne and Margaret Shewring (Cambridge: Cambridge University Press, 1993), pp. 190–216

Gent, L., ed. *Albion's Classicism: The Visual Arts in Britain, 1550–1660* (New Haven and London: Yale University Press, 1995)

Gentilcore, David, *From Bishop to Witch: The System of the Sacred in Early Modern Terra d'Otranto* (Manchester: Manchester University Press, 1992)

Gibbons, Brian, 'Romance and the heroic play', in *The Cambridge Companion to English Renaissance Drama*, eds A. R. Braunmuller and Michael Hattaway (Cambridge: Cambridge University Press, 1990)

Gilman, E. B., '"All eyes": Prospero's inverted masque', *Renaissance Quarterly*, 33 (1980), 214–30

Gilman, Sander, *Disease and Representation: Images of Illness from Madness to Aids* (Ithaca, N.Y., and London: Cornell University Press, 1988)

Goldberg, Jonathan, *James I and the Politics of Literature: Jonson, Shakespeare, Donne, and their Contemporaries* (Baltimore and London: Johns Hopkins University Press, 1983)

Grafton, Anthony, and Lisa Jardine, '"Studied for action": how Gabriel Harvey read his Livy', *Past and Present*, 129 (1990), 30–78

Grundin, R., 'Prospero's masque and the structure of *The Tempest*', *South Atlantic Quarterly*, 71 (1972), 401–9

Gurr, Andrew, *Playgoing in Shakespeare's London* (Cambridge: Cambridge University Press, 1987)

Gurr, Andrew, *The Shakespearean Stage, 1574–1642* (Cambridge: Cambridge University Press, 1992, 3rd edn)

Gurr, Andrew, 'The *Tempest*'s tempest at the Blackfriars', *Shakespeare Survey*, 42 (1992), 91–102

Gurr, Andrew, *The Shakespearian Playing Companies* (Oxford: Clarendon Press, 1996)

Haigh, Christopher, *English Reformations: Religion, Politics and Society under the Tudors* (Oxford: Oxford University Press, 1993)

Hall Jr, Vernon, *Renaissance Literary Criticism: A Study of its Social Contexts* (New York: Columbia University Press, 1945)

Haller, William, *Foxe's Book of Martyrs and the Elect Nation* (London: Jonathan Cape, 1963)

Hamilton, Donna B., '*The Winter's Tale* and the language of union, 1604–1610', *Shakespeare Studies*, 21 (1993), 228–50

Harris, Bernard, '"What's past is prologue": *Cymbeline* and *Henry VIII*', in *Later Shakespeare*, eds John Russell Brown and Bernard Harris (London: Edward Arnold, 1966), pp. 203–34

Hawkes, Terence, 'Swisser-Swatter: making a man of English letters', in *Alternative Shakespeares*, ed. John Drakakis (London: Methuen, 1985), pp. 26–46

Hawkes, Terence, 'Lear's maps', in *Meaning by Shakespeare* (London: Routledge, 1992), pp. 121–40

Heal, Felicity, *Hospitality in Early Modern England* (Oxford: Clarendon Press, 1990)

Helms, Lorraine, 'The saint in the brothel: or, eloquence rewarded', *Shakespeare Quarterly*, 41 (1990), 319–32

Highley, Christopher, *Shakespeare, Spenser, and the Crisis in Ireland* (Cambridge: Cambridge University Press, 1997)

Hillman, Richard, 'Shakespeare's romantic innocents and the misappropriation of the romance past: the case of *The Two Noble Kinsmen*', *Shakespeare Survey*, 43 (1991), 69–80

Hirst, David L., *Tragicomedy* (London: Methuen, 1984)

Hoeniger, F. David, 'Gower and Shakespeare in *Pericles*', *Shakespeare Quarterly*, 33 (1982), 461–79

Holderness, Graham, '"What ish my nation?": Shakespeare and national identities', *Textual Practice*, 5 (1991), 74–93

Holderness, Graham, Nick Potter and John Turner, *Shakespeare Out of Court: Dramatizations of Court Society* (Basingstoke and London: Macmillan, 1990)

Hope, Jonathan, *The Authorship of Shakespeare's Plays: A Socio-Linguistic Study* (Cambridge: Cambridge University Press, 1994)

Hoy, Cyrus, 'The shares of Fletcher and his collaborators in the Beaumont and Fletcher canon (I–VII)', *Studies in Bibliography*, 8–15 (1956–62)

Huth, Alfred H., *The Huth Bequest: Catalogue of the Fifty Manuscripts and Printed Books Bequeathed to the British Museum by Alfred H. Huth* (Oxford: Oxford University Press for the Trustees of the British Museum, 1912)

Hutson, Lorna, *The Usurer's Daughter: Male Friendship and Fictions of Women in Sixteenth-Century England* (London and New York: Routledge, 1994)

Hutson, Lorna, 'Chivalry for merchants; or, knights of temperance in the realms of gold', *Journal of Medieval and Early Modern Studies*, 26 (1996), 29–59

Ingram, Martin, *Church Courts, Sex and Marriage in England, 1570–1640* (Cambridge: Cambridge University Press, 1987)

James, Mervyn, *Society, Politics and Culture: Studies in Early Modern England* (Cambridge: Cambridge University Press, 1986)

Jardine, Lisa, 'Reading and the technology of textual affect: Erasmus's familiar letters and

Shakespeare's *King Lear*', in *Reading Shakespeare Historically* (Routledge: London and New York, 1996), pp. 78–97

Jardine, Lisa, and Alan Stewart, *Hostage to Fortune: The Troubled Life of Francis Bacon 1561–1626* (London: Gollancz, 1998)

Jarvis, Simon, *Scholars and Gentlemen: Shakespearian Textual Criticism and Representations of Scholarly Labour, 1725–65* (Oxford: Clarendon Press, 1995)

Javitch, Daniel, *Poetry and Courtliness in Renaissance England* (Princeton, N.J.: Princeton University Press, 1987)

Jones, Emrys, 'Stuart *Cymbeline*', *Essays in Criticism*, 11 (1961), 84–99

Jowett, John, 'New created creatures: Ralph Crane and the directions in *The Tempest*', *Shakespeare Survey*, 36 (1983), 107–20

Kahn, Coppelia, *Roman Shakespeare: Warriors, Wounds, and Women* (London and New York: Routledge, 1997)

Kahn, Victoria, *Rhetoric, Prudence, and Skepticism in the Renaissance* (Ithaca, N.Y. and London: Cornell University Press, 1985)

Kay, Dennis, '"To hear the rest untold": Shakespeare's postponed endings', *Renaissance Quarterly*, 37 (1984), 207–77

Kermode, Frank 'What is Shakespeare's *Henry VIII* about?', *Durham University Journal*, new series, 9 (1948), 48–55

Kernan, Alvin, *Shakespeare, the King's Playwright: Theater in the Stuart Court, 1603–1613* (New Haven: Yale University Press, 1995)

Kiessling, Nicholas K., '*The Winter's Tale*, II.iii.103–7; an allusion to the hag-incubus', *Shakespeare Quarterly*, 28 (1977), 93–5

King, John, *English Reformation Literature: The Tudor Origins of the Protestant Tradition* (Princeton, N.J.: Princeton University Press, 1982)

Kirsch, Arthur, *Shakespeare and the Experience of Love* (Cambridge: Cambridge University Press, 1981)

Kittredge, G. L., *Witchcraft in Old and New England* (Cambridge, Mass.: Harvard University Press, 1912)

Klapisch-Zuber, Christiane, *Women, Family, and Ritual in Renaissance Italy*, trans. Lydia Cochrane (Chicago and London: University of Chicago Press, 1985)

Knight, George Wilson, *The Olive and the Sword: A Study of England's Shakespeare* (Oxford: Oxford University Press, 1944)

Knight, George Wilson, *The Crown of Life: Essays in Interpretation of Shakespeare's Final Plays* (Oxford: Oxford University Press, 1947)

Knight, George Wilson, *Principles of Shakespearian Production: With Especial Reference to the Tragedies* (London: Faber, 1964)

Knight, George Wilson, *Shakespeare and Religion: Essays of Forty Years* (London: Routledge and Kegan Paul, 1967)

Knowles, James, 'Marston, Skipwith and *The Entertainment at Ashby*', *English Manuscript Studies*, 3 (1992), 137–92

Knowles, James, 'Shopping with Cecil: a new Ben Jonson masque discovered', *Times Literary Supplement*, 4897 (7 February 1997), 14–15

Knowles, Ronald, ed., *Shakespeare and Carnival: After Bakhtin* (Houndmills, Basingstoke and London: Macmillan, 1998)

Krontiris, Tina, 'Breaking barriers of genre and gender: Margaret Tyler's translation of *The Mirrour of Knighthood*', in *Women in the Renaissance: Selections from 'English Literary Renaissance'*, eds Kirby Farrell, Elizabeth H. Hageman and Arthur F. Kinney

(Amherst: University of Massachusetts Press, 1990), pp. 48–68

Kuchta, David, 'The semiotics of masculinity in Renaissance England', in *Sexuality and Gender in Early Modern Europe: Institutions, Texts, Images*, ed. James G. Turner (Cambridge: Cambridge University Press, 1993), pp. 233–46

Kukowski, Stephen, 'The hand of John Fletcher in *Double Falsehood*', *Shakespeare Survey*, 43 (1991), 81–9

Kurland, Stuart M., '*Henry VIII* and James I: Shakespeare and Jacobean politics', *Shakespeare Studies*, 19 (1987), 203–18

Kurland, Stuart M., '*Hamlet* and the Scottish succession?', *Studies in English Literature*, 34 (1994), 279–300

Lacan, Jacques, 'The insistence of the letter in the unconcious' (1957), repr. in *Modern Criticism and Theory: A Reader*, ed. David Lodge (London and New York: Longman, 1988), pp. 79–106

Lake, Peter, *Anglicans and Puritans? Presbyterianism and English Conformist Thought from Whitgift to Hooker* (London: Unwin Hyman, 1988)

Lake, Peter, 'Anti-popery: the structure of a prejudice', in *Conflict in Early Stuart England: Studies in Religion and Politics, 1603–1642*, eds Richard Cust and Ann Hughes (Harlow and New York: Longman, 1989), pp. 72–106

Lancaster, H. Carrington, 'Hermione's statue', *Studies in Philology*, 29 (1932), 233–8

Landry, D. E., 'Dreams as history: the strange unity of *Cymbeline*', *Shakespeare Quarterly*, 33 (1982), 68–79

Laqueur, Thomas, *Making Sex: Body and Gender from the Greeks to Freud* (Cambridge, Mass.: Harvard University Press, 1990)

Latham, Jacqueline E. M., '*The Tempest* and King James's *Dæmnologie*', *Shakespeare Survey*, 28 (1975), 117–23

Leech, Clifford, *The John Fletcher Plays* (London: Chatto and Windus, 1962)

Levack, Brian, *The Formation of the British State: England, Scotland, and the Union, 1603–1707* (Oxford: Clarendon Press, 1987)

Levin, Richard, 'The King James version of *Measure for Measure*', *Clio*, 3 (1974), 129–63

Levy, F. J., *Tudor Historical Thought* (San Marino, Calif.: Huntington Library, 1967)

Lewalski, Barbara, *Writing Women in Jacobean England* (Cambridge, Mass.: Harvard University Press, 1993), pp. 15–43

Lewis, C. S., *Studies in Words* (Cambridge: Cambridge University Press, 1967)

Lief, Madelon, and Nicholas F. Radel, 'Linguistic subversion and the artifice of rhetoric in *The Two Noble Kinsmen*', *Shakespeare Quarterly*, 38 (1987), 405–25

Limon, Jerzy, 'The masque of Stuart culture', in *The Mental World of the Jacobean Court*, ed. Linda Levy Peck (Cambridge: Cambridge University Press, 1991), pp. 209–29

Lindley, David, 'Music, masque and meaning in *The Tempest*', in *The Court Masque*, ed. David Lindley (Manchester: Manchester University Press, 1984), pp. 47–59

Lindley, David, *The Trials of Frances Howard: Fact and Fiction at the Court of King James* (London and New York: Routledge, 1993)

Loades, David, ed. *John Foxe and the English Reformation* (Aldershot: Scolar Press, 1997)

London Theatre Record, Reviews of *Pericles*, RSC 1990 and RNT 1994, *London Theatre Record*, 9–22 April 1990 and 7–20 May 1994

Lowenstein, Joseph, 'Printing and the "multitudinous presse": the contentious texts of Jonson's masques', in *Ben Jonson's 1616 Folio*, eds J. Brady and W. H. Herendeen (Newark, N.J.: University of Delaware Press, 1991), pp. 168–91

Lucas, Caroline, *Writing for Women: The Example of Woman as Reader in Elizabethan*

Romance (Milton Keynes and Philadelphia: Open University Press, 1989)

McAlindon, T., *Shakespeare and Decorum* (London and Basingstoke: Macmillan, 1973)

McCabe, Richard, *Incest, Drama and Nature's Law, 1550–1700* (Cambridge: Cambridge University Press, 1993)

McClung, William, and Rodney Simard, 'Donne's Somerset Epithalamium and the erotics of criticism', *Huntington Library Quarterly*, 50 (1987), 95–106

McEachern, Claire, *The Poetics of English Nationhood, 1590–1612* (Cambridge: Cambridge University Press, 1996)

McGinnis, Kay, and Henry E. Jacobs, eds *Shakespeare's Romances Reconsidered* (Lincoln, Nebr., and London: University of Nebraska Press, 1978)

McLuskie, Kathleen E., 'The poets' Royal Exchange: patronage and commerce in early modern drama', *Yearbook of English Studies*, 21 (1991), 53–62

McLuskie, Kathleen E., *Dekker and Heywood: Professional Dramatists* (Houndmills, Basingstoke and London: Macmillan; New York: St Martin's Press, 1994)

McMullan, Gordon, *The Politics of Unease in the Plays of John Fletcher* (Amherst: University of Massachusetts Press, 1994)

McMullan, Gordon, 'Shakespeare and the end of history', *Essays and Studies*, 48 (1995), 16–37

McMullan, Gordon, '"Our whole life is like a play": collaboration and the problem of editing', *Textus*, 9 (1996), 437–60

McMullan, Gordon, '"Swimming on bladders": the dialogics of Reformation in Shakespeare and Fletcher's *Henry VIII*', *Shakespeare and Carnival: After Bakhtin*, ed. Ronald Knowles (Houndmills, Basingstoke and London: Macmillan, 1998), pp. 211–67.

McMullan, Gordon, and Jonathan Hope, eds, *The Politics of Tragicomedy: Shakespeare and After* (London and New York: Routledge, 1992)

McRae, Andrew, *God Speed the Plough: The Representation of Agrarian England* (Cambridge: Cambridge University Press, 1996)

Mack, Phyllis, 'Women as prophets during the English Civil War', in *The Origins of Anglo-American Radicalism*, eds Margaret C. Jacob and James Jacob (London: Allen and Unwin, 1984), pp. 214–30

Maguire, Nancy Klein, ed. *Renaissance Tragicomedy: Explorations in Genre and Politics* (New York: AMS Press, 1987)

Marcus, Leah, *Puzzling Shakespeare: Local Reading and its Discontents* (Berkeley, Calif., Los Angeles and London: University of California Press, 1988)

Martin, Ruth, *Witchcraft and the Inquisition in Venice, 1550–1650* (Oxford: Basil Blackwell, 1989)

Martinez, Roland L., 'Benefit of absence: Machiavellian valediction in *Clizia*', in *Machiavelli and the Discourses of Literature*, eds Albert R. Ascoli and Victoria Kahn (Ithaca, N.Y., and London: Cornell Univerity Press, 1993), pp. 129–36

Masten, Jeffrey A., 'Beaumont and/or Fletcher: collaboration and the interpretation of Renaissance drama', *English Literary History*, 59 (1992), 337–56

Masten, Jeffrey, *Textual Intercourse: Collaboration, Authorship, and Sexualities in Renaissance Drama* (Cambridge: Cambridge University Press, 1997)

Metz, Harold, *Sources of Four Plays Ascribed to Shakespeare* (Columbia: University of Missouri Press, 1989)

Mikalachki, Jodi, 'The masculine romance of Roman Britain: *Cymbeline* and early modern English nationalism', *Shakespeare Quarterly*, 46 (1995), 301–22

Miller, Carl, *Stages of Desire: Gay Theatre's Hidden History* (London: Cassell, 1996)

Mills, Lauren J., *One Soul in Bodies Twain: Friendship in Tudor Literature and Tudor Drama* (Bloomington, Ind.: Principia Press, 1937)

Moore-Gilbert, Bart, Gareth Stanton and Willy Maley, eds *Postcolonial Criticism* (Addison, Wesley and Longman: London, 1997)

Morse, William R., 'Metacriticism and materiality: the case of Shakespeare's *The Winter's Tale*', *English Literary History*, 58 (1991), 283–304

Mowat, Barbara A., 'Shakesperean tragicomedy', in *Renaissance Tragicomedy: Explorations in Genre and Politics*, ed. Nancy Klein Maguire (New York: AMS Press, 1987), pp. 80–96

Muir, Kenneth, *Shakespeare as Collaborator* (London: Methuen, 1960)

Mullaney, Steven, *The Place of the Stage: License, Play, and Power in Renaissance England* (Chicago and London: University of Chicago Press, 1988)

Neely, Carol Thomas, '*The Winter's Tale*: the triumph of speech', *Studies in English Language and Literature*, 15 (1975), 321–38

Neely, Carol Thomas, *Broken Nuptials in Shakespeare's Plays* (Chicago: University of Chicago Press, 1993)

Nevo, Ruth, *Shakespeare's Other Language* (New York and London: Methuen, 1987)

Norbrook, David, 'The reformation of the masque', in *The Court Masque*, ed. David Lindley (Manchester: Manchester University Press, 1984), pp. 94–110

Norbrook, David, '*Macbeth* and the politics of historiography', in *Politics of Discourse: The Literature and History of Seventeenth-Century England*, eds K. Sharpe and S. N. Zwicker (Berkeley, Calif.: University of California Press, 1987), pp. 78–116

Norbrook, David, '"What cares these roarers for the name of king?": language and utopia in *The Tempest*', in *The Politics of Tragicomedy: Shakespeare and After*, ed. G. McMullan and Jonathan Hope (London: Routledge, 1992), pp. 21–54

Nuttall, A. D., *Two Concepts of Allegory: A Study of Shakespeare's 'The Tempest' and the Logic of Allegorical Expression* (London: Routledge and Kegan Paul, 1967)

O'Connor, John J., '*Amadis de Gaule*' and its Influence on Elizabethan Literature (New Brunswick, N.J.: Rutgers University Press, 1970)

Odell, George C. D., *Shakespeare from Betterton to Irving*, 2 vols (London: Constable, 1921)

Oman, Carola, *Elizabeth of Bohemia* (London: Hodder & Stoughton, 1938)

O'Neil, M. P., 'Sacerdote overro strione: ecclesiastical and superstitious remedies in sixteenth century Italy', in *Understanding Popular Culture*, ed. S. Kaplan (Berlin: Mouton, 1984), pp. 53–83

Orgel, Stephen, and Roy Strong, *Inigo Jones and the Theatre of the Stuart Court*, 2 vols (Berkeley, Calif., and London: University of California Press and Sotheby Parke Bernet, 1973)

Orgel, Stephen, 'Jonson and the Amazons', in *Soliciting Interpretation*, eds E. Harvey and K. E. Maus (Chicago: University of Chicago Press, 1990), pp. 119–39

Orkin, Martin, 'A sad tale's best for South Africa?', *Textual Practice*, 11 (1997), 1–23

Orrell, John, *The Theatres of Inigo Jones and John Webb* (Cambridge: Cambridge University Press, 1985)

Orrell, John, *The Human Stage: English Theatre Design, 1567–1640* (Cambridge: Cambridge University Press, 1988)

Palfrey, Simon, *Late Shakespeare: A New World of Words* (Oxford: Clarendon Press, 1997)

Palmer, D. J., ed. *Shakespeare's Later Comedies: An Anthology of Modern Criticism* (Harmondsworth: Penguin, 1971)

Parker, Patricia, *Literary Fat Ladies: Rhetoric, Gender, Property* (London and New York: Methuen, 1987)

Parker, Patricia, 'Romance and empire: anachronistic *Cymbeline*', in *Unfolded Tales: Essays on Renaissance Romance*, eds George M. Logan and Gordon Teskey (Ithaca, N.Y.: Cornell University Press, 1989), pp. 189–207

Parker, Patricia, 'Preposterous estates, preposterous events: from late to early Shakespeare', in *Shakespeare from the Margins: Language, Culture, Context* (Chicago and London: University of Chicago Press, 1996), pp. 20–55

Parker, R. B., and S. P. Zitner, eds *Elizabethan Theater: Essays in Honor of S. Schoenbaum* (Newark: University of Delaware Press, 1996)

Parry, Graham, 'The Great Picture of Lady Anne Clifford', in *Art and Patronage in the Caroline Courts: Essays in Honour of Sir Oliver Millar*, ed. David Howarth (Cambridge: Cambridge University Press, 1993), pp. 202–19

Patterson, Annabel, *Censorship and Interpretation* (Madison: University of Wisconsin Press, 1984)

Patterson, Annabel, *Reading Between the Lines* (London: Routledge, 1993)

Patterson, Annabel, *Reading Holinshed's Chronicles* (Chicago and London: University of Chicago Press, 1994)

Patterson, Annabel, '"All is true": negotiating the past in *Henry VIII*', in *Elizabethan Theater: Essays in Honor of S. Schoenbaum*, eds R. B. Parker and S. P. Zinter (Newark: University of Delaware Press; London: Associated University Presses, 1996), pp. 147–66

Pearson, D'Orsay W., 'Witchcraft in *The Winter's Tale*: Paulina as "alcahueta y un poquito hechizera"', *Shakespeare Studies*, 12 (1979), 195–213

Peck, Linda Levy, *Northampton: Patronage and Policy at the Court of James I* (London: George Allen & Unwin, 1982)

Peck, Linda Levy, 'The mentality of a Jacobean grandee', in *The Mental World of the Jacobean Court*, ed. Linda Levy Peck (Cambridge: Cambridge University Press, 1991), pp. 148–68

Pittock, Murray, *Inventing and Resisting Britain: Cultural Identities in Britain and Ireland, 1685–1789* (Basingstoke and London: Macmillan, 1997)

Potter, Lois, '"True tragicomedies" of the Civil War and the Commonwealth', in *Renaissance Tragicomedy: Explorations in Genre and Politics*, ed. Nancy Klein Maguire (New York: AMS Press, 1987), pp. 195–216

Potter, Lois, 'Topicality or politics? *The Two Noble Kinsmen*, 1613–34', in *The Politics of Tragicomedy: Shakespeare and After*, ed. G. McMullan and Jonathan Hope (London: Routledge, 1992), pp. 77–91

Proudfoot, G. R., 'Shakespeare and the new dramatists of the King's Men, 1609–1613', in *Later Shakespeare*, Stratford upon Avon Studies 8, eds J. R. Brown and B. Harris (London: Edward Arnold, 1966), pp. 235–61

Proudfoot, G. R., '*Henry VIII (All Is True), The Two Noble Kinsmen*, and the apocryphal plays', in *Shakespeare: A Bibliographical Guide*, ed. Stanley Wells (Oxford: Oxford University Press, 1990), pp. 381–403

Rackin, Phyllis, *Stages of History: Shakespeare's English Chronicles* (Ithaca, N.Y.: Cornell University Press, 1990)

Richmond, Hugh M., *Henry VIII: Shakespeare in Performance* (Manchester: Manchester University Press, 1994)

Relihan, Constance C, 'Liminal geography: *Pericles* and the politics of place', *Philological Quarterly*, 71 (1992), 281–99

Reynolds, George, *The Staging of Elizabethan Plays at the Red Bull Theater, 1605–1625* (New York: MLAA; London: Oxford University Press, 1940)

Riskine, F. H., *English Tragicomedy, its Origin and History* (New York: Columbia University Press, 1910)

Roberts, Gareth, 'The descendants of Circe: witches and Renaissance fictions', in *Witchcraft in Early Modern Europe: Studies in Culture and Belief*, eds Jonathan Barry, Marianne Hester and Gareth Roberts (Cambridge: Cambridge University Press, 1996), pp. 183–206

Roberts, Jeanne Addison, 'Ralph Crane and the text of *The Tempest*', *Shakespeare Studies*, 13 (1980), 213–33

Rosen, Barbara, *Witchcraft in England, 1558–1618* (Amherst: University of Massachusetts Press, 1991)

Rubin, Gayle, 'The traffic in women: notes on a "political economy" of sex', in *Towards an Anthropology of Women*, ed. Rayna Reiter (New York: Monthly Review Press, 1975)

Rublack, Ulinka, 'Pregnancy, childbirth and the female body in early modern Germany', *Past and Present*, 150 (1996), 84–110

Ruggiero, Guido, *Binding Passions: Tales of Magic, Marriage and Power at the End of the Renaissance* (Oxford: Oxford University Press, 1993)

Russell, Conrad, *The Fall of the British Monarchies, 1637–1642* (Oxford: Clarendon Press, 1992)

Saccone, Eduardo, '*Grazia, sprezzatura, affettazione* in the *Courtier*', in *Castiglione: The Ideal and the Real in Reniassance Culture*, eds Robert W. Hanning and David Rosand (New Haven and London: Yale University Press, 1983), pp. 45–67

Saslow, James M., *Ganymede in the Renaissance: Homosexuality in Art and Society* (New Haven: Yale University Press, 1986)

Scarisbrick, J. J., *The Reformation and the English People* (Oxford: Oxford University Press, 1984)

Schmidgall, Gary, *Shakespeare and the Courtly Aesthetic* (Berkeley, Calif., Los Angeles and London: University of California Press, 1981)

Schoenbaum, S., *William Shakespeare: A Compact Documentary Life* (Oxford: Clarendon Press, 1977)

Schwartz, Murray M., 'Between fantasy and imagination: a psycho-logical exploration of *Cymbeline*', in *Pyschoanalysis and Literary Process*, ed. Frederick Crews (Cambridge, Mass.: Winthrop Publishers, 1970), pp. 219–83

Scragg, Leah, *Shakespeare's Mouldy Tales: Recurrent Plot Motifs in Shakespearian Drama* (London and New York: Longman, 1992)

Scribner, Robert W., 'The Reformation, popular magic and the "disenchantment of the world"', *Journal of Interdisciplinary History*, 23 (1993), 475–94

Seary, Peter, *Lewis Theobald and the Editing of Shakespeare* (Oxford: Clarendon Press, 1990)

Sedgwick, Eve Kosofsky, *Between Men: English Literature and Male Homosocial Desire* (New York: Columbia University Press, 1985)

Shulman, Milton, 'Review of *Pericles* (RSC)', *Evening Standard*, 17 April, 1990

Sisson, Charles J., 'Shakespeare quartos as prompt-copies', *Review of English Studies*, 18 (1942), 129–43

Smith, Bruce R., *Homosexual Desire in Shakespeare's England: A Cultural Poetics* (Chicago and London: University of Chicago Press, 1991)

Smith, Jonathan, 'The language of Leontes', *Shakespeare Quarterly*, 19 (1968), 317–27

Smuts, Malcolm, 'Cultural diversity and cultural change at the court of James I', in *The Mental World of the Jacobean Court*, ed. Linda Levy Peck (Cambridge: Cambridge University Press, 1991), pp. 99–113

Sokol, B. J., *Art and Illusion in 'The Winter's Tale'* (Manchester and New York: Manchester University Press, 1994)

Somerset, Anne, *Unnatural Murder: Poison at the Court of James I* (London: Weidenfeld and Nicolson, 1997)

Spalding, William, *A Letter on Shakespeare's Authorship of 'The Two Noble Kinsmen'* (Edinburgh, 1833), ed. J. H. Burton, foreword F. J. Furnivall, *New Shakspeare Society*, Series VIII, no. 1 (1876)

Spedding, James, 'Who wrote Shakespeare's *Henry VIII*?', *Gentleman's Magazine*, clxxviii (August–October 1850), 115–24 and 381–2

Spencer, Theodore, '*The Two Noble Kinsmen*', *Modern Philology*, 36 (1938–9), 255–76

Spikes, Judith Doolin, 'The Jacobean history play and the myth of the elect nation', *Renaissance Drama*, new series, 7 (1977), 117–50

Sprague, Arthur C., *Shakespeare's Histories: Plays for the Stage* (London: Society for Theatre Research, 1964)

Spufford, Margaret, *Small Books and Pleasant Histories: Popular Fiction and its Readership in Seventeenth-Century England* (Cambridge: Cambridge University Press, 1985)

Stallybrass, Peter, and Allon White, *The Politics and Poetics of Transgression* (London: Methuen, 1986)

Strong, Roy, *Henry, Prince of Wales, and England's Lost Renaissance* (London: Thames and Hudson, 1986)

Taylor, Michael, 'The late comedies', in *Shakespeare: A Bibliographical Guide*, ed. Stanley Wells (Oxford: Clarendon Press, 1990)

Tennenhouse, Leonard, *Power on Display: The Politics of Shakespeare's Genres* (London: Methuen, 1986)

Thomas, Keith, *Religion and the Decline of Magic: Studies in Popular Belief in Sixteenth- and Seventeenth-Century England* (Harmondsworth: Penguin, 1973)

Thompson, Ann, *Shakespeare's Chaucer: A Study in Literary Origins* (Liverpool: Liverpool University Press, 1978)

Tillyard, E. M. W., *Shakespeare's Last Plays* (London: Chatto & Windus, 1938, repr. 1964)

Traub, Valerie, *Desire and Anxiety: Circulations of Sexuality in Shakespearean Drama* (Routledge: London, 1992)

Trimpi, Wesley, *Ben Jonson's Poems: A Study of the Plain Style* (Stanford, Calif.: Stanford University Press, 1962)

Tyacke, Nicholas, *Anti-Calvinists: The Rise of English Arminianism, c. 1590–1640* (Oxford: Clarendon Press, 1987)

Vickers, Nancy, '"The blazon of sweet beauty's best": Shakespeare's *Lucrece*', in *Shakespeare and the Question of Theory*, eds Patricia Parker and Geoffrey Hartman (New York and London: Methuen, 1985), pp. 95–115

Waith, Eugene, *The Pattern of Tragicomedy in Beaumont and Fletcher* (New York: Archon Books, 1969)

Waith, Eugene M., 'Shakespeare and Fletcher on love and friendship', *Shakespeare Studies*, 18 (1986), 235–50

Walker, D. P., *Spiritual and Demonic Magic from Ficino to Campanella* (London: Warburg Institute, 1958)

Walker, D. P., 'La cessazione dei miracoli', *Intersezioni*, 3 (1983), 285–301

Wall, Wendy, *The Imprint of Gender: Authorship and Publication in the English Renaissance* (Ithaca, N.Y., and London: Cornell University Press, 1993)

Watson, Foster, *The English Grammar Schools to 1660* (London: Frank Cass, 1968)

Watson, George J., *Irish Identity and the Literary Revival: Synge, Yeats, O'Casey* (Washington, D. C.: Catholic University of America Press, 1994)

Wells, Stanley, 'Shakespeare and romance', in *Later Shakespeare*, eds John Russell Brown and Bernard Harris, Stratford upon Avon Studies 8 (London: Edward Arnold, 1966, repr. 1973)

Wells, Stanley, ed. *Shakespeare: A Bibliographical Guide* (Oxford: Clarendon Press, 1990)

Wells, Stanley, and Gary Taylor, eds, *William Shakespeare: A Textual Companion* (Oxford: Oxford University Press, 1987)

West, Cornel, *Prophesy Deliverance! An Afro-American Revolutionary Christianity* (Philadelphia: Mentor, 1982)

Whigham, Frank, *Ambition and Privilege: The Social Tropes of Elizabethan Courtesy Theory* (Berkeley, Calif., Los Angeles and London: University of California Press, 1984)

White, Beatrice, *Cast of Ravens: The Strange Case of Sir Thomas Overbury* (London: John Murray, 1965)

White, Paul Whitfield, *Theatre and Reformation: Protestantism, Patronage, and Playing in Tudor England* (Cambridge: Cambridge University Press, 1993)

White, R. S., *'Let Wonder Seem Familiar': Endings in Shakespeare's Romance Vision* (London: Athlone Press; N.J.: Humanities Press, 1985)

White, R. S., *Natural Law in English Renaissance Literature* (Cambridge: Cambridge University Press, 1996)

Wickham, Glynne, *Early English Stages, 1300–1660* (London: Routledge and Kegan and Paul, 1959–81), vol. II, part II

Wickham, Glynne, 'From tragedy to tragi-comedy: *King Lear* as prologue', *Shakespeare Survey*, 26 (1973), 33–48

Wickham, Glynne, 'Masque and anti-masque in *The Tempest*', *Essays and Studies*, 28 (1975), 1–14

Wickham, Glynne, '"Heavens", machinery, and pillars in the theatre and other early playhouses', in *The First Public Playhouse: The Theatre in Shoreditch, 1576–1598*, ed. H. Berry (Montreal: McGill-Queen's University Press, 1979), pp. 1–15

Wickham, Glynne, '*The Two Noble Kinsmen* or *A Midsummer Night's Dream, Part II*?', in *The Elizabethan Theatre VII: Papers given at the Seventh International Conference on Elizabethan Theatre held at the University of Waterloo, Ontario, in July 1977*, ed. G. R. Hibbard (London and Basingstoke: Macmillan, 1980), pp. 167–96

Wilcox, Helen, 'Gender and genre in Shakespeare's tragicomedies', in *Reclamations of Shakespeare*, *DQR Studies in Literature* 15, ed. A. J. Hoenselaars (Amsterdam: Rodopi, 1994), pp. 129–38

Wilson, Richard, 'Observations on English bodies: licensing maternity in Shakespeare's late plays', in *Enclosure Acts: Sexuality, Property, and Culture in Early Modern England*, eds Richard Burt and John Michael Archer (Ithaca, N.Y., and London: Cornell University Press, 1994), pp. 121–50

Wilson, Richard, 'Voyage to Tunis: new history and the old world of *The Tempest*', *English Literary History*, 64 (1997), 333–57

Winkler, John J., *The Constraints of Desire: The Anthropology of Sex and Gender in Ancient Greece* (London and New York: Routledge, 1990)

Wooden, Warren W., *John Foxe*, Twayne English Authors Series 345 (Boston: G. K. Hall, 1983)

Woodhuysen, Henry R., '*King Henry VIII* and *All Is True*', *Notes and Queries*, 229 (1984), 217–18

Wortham, Christopher, 'Shakespeare, James I and the Matter of Britain', *English*, 45 (1996), 97–122

Wright, Louis B., *Middle-Class Culture in Elizabethan England* (Chapel Hill: University of North Carolina Press, 1935)

Wrightson, Keith, *English Society 1580–1680* (London: Hutchinson, 1982)

Wrightson, Keith, 'Estates, degrees and sorts in Tudor and Stuart England', *History Today* (January 1987), 17–22

Yates, Frances A., *Giordano Bruno and the Hermetic Tradition* (London and Henley: Routledge and Kegan Paul, 1964)

Yates, Frances A., *Theatre of the World* (London and Henley: Routledge and Kegan Paul, 1969)

Yates, Frances A., *Shakespeare's Last Plays: A New Approach* (London and Henley: Routledge and Kegan Paul, 1975)

Yoch, James J., 'The Renaissance dramatization of temperance: the Italian revival of tragicomedy and *The Faithful Shepherdess*', in *Renaissance Tragicomedy: Explorations in Genre and Politics*, ed. Nancy Klein Maguire (New York: AMS Press, 1987), pp. 114–37

INDEX

Page numbers in italics refer to illustrations.